Getting Over The X

GETTING OVER THE X

STEVE BROOKSTEIN

Matador
9 Priory Business Park
Kibworth Beauchamp
Leicestershire LE8 0RX, UK
Tel: (+44) 116 279 2299
Fax: (+44) 116 279 2277
Email: books@troubador.co.uk
Web: www.troubador.co.uk/matador

ISBN 978 1784621 544

British Library Cataloguing in Publication Data.
A catalogue record for this book is available from the British Library.

Typeset in Adobe Garamond Pro by Troubador Publishing Ltd
Printed and bound in the UK by CPI Group (UK) Ltd, Croydon, CR0 4YY

Matador is an imprint of Troubador Publishing Ltd

This book is dedicated to

my wonderful wife Eileen

and my beautiful children

Hamish and Esmé

Acknowledgements

Mum, Dad, Sis, Rob and the rest of the family. You know how much I love you.

The one innocent person who was dragged into my *X Factor* experience was my then girlfriend, Eileen. Through good and bad we've come a long way, and now married, we've been blessed with Hamish and Esmé. I wouldn't have made it without you.

Let our life really begin.

When contemplating writing this book over many years I could never quite bring myself to do it. After the Max Clifford conviction I felt stronger, but it was still with much trepidation that I contacted broadcaster and ghostwriter Tony Horne, even though he was highly recommended by a friend on Facebook, Victoria Hockley. Once we met I was sure that it was time to finally put things behind me the best way I knew how – by dealing with it. Against the clock, but with incredible discipline and expertise, Tony has helped share something that was emotionally too heavy a task to take on alone. Warm, considerate and honest: I can't thank you enough.

To John Iley, a man whom I have never met, I thank you for piecing together some bits we couldn't.

To Matt Rance @ProofProfessor, your genius, software and speed make you a must for any writer and publisher.

To the team at Matador, we had a deadline and you delivered where nobody else could. Thank you.

I will state for the record that some of my thoughts expressed herein are feelings that I had at the time; others are conclusions that I have drawn through the passing of time. I hope we make that clear in the book. Equally, in the sections concerning the live TV shows, the date used as a chapter heading invariably represents both that night's show and the week leading up to it. I say that for the avoidance of doubt in the unlikely event that there are grey areas over specific days.

Then came people who have made a direct contribution through supporting me and the book.

You all know how you have helped, and I want you all to understand how grateful I am. Without true friends, supporters and contributors neither my book nor my new album would have happened:

Morag Livingstone
Chris Hayden
David Bradford
Niki Wibrow
Ryan Lee
Lynn Turley
Sandra Ford
Jenny Fortnam
Geraldine Coen
Michael Lamb
Loz Stokley
Connie Gurney
Sandra Colston
Toby Croney

Then there are the unsung heroes – and I know a few too many of you by name. If you are in the millions who picked up the phone and voted even just once, I, of course, thank you, especially if you have stayed the course since 2004.

Old friends Clive, Eric and Linda: I'm thinking of you.

'After 50,000 applicants and sixteen weeks of fierce competition, this is it. Only two acts remain – Steve and G4.'

'One of them is about to become the winner of *The X Factor*. The other leaves with nothing.'

'The public have been voting all night and I'm about to deliver their verdict. Good luck to you both. Can I ask the official adjudicator for the vote, please?'

Kate announced that it was now 8 million votes.

'OK, you ready?' she asked.

'The winner of *The X Factor* is…'

Then…nothing…twenty seconds of silence interspersed with a crowd holding their breath before bursting into a frenzy.

I looked skywards, closing my eyes. Louis was smiling, shaking his head. The G4 boys were all linked – their arms around each other's shoulders. Simon looked calmly into the distance, whilst Sharon was chatting to her vocal coach in the audience.

'Steve', she shouted…

4 June 2004

A plain white envelope sat on the floor. There was no obvious branding. If I had opened it on the day it arrived I wouldn't have been so surprised by what it said.

My dad, who had always been one of my biggest supporters, accompanying me on so many of my late nights, had seen an ad on the TV with Simon Cowell asking people to audition for his new show.

My girlfriend Eileen had also seen it and, as ever, been nothing but encouraging.

I wasn't so sure.

I had been here before in 1997 as runner-up on Jonathan Ross's *Big Big Talent Show* and little had come from that. I had been too old for *Pop Idol* when that aired in 2002, and I couldn't even get past the first audition stage of *Fame Academy* a year later.

All I really wanted was to make music and keep getting more and better gigs. Despite the best intentions of those closest to me, that was my only motivation for entering.

In fact, I was so blasé about the whole thing that I had totally forgotten about ringing up for it and requesting an audition.

I only opened the letter that morning because it didn't look like a bill.

I read it and laughed to myself. The letter had sat there for weeks and now I see I have just three days to prepare. I was an *X Factor* contestant.

Of course, over the years and through that first series, I have come to know many of the hopefuls hanging on such news, and subsequently witnessed some of the tricks TV plays to portray this life-changing moment.

But in 2004, with nobody really knowing what *X Factor* was going to be in relation to its predecessor, *Pop Idol,* we were still realistically at the dawn of this era.

I knew one thing only about the new show. Simon Cowell had to have a point of difference from *Idol,* and that seemed to be that age limits were lifted. There was, for the first time, a real chance for the Over 25s.

This *wasn't* a defining moment in my life as it would have been for so many others. I didn't even tell one of my closest friends, Livingstone Brown. He first knew when he saw me on TV and later when the audition stages went out, and at every point after that I just lied to him that I had left the competition in a bid to play down expectations. I couldn't hide it anymore obviously by the time the live shows came around.

My life *had* changed but not because of this moment. I had been badly burnt by a couple of record deals that just fell away due to changes in personnel at the labels.

When I passed 30, some five years back, I had given up on being a recording artist. I had become very realistic about being too old already to be a popstar. That ship had long since sailed.

The years of taking three buses to get to singing lessons, the lunch breaks sitting in my company car covered in crumbs eating a sandwich and doing my scales, the sending in of endless demos that I knew just went straight in an A&R man's bin were all part of life. Some things are meant to be and some things are not. I still had that dream but it was just that. The most important thing was to be happy and in a good relationship. I was hoping I had found that in my girlfriend Eileen.

So, when I arrived for my first audition, I was pretty

chilled. On the train to Wembley, I listened to Jaheim on my headphones. "Back Tight" was my song. It helped me get through the six months Eileen had been away working abroad. It made me feel everything is OK.

I arrived at Wembley to a long queue. I felt like I was standing outside the Odeon on opening night of *Return Of The Jedi*. 'Fuckin' hell!'

Luckily I had my headphones. All these people talking, laughing and singing like old friends. No thank you.

I recall seeing one guy in a football shirt and jeans, his leg in plaster, and thinking he had better be good when he started singing "I Believe I Can Fly" – 'Fuckin' hell'.

The only thing I could do was stay relaxed – and this helped – and just be professional with my warm-ups. After an hour or two queuing outside I was given a number, so I made for the stairwell and designated that my spot to wait for a call, keeping myself to myself.

By the time it came to face the music, I had already been there half a day. Some great singers and some not so great singers had inevitably come and gone – one in particular, Lloyd Wade stood out physically.

Big and black, he just said gospel, soul and R & B. I could tell he could sing. I just knew he had a voice. It was way too early to be thinking of Lloyd in terms of competition, but I did clock the fact that they were filming an interview with him. From even that moment, it seemed they had an idea of who was going to the judges' houses.

And then it was my turn.

My first audition was with Nigel Hall. I had no idea who he was or how important he would become, both for Simon's company Syco and as a global player with their American shows. I still look back at that first audition and meeting with great fondness.

I remained calm. Not too calm, but quietly confident. I

had long accepted being judged was subjective and was not the reality.

What happened next has replayed in my mind so many times over the years, and to this day I am probably the only applicant to have done this.

I was so unfazed by the process that when Nigel asked me what I was going to sing, I handed him five folded-up pieces of paper with song titles hidden inside.

'You pick,' I told him.

Nigel seemed intrigued by this introduction. He smiled which made me feel even more at ease. He opened a piece of paper and read out "Part Time Love".

I love Gladys Knight. This was good.

Before I began I quickly warmed up with a line: "I've been so many places in my life and time…"

'What's that? I love that song,' he said, still smiling.

I had sung Donny Hathaway's "A Song For You" for some clean-shaven young man at *Fame Academy* and either he didn't get it or just thought 'Get lost, grandad' so when Nigel interrupted me I was relieved he had.

I delivered a verse and chorus and was through. Simple. He handed me a red letter. This was a badge of honour. I had seen a few people running out waving their red letters throughout the day. People crying didn't have one. I had worked out on my own what it meant. So I held it proudly and left the room.

2:30 pm on 17 June would be my next audition.

It wasn't me at all to sit at home for the next ten days waiting and wondering what might be, but I had to consider it. I had an autumn full of dates including many couples' big days – weddings. I had to warn people that I might have to cancel. I never cancel.

I knew I was one of many whom they had said yes to at this point, and that is as carried away as I could allow myself to be.

For the moment, I had bigger fish to fry.

By the time I performed my next gig at Wentworth Golf Club in one of those long-standing bookings, word was out that I had entered the show. They didn't know I was going to be on the telly in the autumn, but everyone was telling me I had the voice to win it. In time, my fee might go up, but that was for later. I was so far away from any notion of winning that I dismissed it from my mind.

There was something in me as a professional which would always honour a function to the level that we had agreed at the booking. That wasn't changing overnight.

Nor was I a musical snob – live TV or a social club in the back of beyond – it didn't matter. I loved singing and performing, and it was the best way I knew to make a living. Once you've worked in the video shop, or as a gardener, an intern at a graphic designers or even selling houses, this was what it was all about. I adored what I did.

By the time of the second audition, I was much more concerned with my schedule than the show.

After an open mic night in London, I had been approached by a booker called Alan Shepherd who had heard me sing a Teddy Pendergrass track.

'Would you like to support Dionne Warwick at the Fairfield Halls in Croydon at the end of July?' he asked.

This is why, amongst thousands of people entering, and despite impressing Nigel Hall, I genuinely, at that point, did have better irons in the fire.

In the rare moments when I had relived my first audition in my head, it still came down to a couple of things. TV exposure meant better gigs but the odds of winning were huge and to make the live shows was almost as unlikely.

So, at that point Dionne Warwick, an artist I had always admired, was both exciting and definitely happening.

That was what kept me going.

But soon 17 June arrived and I was back at Wembley. Again

I kept my own company, the odd conversation, hanging around aplenty, and really only speaking to the runners on the show.

Once in the audition, Nigel Hall was there again but on this occasion he had been joined by two more people who I expect were also producers. The red letter had said if I made it through this audition I would face the judges Sharon Osbourne, Louis Walsh or Simon Cowell. I knew how close I could be.

From a practical point of view, there were simply too many people to go through and they were still whittling down numbers at high speed. It was clear you would only get to sing at the top table if you were really good…or really crap.

The second audition was as straightforward as the first. I was asked to sing "A Song For You" again, and seeing how Nigel enjoyed it before I thought I had a good chance. This was turning into an eventful month. The biggest gig of my life, supporting Dionne Warwick, was just around the corner and now I'm just hours away from meeting *The X Factor* judges.

***

'Hello, smiley,' Sharon purred at me.

At this point I was simply number 7688.

'This is surreal,' I laughed back at them. I had walked through a door into a room filled with cameras, production team, a table and three very famous people smiling at me.

I remember again feeling uncomfortable at being so exposed. This was totally different to the previous two dimly lit auditions. Now it was bright and colourful. X marked the spot and all of sudden I was having an out-of-body experience. I had an audience but no mic, no mic stand and no PA. I had no nerves at performing but suddenly I was all too well aware that this was a TV show.

In the edit, I had gone from being just another number to acquiring a narrative which began there and never ever left me since.

After singing on camera for Kate Thornton, the presenter in the opening series, the voice-over (added later) plays the pub singer card for the first time. It also underlines my age, and with that comes immediately the message that my career is in the last chance saloon.

Here was a show, whose point of difference was extending the age category, and yet they were now positioning me in the make-or-break phase as an artist because of that very age. And yet, how last chance saloon could I be? I had just landed a support slot for Dionne Warwick.

Besides, I liked playing in pubs!

Though only through the passage of time can I *understand* the true juxtaposition of trying to win a singing competition against the needs to make a compelling TV show, I *was* brutally aware of it from the off.

This was where the fun – and games – truly started.

'I liked the voice …not sure about the whole package.' Louis put image on the table.

'You've a defeatist attitude before you've begun,' Sharon piled in.

'I wouldn't want you in my group,' Louis closed the door shut on me.

Deep down, I was grateful because as vast as his expertise in the biz was, I couldn't see myself sitting on a stool next to three or four guys murdering a classic song.

But that does not explain where all this tone came from. I sang well, but they slaughtered me on everything that was irrelevant. It sent me recoiling into that defeatist attitude of which I had shown no real signs! They told me I was something just for the cameras. The result was that I acquired those traits.

'Yay or nay? I am 35, aren't I? I drink too much beer.' I knew I was 35, I knew I was past the age of being a popstar. I thought this was about singing.

Simon wanted me through, telling me that not many had a voice like me, but then dropped the bombshell.

'I gotta tell you. You blew it on the interview.'

I had been here before in life and I knew not to take that personally. My arms were folded and I listened, rubbing my chin. 'Oh well, thanks' was all I could offer back.

I had been right all along to not get excited about something that might not happen. The game was up. I would continue to gig and if they didn't want to work with me, so be it. Other people did. It was just their opinion and they were trying to make a TV show. It was over.

I left the room and the cameras were still rolling as Kate consoled me, agreeing that it shouldn't be about the interview. Her remark was genuine, and *not* for the cameras as she couldn't have known what I would say when I walked out of the room.

Back inside, Louis was slating me, suggesting that if we were on tour I would be an hour late for the bus. In that split second or two, he made an instant judgement on me that time would show never left him.

As I was talking to Kate by the door a researcher came up to me. I thought he wanted me to move along so the next dummy could get mugged off. I was a little confused and didn't know what was happening. Then Kate told me they wanted me back in the room and Simon expressed Louis's viewpoint to my face. I couldn't believe it. In fact, it became a line in the sand. "Hello, Smiley" acquired attitude.

I had been very laid-back about the whole thing, but when that accusation came from nowhere, if they wanted to provoke me they did.

'I don't think you care enough,' Louis levelled at me.

"You don't know me," I said. I wasn't smiling.

'Stay out of the pub, pisshead,' Sharon taunted as Simon asked me to come back tomorrow.

I hadn't seen any of this coming.

I didn't get it. I had queued for hours for two days, travelled to Wembley and was still gigging full-time at the age of 35. I didn't need to prove I could sing. I had done that in 1997. I really felt like they were messing me about. Nigel managed to work out I was talented, but these three numpties were wondering what my timekeeping was like. It was crazy. I couldn't work out what they were playing at. Was I really going to travel back to Wembley for a third time to be told 'no' again?

I doubt it.

***

'Tell us about the last 24 hours,' Simon began.

It was a good question because unlike the previous two auditions with Nigel Hall where I had done my bit and gone, I was stewing overnight.

'I was a little put back by some of the comments,' I held back.

He laughed, asked me which one and then dismissed it.

Maybe it was all part of the game. It was time to sing again.

I went safe in my song choice with one from the list I had given Nigel. "Part Time Love" by Gladys Knight would finally let my voice do the talking.

Or so I thought.

'Wrong choice of song.'

In my head I'm thinking: *'What are you on about? It's amazing.'*

Simon, who had seemed the most supportive 24 hours previously, didn't like it.

'You're going to need a lot of work.'

Again he was laughing, but this time Sharon leapt to my defence.

'You guys are giving him such a hard time.'

They kept on and asked me if I had any other songs. I told

them I even enjoyed big band, then gave them a burst of "Fly Me To The Moon". I resented the accusations about my desire and ability.

It was like dealing with split personalities – each of them unrecognisable from the day before as they rushed to put me through without a moment's conference.

What had it all been about? My belief today is that they were always putting me through. They were just setting a tone and didn't count on how far I would go.

The irony was never greater. I had entered a singing competition and was now through to the next stage. This meant I had to give up singing.

Though I was through to boot camp, whatever that meant, my mind was firmly fixed on the Dionne Warwick gig. Performing to fifteen hundred people in a theatre was to be the biggest show of my life. I had decided to include a song that would go on to haunt me through *The X Factor:* "Dance With My Father."

I had so many people come up to me after the concert to say how much they enjoyed it. I knew I had to do it on the show.

Ms Warwick was kind enough to let Eileen and I visit her in her dressing room and we chatted for a moment. Compliments were exchanged but I was in awe. She wasn't a celeb or someone famous, she was a legend. It doesn't get better than that.

The next day Alan Shepherd called me.

'Great job, how do you fancy supporting Lionel Richie?'

I couldn't believe it. I had stood at the proverbial bus stop for years and here came two.

A one-off gig at Wembley supporting another hero of mine, or trying out for a talent show with a £1 million prize and TV exposure? They were the options.

When we rolled up to boot camp we signed our life away. In short, rules appeared and we were told to cancel all work for the autumn.

In the name of a TV show and a million-pound record contract that would require overcoming huge odds to win, I had to turn down supporting Lionel Richie.

It didn't seem right and both the show and I would have benefited from doing the gigs – except of course, that it would spoil the narrative of *The X Factor*. They couldn't be seen to turn a pub singer into a recording star if indeed that person was already supporting one of the biggest acts of all time.

In many ways, it was a totally illogical risk to proceed on my part. Once again it was guaranteed work, money and profile that could lead anywhere against that old dream of hitting the big time. It was like Bruce Willis in *Sin City*, an old guy falling for something that would ultimately end in tears. It's only that I won the competition in the end that would cloud anyone's viewpoint on the absurdity of staying on *The X Factor* at that point.

This suddenly made things serious. It had now become real. It's not that I was full of fear, but I had no work lined up now, and in our business you always need to work.

I had arrived early at The Landmark Hotel in London with my mum, Eileen and my friend Tony. They wanted to come along and I was pleased to have them there. Until I got the bill for cups of tea and my sandwich! Fifty quid! I'd cancelled all my work.

'I better bloody win this!' I said and we all laughed before saying our goodbyes.

I was sharing a room with a complete stranger, a potential competitor, and we were both in foreign surroundings. I will never forget the moment all my confidence drained away from me in an instant. I was unpacking my clothes and my room-mate John Cabey was warming up. For me, his voice was faultless. He sounded like Will Downing.

In the many hours of waiting around for the production team I also befriended a very attractive older lady who sat quietly on her own. Her name was Verity. I was 35 and felt too old. She was 50.

She was nervous, shy and surprised to be there. We had both been around too long to be taken in totally by the nonsense, though. It was inevitable that everyone would get dragged in at some point. There seemed a lot of bravado in the room. I would try and lighten the mood by going into "The Flintstones" theme like John Candy did in *Planes, Trains and Automobiles*, but only to polite laughter.

Verity and I chatted without pretence or any airs and graces, and I can say meeting her was one of the better things to come out of the show. She had a lovely voice but I just couldn't see where she would fit into the competition. Even though *The X Factor* was a supposedly *new* show with unique parameters, you would have been a fool to believe that ultimately anything would be different, and that meant the 'Overs' category was flawed from the outset because this was an industry driven by image.

Louis Walsh's words at my audition regarding the whole package had served as a gentle reminder.

So the plan was that all the guys would sit in rows of chairs behind Simon and watch the women perform one by one and then it was our turn.

Out stepped this woman with big hair dressed in black. I had no idea Rowetta was from the Happy Mondays.

I wasn't a fan and to be fair to her I can't remember her going on about it either. She did, however, share stories of 'bottom rape' and abusive relationships before we had even heard her sing. Her boot camp performance was edited big time. It was the craziest thing I had ever seen. Talk about blow it on the interview. That's when things started getting all a bit bizarre.

From a professional point of view, I was well aware there were some great singers in the show. I had upped my game slightly to be more aware that this *was* an opportunity, if *not* the last chance saloon, but because of previous experiences, I was a long way away from dreaming.

I knew little about the other categories, but The Overs did seem thin on the ground. I really rated Maria Lawson, Wayne Fernandez, and one of my favourites was a guy Simon had said was 'nearly as good as R. Kelly'. That was Odis Palmer, a cool-looking, guitar-wielding black guy with a good voice. He looked a cert for the live finals. I wasn't so sure about 50-year-old Linda in her wheelchair and 81-year-old Irene who could just about walk up the stairs onto the stage, but this was the cast they had assembled.

They must have had some sort of storyboarding in their head at this point – history has now shown that *The X Factor* divides itself into those who can genuinely win and those who have no chance, scattered with the sob stories and the loose cannons. We just weren't aware of it in 2004, though the signs were there.

Whilst waiting to perform before Simon, mentor for the Overs, there was yet more hanging around than singing. At auditions this was just part of the practicality of so many people wanting to be seen; at boot camp there was more to it.

We were regularly in position when judges weren't. Often we were sitting around in anticipation but doing nothing. With the central heating cranked up to the max in the summer, the silence of inactivity in a stifling environment created a tension that could only lead to TV gold.

It's easy with hindsight to say that so much of these shows are about the footage and not the performance, but you do not think that when most are waiting on their one shot at fame. You can't see that the silence works for the edit, or that the heat and lack of food and water are a device to exude pressure. Or, in my case, me seemingly showing off to loosen up the place would make me look a jerk when it aired.

I stuck to what I knew, choosing Michael McDonald's "That's Why".

For the first time, I was nervous. I knew the song inside out, but the auditions had served notice on me – my self-doubt was at the judging rather than the performance. Obviously, I knew we were being filmed and – worse – edited, but I didn't want to become part of that process. My confidence had been good. I knew I could hold my own. I couldn't anticipate wild card behaviour from Simon, and I was well aware things could go wrong… and they did.

I made a mistake. I don't sing a cappella much and I started in a slightly higher key. I felt I messed up. I had proven before and since that I could handle the cameras but it was the waiting, the stop-start nature of the filming, and the room full of female contestants and a front row consisting of Simon, Sinitta and vocal coach Annie Skates that unnerved me momentarily.

Now all the girls had heard the boys, and the boys had heard the girls. We had to wait and see who made it to Day Two. All day waiting for a one-minute performance. The tension was infectious. People crying or getting angry put a cloud over the room.

John Cabey came up to me. 'I'm going home.'

It didn't register. Was he quitting?

His eyes were filling: he was gutted and I was shocked. For me, the best singer I had heard on the show was out. I didn't know what to say. I didn't feel good about this at all. It just devalued the competition. I can only imagine the long walk to our room to pack up again and leave before even staying the night. It left me hollow – and it wasn't even me.

Once the cull had taken place the remaining contestants had to team up and learn two songs. In the real world professionals would never be expected to learn two new tracks for a TV performance the very next day. But this wasn't the real world. The panic set it in. The following morning, we were all doing duets. Everyone urgently looked around for someone they thought would either make them look good or not ruin their chances. I noticed Lloyd and he looked at me. We both nodded and that was it. We quickly agreed on two songs from the list and went straight to work. Verity didn't look happy. She was stuck with Linda in her wheelchair.

Lloyd was brilliant that night. We practised until the early hours. He was on his A game. Working out his harmonies, he knew the songs well and I thought we sounded great together. Regardless of who went through I was going to enjoy this.

With John gone I had a new room-mate. I can't remember his name but he had been out and I don't think he had practised much that night. He had a few drinks and kept me awake. I didn't complain. I just couldn't sleep. That night I slept from 5 am until 7 am. That was all. I didn't think it was fair that we shared rooms, especially with a stranger who will keep you up all night.

In complete contrast to when I got the trains in for the auditions, I had become sucked in. I was conscious as much with letting friends and family down and embarrassing myself as with the idea of winning. Simply, I didn't want to look silly.

I spent the night with "Ain't No Mountain High Enough" and "Somewhere over the Rainbow" playing in my head on repeat, and some half-cut bloke moaning that he didn't know his songs. Two hours' kip. This was going to be a tough day.

I woke up with my head throbbing. I decided to take Paracetamol. I had never reacted like this. Gigging was what I did. This was different. It's one thing to finger the TV show and say that they caused this through whatever techniques they may or may not have applied, but if you feel it, it is real and remember I had been here before where others hadn't. I was drained like never before. Tension and dehydration were not the ideal combination to prepare for something so important.

I met up with Lloyd and we got straight back to work

running the songs over and over. We would go to the loo regularly to practise and then back to the room to do it all again. Other contestants seemed to like what we had done with the tracks. Poor Verity was in tears. She said that Linda was difficult to work with and she thought she was going home.

By lunch, Lloyd and I had done our songs together and I must say, we did well. I was knackered but we pulled it off.

Lloyd was fantastic both as a singer and as a person, but why singing as a pair would help them decide either of us was a credible recording artist was beyond me, but it gave the show that element of competition. It enables the edit to portray two people bonding, only one of whom goes through. The same song that you perform with a partner can mean victory for one and defeat for another, yet you both contribute to the moment. It truly was set up to be a divisive device. We were lucky. We practised hard and our partnership worked. Others weren't so fortunate.

The whittling down was constant, but I went through again. That just left our solo performances for the early evening before the big reveal. True to form, there was a lot more hanging around before we knew our fate.

Any signs of the supposed me who didn't really care and wouldn't make the tour bus were long gone as we were finally asked to line up onstage at the end of the day to see who was staying on. It was cruel. Nowadays we accept it. Then, we knew no better.

Over the day I had seen others breaking, and the intensity of the situation had left me exhausted. We were all well and truly spent. My time had come and I was called in to sing my solo for Simon. I pulled it together with my song at the ready.

It was my favourite track from my favourite artist. It had to be "Dance With My Father" by Luther Vandross. I knew this song better than anyone except the man himself, and if I still needed to prove myself to Simon, this would do it.

Up to this point, he had been nothing but warm to me. The early signs of trouble had come from Sharon and Louis at the audition. He surely knew by now whom he was putting through.

'Thanks very much,' Simon held up his hand to me.

I was stopped dead in my tracks.

I was barely a verse and a chorus in. He had cut me in my prime. It's the worst of all moments. You can do neither yourself nor the track justice if you only deliver half a chorus.

I was devastated, assuming the worst, and when I left the room they wanted to interview me. All I could think about was I didn't like the pianist playing the song. Maybe that put me off. I was doubting what I had done. The whole long experience had come to this moment. I had no more singing to do and I was finished emotionally.

And this is how TV works its magic. You're singing for ninety seconds to secure the deal to die for, and you're cut short. Already tired and ill, you then have cameras and microphones shoved in your drained face. Even for the coolest of customers, it's nothing but stress, and that's what the TV show wants.

And the narrative began.

'It must mean a lot?' they started.

They would ask that question a thousand times and more to not just me, but everyone over the next few days, weeks and years. All that matters is that pain showed on your face and that you give them the soundbite that captured the dreams of those in the show now and wanting to apply next time around. The question had one purpose – to illustrate desperation and power. How badly you wanted it and how much power they had to make it happen. That was all that mattered.

I was visibly upset. I didn't want that camera near me.

I actually tried to run away from Kate. Of course, they followed. I ran to the bathroom, locked myself in a cubicle and sobbed. I don't even know why.

True to form, there was even more waiting before we knew our fate. I had time to compose myself. The ten final singers were called to line up.

Silence filled the room. Not a soul moved. We just stood there. This was it...again.

The atmosphere that had been created over the last 48 hours and the power that Simon had rather than anything tangible had emptied each and every one of us into a state of bewilderment. You can't stress over something you never had, but the process that took you there can create that emotion.

And we were all in the same boat.

'Can I ask the following to step forward,' Simon began.

The tank was empty. The tension had melted away with the afternoon tears and I just wanted to go home.

'Jermaine, Maria, Wayne, Casita, Angie,' he continued.

'You have no idea how difficult this was.'

When I saw Wayne and Maria step forward I had resigned myself to going home.

Simon applied the *now* tired narrative.

'Verity, Lloyd, Steve, Rowetta, Odis…on the back five.'

His voice hung in the air.

Nobody moved. No one jumped for joy. There were no squeals of excitement.

'It's you five, congratulations.'

We were stunned into an exhausted silence – winners and losers alike. It was as though someone pressed 'Pause' on our story.

Then, in delay, we looked at each other, almost mouthing 'We're going through?'

I didn't hear Simon say another word. We were left to shake hands with those who hadn't made it. Hands became hugs. I just wanted to go home. Maybe I didn't want it enough.

We were through to judges' houses. Another step closer to the live shows, but the drama and the process had made me question everything. Years of quiet confidence and knowing exactly what I was doing and making a decent name for myself suddenly brought on self-doubt and vulnerability which I hadn't seen since my early teens. And yet, I was through. I had made it – to a degree.

So when Kate Thornton accosted me outside for the cameras, I said nothing of any consequence.

'Yeah, really good' was about as much as I could manage.

Yet even this moment of supposed celebration or relief was, of course, stage-managed for the TV. In any normal circumstance you would want to take a moment out and call a loved one, but we were held in a room and Kate was to one side. At the moment of the greatest tension all of us had ever experienced, the making of the programme came first. But I didn't care. Hugging Kate was bliss. Boot camp was over.

I went to my room, collected my things and took a couple more painkillers.

I said my goodbyes to Verity, Rowetta, Lloyd and Odis. We knew it was major to get this far. I recognised that despite my almost disinterest when Dad told me about the show, things had gone up a notch. TV exposure was guaranteed and I was one step from the live shows. I was starting to believe I may have made the right decision about choosing *The X Factor* ahead of Lionel Richie. I had arrived at The Landmark by tube and was going home in a cab.

When I got home my headache had got worse. I had never felt pain like it before or since. Eileen and my mum were waiting, ready with their questions. I just couldn't talk about the day. I took another painkiller. But my headache just got worse. I swear I thought I was going to die. I became delirious. I don't want to make a big thing about them calling an ambulance, and it turned out I had taken too many Paracetamols and was dehydrated.

It was at best a wake-up call for the pressure that lay ahead.

Much of the debate over the last decade has been about exploitation of people on talent shows – none of it is really about the mental health issues that manifest themselves because of the process of making the programme. I was definitely feeling it, and I was considerably more experienced than almost anyone there except Rowetta, and she certainly had her moments. I needed to make sure my head was clear before judges' houses.

I cycled a lot and prepared myself mentally for the next stage. I reminded myself not to get sucked in. This is not reality.

From 50,000, I was now in the final fifteen acts and, even though I suppose I had a chance of winning, my feet were firmly on the ground. The message to contestants that winning was everything was far from subliminal but constant. I thought back to that *Big Big Talent Show*.

I had come second and I thought it should have led to something but, within hours of the final being broadcast, Princess Diana died in a car crash in Paris, which meant that the media was dominated for the next three weeks with her death and the funeral. There was simply no place for stories about any TV show winner. Nobody was interested and the tone wouldn't have been right. Over the years, I had never felt that coming second was the reason I didn't get success from the show. I just blamed circumstance.

At no point did I buy into *The X Factor* narrative that winning was everything. My motivation remained not to embarrass myself, not to let down my folks, and to get something out of this. Winning still felt a long way off.

I had first met Eileen in a coffee shop in Wimbledon. She walked in, bought a coffee, then scanned the room for somewhere to sit. I didn't disguise my interest and she has since told me that she noticed I had clocked her. I watched her take a seat and pull out some sheet music. I knew I had to speak to her. If you want something you have to go for it. I walked over and asked if I could sit down. She said 'No.' I sat down anyway. Today, people may consider it harassment, but I was old school. I kept it brief, made my point, and gave her my number. I'm in music, you're in music, let's make music! I wish I had thought of that line at the time. You can almost smell the Old Spice. Anyway, I was on fire. I returned to my seat an inch taller.

We became friends and began working together. Both of us were nervous about starting something. She had just broken up from a long relationship, and I didn't want to make yet another mistake. For some time we were in that status of not being officially an item. Eileen then got an opportunity to perform on a cruise for six months and so I told her to go – she didn't owe me anything. If she had gone and met someone, so be it. If she came back and we were what we both wanted then we would know it was for real. Once she left, I felt an idiot. I could so easily have lost her.

It wasn't the ideal start to our relationship. Two people in their thirties, both musicians and both independent, but what worked for us is that we both supported each other. I had, and still have, huge respect for Eileen as an artist. She would walk into an *X Factor* final. A real class act and a wonderful person.

We joked together about me winning, but outside the show we could see what it truly was in the context of us. It was something that would help us get to where we wanted to go. We recalled a day we sat in that very coffee shop where we had met and Eileen had remarked 'One of us better do something big!' It appeared that this might be it. I was now at judges' houses.

Simon asked me again.

'Do you want it?'

When I was sitting with him in his garden, he must have asked me a dozen times: 'Do you think you can win this?' He told me to say 'I can win this', but I couldn't say those words.

I don't know if it was personal or just the desired narrative. Simon was saying I didn't want it badly enough. How do you respond to that? They knew I had done a talent show in 1997 and here I was again in 2004. I wanted it, but not to the point that it would consume me. I was 35 and single. I wanted a wife and children more. I had been down this road too many times to know things can go wrong, and even when they go right they don't last. It was a good mindset to not want it too much.

The cameras still rolled of course, and runners and producers dominated, but at least it was somebody's home – though seemingly barely lived in – and there was no shunting around from room to room. There was still a huge amount of waiting but the atmosphere was different. We felt special. Food and drink were easily available. It was a lovely sunny day and a million miles from the pressure of boot camp. The maths were better, too. From an equation of thousands down to 100 now to single figures, five had to go into three and whilst I genuinely felt that the three guys should progress, I sensed that this was not the TV show they were making. They wouldn't want three blokes all taking votes from each other – that would lead to mediocrity and no clear leader week on week. From the moment I met Verity she said she was going home, and yet she was still there. For me, Rowetta blew it in her crazy audition at boot camp and she was also still there. I had no idea what the final three were really going to be.

In many ways this part of the show was easier. I am sure they had their strategy at this point and were well ahead of those of us living the drama.

Yet still, Simon played the game with me one last time before telling me I had made the live finals. He was making me want it. I *had* made it.

Seven years after *The Big Big Talent Show* I was back on ITV doing… a talent show. So bizarre. I never saw that coming.

Everyone else was excited for me. Ben Shephard and Kate

Thornton were so lovely. The production team, the producers, everyone. Except Simon. I don't actually remember talking to him much after the cameras had stopped filming. He was obviously pleased it was a great exchange. I can only imagine he had to get ready for his next scene.

They drove me 'home' to my sister's house – my girlfriend and my parents were there. I had not long sold my house after yet another disastrous relationship, and my parents weren't keen on their house being used for filming. My sister had a lovely home in Reigate and she was happy to use that as the show home. Hey, it's TV!

I didn't necessarily want to share this private moment with a crew but they needed to get their shots. It was no surprise when I was encouraged to stop for a quick one at the pub with Ben Shephard whilst they got my parents ready for my arrival. It was never going to be the spontaneous piece you would see on TV.

I was so excited and I was in a pub. A great combo.

I sat with Ben and we chatted. He was such a nice guy who plays hard and works hard. Totally focussed. I admire how he conducted himself over the years. It was a special moment for me. We drank up and left.

When I walked in the house I was told where my family were and we went to the kitchen while everyone was getting ready to roll. I had just knocked back a pint and was feeling happy. Not drunk, just good. I joked with Ben as to how I was going to break the news. I could tell this was as much fun for the production team as it was for me. Everywhere I looked there were smiles.

The stage was set. I stood in the hall with my family in the living room. The room was eerily silent and I walked in. Nobody walks into a house full of people to find it silent! I was trying not to grin. I told Ben that I was going to pretend that I was sad, but I couldn't hold back the smile so I covered my mouth.

'Well? Well?' Mum broke the silence.

I nodded and my eyes suddenly filled. I felt like crying.

Then the house erupted. The excitement was all theirs. It *was* a great moment, part of a fantastic day, but the moment was for them. Seeing my family's overwhelming happiness was my joy. This was what it was all about to me. My parents were proud. My sister Tanya and my brother-in-law Robert were ecstatic, and Eileen was Eileen. Softly reserved, not giving too much away. A knowing smile and a kiss that said 'Well done'.

I am sure Mum and Dad were dreaming of what might happen when I was trying to take each moment as it came. My focus was purely on doing my best to make them proud and not making a fool of myself. I can only imagine the heartache some people must feel having to share bad news of not making it through. That irrational fear of letting your family down wasn't mine that day.

The crew got what they wanted and stayed for a quick cuppa. We offered them a drink but they had editing to do. I didn't feel this was manipulated. It was genuinely nice.

My sister was the perfect host and the night became a true family gathering. With the champagne open, I could finally unwind. We sat and chatted until the early hours about what I had gone through and what was to come.

We had no idea.

23 October 2004

In 2004, the live shows meant two outings on a Saturday night. There was no Sunday evening second chance. It was all or nothing.

As the first pressure cooker moment approached, I knew I was about to give almost nothing rather than my all. I'd been struck down with laryngitis. It was the worst possible way to make a first impression. My fear was also that Louis and Sharon might try to use it against me, even though I was obviously unwell.

Building up to the show, I was unbelievably tense. We had already started to do many interviews and I was doing more talking than singing.

Talking voice is different to singing. I may be able to sing for hours but talking can be more difficult.

Behind the scenes the game unravelled. We were coached in giving soundbites so the media became the dog with a bone, and Rowetta simply revelled in it.

Verity and I rolled our eyes as she declared she would like to snog the young Irish rocker, Tabby. The press ran the story en masse and, in so doing, she had made it instantly competitive. That was how it worked. There was no word back from Tabby as to the level of his reluctance to engage!

But it was also the judges who were stirring it up. On the day before the show, the *Mirror* ran this story:

"*X Factor* judges Sharon Osbourne and Simon Cowell aren't speaking to each other after she accused him of rigging the show."

"He's a f***ing w***er," she was reported as saying. "I'm not going to leave because I work for ITV and not him. But he's pissed me off. He's rigged it all."

"She thinks I have an unfair advantage but it's tosh," said Cowell. "People are simply more interested in the older contestants. She is desperate to win. It's OTT and ludicrous."

It sowed the seeds of what was to come later.

Media as much as performance dominated before we went live. It *did* feel different to 1997. Back then, you could have come second to a ventriloquist or God knows what. At least here, if you left the competition, there was a level playing field. It was singer versus singer. I just didn't want to be first to go.

Inevitably, I compared the two shows in my head, and yet, even though I had done so well before the reality TV explosion, it was always the incidental detail that I remembered.

Jonathan Ross had made a joke that night about Dodi Fayed. By 3 am as I went to bed, my dad was already waking me up to say Princess Diana and Dodi had died, and like all of us it went from a dent in her car to being the biggest news story of the century.

On the night I had missed out on a Royal performance which was part of the prize, but that didn't matter in the context of her death. Either way, the public wouldn't have had the appetite. For me, circumstance had intervened.

I also could never lose sight of Ross grabbing my girlfriend Katie Jackson's breasts in a photo. I knew I was once again back in a different world where the rules of fame and TV overrode those of the real world of the people watching.

In the run-up this time, Simon had been nothing but onside. And yet, I was thinking of pulling out through illness. My chest voice had gone. I had nothing but falsetto left. Suddenly the week had merged into Saturday, and a now familiar routine had begun where I would go down to Simon's dressing room with my outfits and he would say yes or no.

From a long way out, they began to build my image from the guy who turned up looking so casual at the auditions. I didn't consider it too much at first, as even my soul idols would suit up, but I don't think that was their driving motivation.

I was on fifth after Voices With Soul, Verity, Roberta Howett, and 2 to Go. I really fancied VWS to do well and loved Peter's voice from 2 to Go. I still look back and think the standard of singers was good. Maybe not the best, but nobody was rubbish. It was an interesting line-up for a TV talent show.

Everybody was already aware, though, of the power of going last – and that was Tabby Callaghan tonight – and equally the risk at going first. Voices With Soul had opened the show.

Following 2 to Go became a legendary moment. People will remember the name but forget that, of the two, Peter was blind. I couldn't imagine that a blind person then was going to win a Simon Cowell show, but when he shouted aloud on air 'Just shut up' after Simon labelled their rendition of "I Don't Know Much" as 'Disney', he achieved kudos from the off. It became a theme backstage and a running joke off the air. On small things, fragile camaraderie was built.

I was nervous. I found the stage set exciting in that it reminded me of *The Big Big Talent Show,* but intimidating, too. For the first series it was built in the shape of an X. Worse, though – the audience were on either side of you, literally breathing down your neck.

Add to that, the narrative of the show simply didn't help.

'I am not making excuses. This morning Steve couldn't sing a note,' Simon introduced me honestly.

It really did me no favours. His words were met with laughter and mockery.

But then the VT (videotape) set the tone.

'It's personal now between Louis and Steve,' Simon announced.

I hadn't actually said that it was. This was the other element of the show – the war of the judges.

I had felt goaded into saying earlier in the week that Louis didn't have a clue. Simon backed it up by saying that Louis didn't know about talent. There is a massive difference between the two comments. Louis had been judging me as a person wrongly. Yes, he didn't have a clue about me, but this became 'he didn't have a clue about music' and foolishly I went along with it. The reality is that Simon regularly worked with Louis, so you can see that his comments were purely panto.

And of course, after I had delivered a half-decent version of Percy Sledge's beautiful "When A Man Loves A Woman" Louis couldn't hold back.

'I've had 28 number ones. He hasn't had any.' He was full-on, and so it began.

'27,' Kate interrupted.

'28 next week,' he bit back, referring to Girls Aloud's Children in Need song.

He adopted this stance there and then, and from this point on it would never leave him. His established acts outside of the competition had a new platform.

You could look back and laugh at it, but actually it was disgraceful product placement.

Then he made it personal again.

'You remind me of a cab driver who does cabaret at the weekend.'

That we have all heard comments like this in the years since tells you there is a definitive language to the show, or that the judges have a limited vocabulary.

'I don't think you're a star,' he condemned me.

Then Sharon piled in.

'When you sing about when a man loves a woman, you just grin. You just grin at everything. I could slag you and you just keep on grinning.'

In that series, your mentor stood next to you as you faced the music and, to Simon's credit, when Louis and Sharon were bitching, he defended me. But that was part of the game.

'If this is what he's like at 50%, what's he going to be like at 100%?'

The audience cheered. I sensed they were on our side.

Then he rounded on Louis.

'If you haven't got anything to say, then just shut up.'

I have come to believe since that they later removed this element of the show because it left a lasting image on YouTube etc of the mentor side-by-side with his act, and history has shown that the mentors don't stand by their acts for very long.

I felt supported by Simon but I knew that those two would have a drink after the show and it was all theatre. I was already feeling the heat personally because I was just that – a person, not a guinea pig in their made-for-TV catfight.

Thankfully, I had done enough for the public and it came down to a head-to-head between Roberta and, unbelievably, Voices With Soul.

Roberta was gone before she even had a chance to survive. She really suffered for being given a Carpenters track by Sharon, and that made her departure inevitable. I was just glad it was over for the week, and for me the competition began proper as soon as my voice cleared. I hadn't even seriously entered the fray at this point.

30 October 2004

If this was a competition in which you gained momentum, I hadn't even got out of the starting blocks. It began for real on my second show.

I was due on seventh, which was the last but one performance. I had a lot of time to stew and I watched Cassie Compton deliver a brilliant version of "Alfie" which blew me away only for Simon to dismiss it as a crap song. Ridiculous.

That annoyed me greatly. I had watched her perform it in rehearsals: I thought it was the song and performance of the night. I couldn't know at that point if he really believed it or if it was just part of the judges' war. I felt he was wrong and that left me in a bad position. I began to question my mentor. His business sense was not in doubt, but did he really feel any connection? If he thought this song choice was so misguided, what would this mean for me further down the line?

I just didn't agree with him. I was left unsure if he would make the right calls on me. To emphasise the point, I knew she could win the competition and I believed that they could've shaped her into a winner if she was falling short of votes.

Now, physically better, my mind was sharpening up to what was at stake and the lengths anyone could go to in pursuit of that goal.

I had felt that in a photo shoot in the week up to the live show, too. Tabby, the four-piece poperatic act, G4 and myself were definitely given preferential treatment in front of the lens. It was considerably less for 2 to Go, Rowetta, Verity, and VWS.

On one occasion it made me incredibly uncomfortable. I wasn't aware who the shoot was for: I rarely was. I would just turn up and was put in some new clothes and stood where they told me to stand. It seemed pretty harmless; the clothes seemed OK. What could go wrong? My manager Tim Byrne would oversee things with a female member of the production team. As the session drew to a close they suggested a few open-shirt shots. I immediately said no. Looking back I can see how stupid I was. They started badgering me to open my shirt and sprayed me with water. It was all light-hearted and, although I knew I didn't want to do it, I didn't want to appear hard work. So I let them take a couple of shots. Click, click, click and they were done.

It's funny, when you are in a room with just a few people you need to remember that the photographer is holding a lens that millions of people are looking through. I had forgotten.

On the Saturday I walked into the canteen at Fountain Studios and the other contestants were sitting there with a copy of *The Sun*. I was horrified to see a large picture of me like some aging Page Seven Fella. I was totally mortified. I couldn't believe I had been so stupid. This was selling sex not music. I never considered myself a popstar and I definitely didn't consider myself a sex symbol. I could tell that the other contestants thought I was doing anything to win but it was nothing of the sort.

As the night evolved, nervous, frail Verity finally saw her journey (sorry) end. Simon had supported her 110% (sorry, again) and took her further than she thought possible. If it had been left to our mentor, 2 to Go would have been on their way, but his vote was made redundant. This immediately struck me as something that was wrong with the show. Judges would let better acts go out if they were not mentoring them.

I started to feel concerned, too, for Voices With Soul. Essentially they had Hildia who was a great lead vocalist and then Corene and Grace as backing singers. Unfortunately, they all came out equally in the mix when the backing vocals should have been lower. I felt it wasn't good. If I were Louis, I would have said something.

Now able to relax a little more post-laryngitis, I found moments like this exhilarating, watching and understanding it at the same time. I was in the show but absorbing it from the outside, too.

I had performed "If You Don't Know Me By Now". I knew the song well, loved it and it was a popular choice with the whole team. (Later it even made my debut album.)

Simon said as much in the footage after, telling me to forget about Sharon and Louis, though I couldn't be sure if he was saying the opposite to them. For the moment, it didn't matter. I had delivered.

If I was under pressure or just felt it from the previous Saturday, that had passed. I had come to the party and reminded myself that, on form, I could really compete with any of them. Also, I absolutely loved the choir that backed me that night. That was certainly something I would like to revisit professionally.

But I was also on a TV show.

'Ladies, calm yourself,' Kate announced.

I wanted it to be about me and not about an image. I was laughing, though, because I could see my sister standing up at the front egging everyone on!

'Am I judging the choir or Steve?' Louis piped up.

Any act like mine would revel at some point in a gospel choir – and goodness, Louis has used many gimmicks over the years since – but I didn't see it as that. For me, that was a cheap shot.

I sang with a choir. We complemented each other. It was poor to imply that there were two acts at play and that my performance was anything more or less because of the backing vocals. It was clear that his words were just for the TV show.

'Simon is cheating.' Louis had the audacity to continue whilst looking innocent and hard-done-by on his face.

Then, of course, his own backing vocals piled in.

'Very nice voice, too Vegasy slick,' said Sharon.

This was a stupid comment because 'slick' actually means professional, and those acts who deliver almost every night of the year on cruise ships, pubs and in Nevada itself are often more on the money than some of the acts that people like this manage. They are slick because they have discipline, professionalism and talent. It was meant as an insult, but I also knew it was ignorance on their part.

I didn't expect the borderline racism that followed.

'You're not black. Why sing like a black person? You haven't got soul.'

Sharon's words told me she was clueless.

'An English Michael Bolton...' she continued.

Michael Bolton had been pretty successful, and nobody in the UK had really owned that marketplace since.

Then she went in for the kill. And it was personal.

'Every middle-aged woman would like to spend the night with you...' she said.

'Except me.'

And she was done.

Simon just smiled back.

The truth is I probably do have black blood in me. My dad's side are fairly dark. My aunt, who is only three years older than me, was called 'Paki' as we grew up. My family tree was certainly diverse. My grandfather was from St Helena, and it wouldn't surprise me if some of that Chinese slave trade had got mixed in.

I do not recall anyone else having this character assassination and, as I write this, there is no way Sharon would get away with it today. Yet, they would have known from the voting figures that I was winning hands down. That can only lead to two conclusions – that the judges were on order to be divisive or it was in their personalities to be so and that Louis and Sharon weren't acting up and what they said for the TV was what they really felt. At the end of the day, even if the production company suggests you say X, Y and Z, you can say those words but only you deliver the tone. There was no doubting the poison in the voice of these words.

Simon looked taken aback, too.

'I didn't think it was possible for Louis Walsh to outdo himself on banality,' he replied.

I was dying to dive in.

'I think he's a great singer,' Simon continued. 'It's obvious he needed a confidence boost after last week.'

The truth is I knew what I could do but I had to be well. But now, I bit back at Sharon, telling her I had listened to Al Green since the age of four – only to then end up apologising to her! It really was just an ugly shouting match, but it seemed reserved especially for me.

As we said goodbye to Verity, I could see the pain already in those leaving the competition. She had cancelled a lot of teaching work to do the show – she had even been written up in the press as though she had told her pupils to look for a new teacher. Simon was saying she was the new Olivia Newton-John! She had really overcome a natural shyness to perform and then, in an instant, it was over.

By now, the week began to take a routine shape. After the show Simon would call me to his dressing room and we would discuss next week's song.

The next morning, we would all meet at a theatre in London and work with the musical director Nigel Wright – we would get half-hour slots and work on the arrangement. The only problem was that, vocally, I was at my worst in the morning. I always have been. Choosing a key was awkward and I had to take a calculated punt.

On Monday and Tuesday I would practise and by Wednesday there would be a rough track laid down on CD and perhaps on a Thursday, I would go home from the communal digs.

Friday meant rehearsal and *The Xtra Factor Live* – the schedule was relentless. I would have perhaps one meeting a week with Simon. The rest of the time was spent making VTs. Generally that meant a lot of time for a small amount of footage that aired. That aside, wardrobe ate into the schedule.

And then it would be Saturday again.

6 November 2004

It was decided I would sing Charlie Chaplin's "Smile". I told Sinitta that, as Sharon had made such a big thing about my smile, it would be a fun choice.

By the time I watched the tape just before I went on third after Tabby and Voices With Soul, Simon was taking the credit for it! That really didn't bother me, but I disagreed wholeheartedly that he only rated me as 7/10 the previous week, saying 'some of my ad-libs were a bit over the top'.

I did laugh, though, when Simon and Sinitta agreed with me after I had said that Sharon had spent too long in the States and all she knew was rock music.

At the same time, Simon was telling me again to ignore the criticism as he could see it playing on my mind, yet that was the very dynamic that they needed for the show. They wanted the judges going at each other. It was mind-blowing how any of them could say one thing for the tape or privately and then a completely different thing in the studio during the show.

Simon stated the obvious. He didn't want me to become a one-trick pony, although it had worked for Westlife for years.

After a huge pause when prompted to give her comments, Sharon suddenly blurted out:

'Sorry, I thought I was back in America then.'

But that was all she had because I had done a really good job on it. It might have helped, too, that Voices With Soul had just attempted one of the hardest songs ever in "Bridge Over Troubled Water" which sadly put them in the bottom two.

'You've actually achieved to sing with some soul tonight. You are singing a song where you've listened to the words you were singing...not trying to be a crooner or a flash guy... 10/10.'

She still patronised me, punctuating her monologue with 'Listen' as if she were a deity in soul herself.

Louis also found himself in the same boat.

'I liked it. You pulled it off,' he said whilst reminding everyone that I had no voice on Week One and 'the choir did most of the work' last week.

'If you want to hear a better version of the song, it's on the new Westlife album. It's a much better version. It's out tomorrow.'

I had no choice but to laugh. It was the second time he had done this.

Simon laughed, too, but Westlife was his act: it was his show and for all I knew Louis was reading his script.

'He's had a tough time from these two, but tonight they were fair.'

I had sung it well so they had no place to go, but it was as though it was a team message to back off.

'He not only wants to win. He deserves to win,' Simon ended. We would get to hear that line a few more times over the years.

But it was still only the third week. A lot could happen, even though he had made his mind up. Sharon and Louis both added that tonight they had seen the real me.

Nothing had changed on my part!

They had to have seen the votes if Simon was already positioning me as the winner.

Voices With Soul lived to fight another day, but it was the end of the road for 2 to Go. Like Verity, I was affected by their departure. I felt they had been harshly treated – bigged up in rehearsals and let down on-screen. I loved Peter's voice a lot but

I didn't feel his styling or presentation had been helped much, and by now we were all very aware that they also wanted image. Peter was quite strong-willed in what he wanted to do, too. I also felt the name was wrong. Again, Louis should've dealt with this from the beginning. *2 to Go* had 'exit' written all over it.

With the right name, songs and image they might have had a chance, but too many things were wrong or perceived to be wrong. I can never understand how these mentors put people through so many auditions only to insult them in the live finals.

13 November 2004

By now, there were seven of us left in the competition. (There were a lot fewer acts in the live shows back in 2004.) This, however, had been a pivotal week for three reasons.

Firstly, Verity had broken ranks. She had done a piece with *Now* magazine in which she had said Sharon had stabbed her in the back. This didn't sound like the Verity that we had been just starting to get to know. Either her words were twisted or she really was hurting – probably a bit of both. It was written up that the judges' feuds had shattered her dreams and that she knew she was going out before she even sang, citing that, earlier in the competition, Sharon had said how much she empathised with her, but ended up just staring in her direction. That told her it was home time.

It didn't seem very Verity to be letting rip publicly. Everybody took note. This was the first dissenting voice from within the show. Yes, there had been the odd piece here or there, but generally the show was pretty much in control of its own media. If you read something in the press up to now, they would have been happy for you to do so.

Just seven days before, Simon was positioning me as a winner, and G4 and Tabby looked like the serious competition. I was just trying to get through each week, and hang on. The longer I was in, the greater chance of better gigs I had. There was still a month to go before any of us could really start believing.

There was the issue of song choice. I was always onto Simon to let me do Luther's "Dance With My Father". It was the song more than any other that I wanted to do. I was constantly pleading with him, but right after the previous week's show, he sat me down with Sinitta and Annie and changed his mind.

'I don't want you to do it,' he said. 'Sharon says you are copying soul singers. Tonight you took a song and made it into a soul song. It sounded like your song. We mustn't offer comparisons anymore.'

I didn't agree. It was part two of the previous one-trick pony comment.

It was also patronising because I simply hadn't got to my mid-thirties by just singing soul or ballads.

They were also now seriously working on my image – any trace of my old look were gone. All the necklaces were off.

By the time I came to sing, I had parked my Luther moment. That conversation would come again, I was sure. The most important thing was that I delivered on this track and gave Sharon and Louis nothing to go at.

That, of course, was asking the impossible.

'Beautiful song…you sang it well,' she began, and then started going on about the lyrics, which was pointless as I didn't write them.

'But…' she continued. 'There's always a but…'

I began to smile. She couldn't stop herself. I think the look on my face showed that I felt less venom in her words by the sheer nature of them being constant. Even on a good week, she had to have her say. I hoped I was turning the corner and it wasn't going to get to me.

'But…four ballads…four crooning songs…are we a one-trick pony?'

For whatever reason, the tabloid press were happy to discuss everything in my personal life, but not my musical past. If they had, they would have known that in 1996 I had signed a club track to MCA Records. My old friend Ryan Lee and I had recorded a dance version of the Teddy Pendergrass classic, "Only You". It was BBC Radio 1 DJ Judge Jules' Record of the Week. Any question that I could be a 'one-trick pony' was laughable.

There was that language again. It was the only card she had to play.

Kate turned to me and asked me the same. I tried to make the point that people can vote, and if they don't like what I do I'll be gone, but Sharon cut across me, saying she didn't ask that. I had no choice but to meekly deny that I was as she described me. I didn't have to tell her what I was capable of. Judge what I do, I thought, not what you want me to do. What next? Can you juggle? I couldn't just pull out my CV when TV allows me fifteen seconds to sell myself.

Even when Kate then asked for confirmation of whether I had nailed it, Sharon could only offer 'beautiful song and you sang it well'. Full-on praise was beyond her; begrudging was all I was going to get.

Louis added that he got a little bit bored in the middle. One minute Sharon is saying the song is great, and now Louis thinks the song is boring. I was hitting the notes. Was it the production? Was it the lyric? The melody? Louis never said. I think he was just trying to find fault.

Nothing underlined this more than when he criticised my image.

'I don't know why you didn't bother dressing up for the show,' he mocked. 'It just looks very casual.'

I was now wearing the white shirt over some blue jeans. It could've come out of Simon Cowell's wardrobe. I had been given this to wear by stylists. Maybe Louis was looking to do some moonlighting.

This is what happened. You make changes with your mentor – over image and to avoid being a one-trick pony – and they just throw it back at you. None of the criticism is about the vocal. Everybody knows how it works now, but then it was all new.

Louis also adopted the crooning theme, calling for me to sing something uptempo. Again I thought of Westlife.

Simon, to his credit, gave a smug smile.

'I always believe in giving the public what they want.'

Sharon couldn't even stop herself when Kate was asking me about the song choice. I had been pretty happy with it in the end.

'When it comes to make an album, are you going to be a crooner?'

She couldn't know then the issues I would later have about my only release for Simon's label, but I felt the only thing to do was to let my voice do the talking.

'I just don't wanna stop oh my love…' I burst into "Never Too Much".

The audience erupted into applause. I had knocked her dead. They were with me even if Sharon wasn't. I left the stage showing Sharon and Louis the palm of my hand with Simon smiling. It was brilliant.

In the bigger picture, G4 were in trouble. Everybody was shocked. It's largely forgotten that this was the week they made the bottom two.

For an act to go on and have the success that they did yet end up so close to going out with six other acts in the competition is a sobering thought. They did nothing different on the night, and voting patterns can throw you the odd curve ball. Anything can explain a one-off visit to the bottom two. It was widely believed amongst the people working on the show that it was a backlash after murdering a Britney song the week before.

Even Simon tried to get them out. To my surprise, Sharon and Louis binned a tearful Voices With Soul.

G4 were off the hook.

20 November 2004

I was now conscious that I was doing as much for the show as I was for my singing. They had upped the PR ante. The constant cameras meant there was always a film to make. Much of that would get lost in the edit but it was easy to take your eye off the dream of the recording contract for the five of us left in the show, given the demands to make the programme. I was now sharing magazine space with Peter Andre and Katie Price flashing her knickers, and Kerry was still in love with Brian. What joy!

From Day One, the 'million-pound record deal' was being spun out on every show and this was no exception. That only the winner would get a deal seemed really harsh, but it focussed the minds of both the viewers and the contestants.

As far as I was concerned, all the PR I was doing was to get me more votes. It never occurred to me that my main job was promoting the show.

So when Simon's VT aired before my performance, nothing drummed this point home more as he staged a call to his 'angels' Annie and Sinitta, saying they needed to raise my profile. He must have known I was winning each week, so this was to make it look like he was working to help me, but also to get more bums on seats.

The girls had three days to book me in as the host at the official Christmas lights turn-on in Covent Garden.

It was probably booked weeks ago that an *X Factor* contestant would turn on the lights.

Lots of women whom I had never met wanted kisses. I felt uncomfortable with the whole thing. They had clearly fallen for a Steve Brookstein on the telly who, at this point, I didn't recognise. I hadn't changed one iota but people were changing towards me. Kate's voice-over continued the narrative that almost implied I was something of a lady's man.

'Steve seems to be enjoying himself,' she said as the footage only showed women shouting my name amidst cries of 'I love you, Steve.'

I didn't mind, of course, but it was the first time I felt I was moving into that housewives' choice demographic. Either way, image-building was in full swing. They were creating something out of me.

Fame didn't interest me in this way anymore. Not this sort of fame. If it had come along ten years earlier, things might have been different. In fact, at events like this I felt very self-conscious. Wearing a borrowed £500 leather jacket was just fake. I was still clear in my mind that I wanted to be something of substance rather than someone who was famous without anyone knowing why.

'I can't believe how things have changed in a year,' I said on the VT. And I really couldn't.

Then, performing "Let's Stay Together" was special. I had sung it back in the days of Rocky's in Cobham in Surrey where it all really started for me. That was where my friend Ryan Lee heard me singing and said:

'You could be great if you had singing lessons.'

He gave me the number of a vocal coach Glyn Jones, an old Welshman, who lived in Turnham Green, West London. Glyn had taught many top stars from Shirley Bassey to Patti LaBelle. He had also had spells working with Luther Vandross and Prince. His CV was unbelievable, but that didn't come cheap. On average it was an hour there and an hour back for just a 45-minute lesson costing nearly a third of my week's wages. My dad thought I was mad. After giving up on football in my teens I had finally found something I loved again, and this time I wasn't going to give up easily.

So "Let's Stay Together" was a song full of happy memories. I wasn't even thinking about what the judges would say about me. I was just relieved to get back out there. Up to now, the whole week had been about the Saturday, but now the week had taken over. To be back singing again live onstage and on TV, despite the inevitable grief that would follow from Sharon and Louis, was actually a new comfort zone, whereas it hadn't been before. It was easy to see how fame became more important than content, and yet people like Simon could sell product on the back of it, sometimes without lasting value.

I felt instantly relaxed when I took to the stage – the camera was panning to the audience and, even though it was November, I could see four of my mates dressed as Santa in the audience. The fact that we were all prepared to mess about a bit was a good tension-reliever, but also a great feet-on-the-ground moment: it was only TV after all and they were still very much my friends.

Oddly, both Sharon and Louis said I had delivered. Louis said it was his favourite performance so far, despite doubting I would be able to pull it off. He couldn't resist a few 'but but buts' and resorted to calling me a 'Simon clone', as that night we dressed a little similar.

This is what it had now been reduced to. Simon loved it, of course. The previous week he had ridiculed the idea of taking fashion advice from Louis, now, as it was all about him, he was endorsing it.

Simon did go on to say that I was singing as well as anyone who was selling records in the country at that point, prompting Kate to ask me what I had learned from Simon.

I couldn't answer immediately – not because I had nothing to say. I just wasn't expecting the question. It wasn't about

Simon being amazing – was it? – it was about the remaining acts progressing.

I replied that it was a pleasure, amazing, and that I didn't like to big him up but it had been incredible. At that point, I really could have seen us working together for a long time. He seemed to be backing me, and there was no way I could be doing anything with Sharon and Louis. We were in a good place.

And when the camera crossed backstage to us – as Kate routinely did in 2004 – she told us we were all in danger of being in the bottom two. Looking back now, this sounds unlikely.

The camera went up the line of G4, Rowetta, Tabby, Cassie and then me. All faces seemed worried expect mine. I was getting into the show like a viewer. This was exciting.

I had given it my all in performance; I wanted to progress. Yet, when the pressure was off, I was back to normal. In 1997 I looked so nervous backstage when votes were coming in that I wanted to enjoy it this time. I was the only one messing with Kate on the live cross. In fact, she accused me of being in the bar, which I didn't deny but I was well aware that you had to be so careful of any soundbite you could give them. They would latch onto anything and it would just give Sharon and Louis closure on what they said to me at auditions.

Rowetta and Tabby looked particularly tense; all but Jonathan from G4 seemed caught in the moment, Cassie had a tissue in her hand after having a hard time with her song.

During the week when she was doing her VT for the show, Cassie didn't really know what to say. She was given "All By Myself", which Simon had originally chosen for Rowetta, but after she struggled to pull it off, it became Cassie's. The VT producer said, 'Why don't you just say that you are worried that the song is too big for you so when you deliver it on the night everyone will be blown away?'

Not thinking any more of it, Cassie simply repeated the line to camera.

'I hope this song isn't too big for me,' she said as I watched on, knowing she didn't feel this.

When it came to the live show, it gave Simon the line he wanted and instead of congratulating Cassie for taking on a song that Rowetta failed to perform, he simply said:

'I think the song was inappropriate and too big for you.'

Sharon was surprisingly tactful in her response.

'She hit all the notes, unlike one of your contestants that couldn't hit the notes, and that is why it was available to sing... Yeah baby! And we didn't get somebody in the studio to help her hit the notes!'

The audience cheered and Kate Thornton laughed, but nobody understood what she was saying.

Sharon made it clear. Rowetta couldn't sing the song and they even tried to put backing vocals on the track in the studio to cover the fact.

People would only remember Cassie and Simon questioning if the song was too big for her. She was left to regret the VT.

She soon let herself go when I pretended to flee the corridor joking that it was all too much. It wasn't that I was messing because I didn't want it. I just could see it for what it was.

Tabby was right to be concerned. He was in the bottom two with Cassie. I loved them both and again felt song choices had let them down. Personally I thought either were potential winners.

When it came to sending an act home, Sharon refused to play ball. She would send neither of her acts on their way. This set a precedent, of course, for the future, but just reeked of spoilt child. You had to show some manners and decency in moments like this, but it was left to Louis and Simon to send Cassie out. I felt sick. We had become close friends and I thought she was capable of a pop career, regardless of not winning. She reminded me of Lydia Griffiths who beat me to win *The Big Big Talent Show*, so there was no reason Cassie couldn't have won this talent show. Still, both have since gone on to have careers starring in the West End, and thankfully she's one of the success stories from 2004.

There were now just four of us left.

27 November 2004

The difference in going down to just four acts was a hell of a leap. Suddenly we were in touching distance. We all knew that when an act went out someone else would possibly get some of those votes. I thought I stood a better chance of getting Cassie's, though I had no idea if I needed them. For her, it was probably the right time to go before all the tabloid nonsense really started. It had begun to get ugly. Sharon and Louis could no longer kick me out, as only the bottom act would go. That would have hurt them. I always knew if I had ever been in the bottom two I would be going home, but in many ways I wanted to be there. I found the tension in that part of the show fascinating. There's nothing like the life-or-death drama of an *X Factor* sing-off. I've often thought about how my life would have turned out if I hadn't won the whole thing but Louis or Sharon had instead.

For the show, it pretty much had what it needed. The poperatic of G4, Tabby's rock, my soul, and Rowetta being seen as slightly unpredictable.

We now had to sing twice and I didn't want to do either of the songs given to me.

The discussions regarding songs were becoming more prolonged. Simon had chosen "I Get The Sweetest Feeling" and "If I Could Turn Back The Hands Of Time". "Sweetest Feeling" was not a song I would normally perform and I had to spend a lot of time on it. The R. Kelly track was a huge disappointment. I hated it and I told him it was a rip-off of

"Unchained Melody". That's why he loved it – "Unchained Melody" was one of his all-time favourites! He insisted I did it, but I wish I had just said no. This was the first point where I lost control of my career. It was a defining moment that needed me to stand tall and explain to Simon the sort of artist I wanted to be. It was now clear he didn't get me and we didn't share the same taste in music.

I had been in many fights with various managements over the years, making bad decisions, and now I was keen to just get through the show with as little fuss as possible, even when I knew the song choices were wrong.

On the live show, they gave it all that 'you made it your own' nonsense, but my confidence took a bashing as I just felt I hadn't done myself justice at all. My nan loved them both but that wasn't a career plan of any substance, having her as my key demographic. In truth, I probably did a good job on the songs, but you can't get over that nagging feeling in your head that you had let yourself down, and through no fault of your own. I didn't want to bail out of the show having performed two tracks I didn't believe in. I still hadn't done "Dance With My Father" and after shrugging it off with humour for a couple of weeks, it was eating away at me.

As a result, having to sing songs that were alien meant working even harder. I spent hours re-working the melody for the R. Kelly track to the point where I actually liked it. Then in rehearsal Simon told me to sing it like the original. My mood was changing.

The niggles had started. I began to question absolutely everything. What is going on here? Why are they doing this? What are they trying to make me? All I could think was Robson and Jerome.

Things went from bad to worse on the night. The noise in the studio just seemed to get louder every week and I had no in-ear monitors. I missed the opening line of "Sweetest Feeling" simply because I couldn't hear. People at home would have no sense of the volume on the studio floor by the time it came out of their TV. I was annoyed that I couldn't hear the on-set monitors. It was a crucifying moment. What do I do? In an instant I'm thinking will they stop the music? It became clear that wasn't going to happen.

It all happened so fast but I looked down and saw my saviour and vocal coach Annie Skates who was mouthing the lyrics at me. It was an unbelievable moment to be so out of control and having to take it on trust. Of all the gigs I had done over the years where something had gone wrong, this topped the lot. It hung over me for the rest of the night and much of the week that followed.

In the grand scheme of things it didn't make a big impact. I was safe and Rowetta did leave the competition as expected. She was favourite to go and the bookies were right. It was now to be decided only by the fewest public votes and she was automatically eliminated. It made me sad not to get on with her. I never entered the show to make enemies but I was glad to see the back of her.

Saying goodbye to whoever was leaving was pretty standard every week, but I now also had my own little ritual with Louis, too.

Each Saturday, I would go to shake his hand and then pull it away lifting my thumb to my nose. Every time he would fall for it. I also said I wouldn't do it the next week, but I couldn't resist. It was a very small victory against the bigger picture that released the tension but what lay ahead was enormous.

4 December 2004

Semi-final time.

It was set up perfectly as a competition, and as a competition within the competition. That's to say, three different styles of music and each judge with a perceived chance of winning. Remember, in 2004, the judges' rivalry had been a key point of difference in the creation of the show. I was pretty confident they now had the final three that they wanted.

For me personally, I wouldn't have minded leaving the show at any point after the first week but there was always something that drove me on. At first, I just wanted to make the live finals, then I wanted to get over my laryngitis. After that, if I stayed another week, I could make the semi and now that we were here, obviously I could see the final and all that meant. It was only here that I really began to want the final prize, probably because you could see it for the first time. I could feel my ambition changing from wanting more and better gigs to the very real possibility that I could jump a few steps straight into a record deal... again.

But we had problems. Simon said that he had noticed that I had been down for much of the week because of last week's show. That error couldn't happen again, though in theory it was only going to get louder and there was every chance it might.

Simon hadn't noticed anything! All the VTs we had made together were choreographed. The cameras would be set up, I would sit and wait while Simon talked to producers in another room, and then he would come in and they would roll. He would then say goodbye. Yes, I was annoyed about the monitors and prayed that it wouldn't be an issue again, but the real tension was about how big this was getting and the uncertainty of what I had got myself into. I wasn't going to suddenly turn to the camera and say 'Simon, this week your song choices sucked!' I had to play the game.

I could never understand that expression "play the game". It makes out that it's fun when it never is.

On the VT that night, it was clear the tension was getting to me.

'I never thought I could get this far,' I began.

Then I confessed it was nerve-racking. I hadn't really felt like this just a fortnight before.

'All he ever talks about is letting people down,' Simon added.

It is true that this always played on my mind. Last week I came so close to blowing it in a way that would have only been humiliating. These were the type of things I feared. Going out after singing well is OK. You give it your best and nobody can have a go about that. Winning *was* now a realistic possibility, but truly I was happy. I had achieved what I had set out to achieve. I had reached the live shows and survived a few rounds... but next week was the final. And there I go again wanting a little more. It had you wanting it. Finally, I wanted it.

I opened up with "Have I Told You Lately". I didn't know the song well but learned it that week and now love it. It was Simon's choice and it was a great one, more than making up for last week. There were no judges' comments after your first vocal so I was spared that mauling from Louis and Sharon and that was a massive moment because the audience rose for me and I realised I had a great relationship with them. I had been well received throughout in the studio, but it meant a lot to strip away the nonsense. I was back doing what I do best – connecting with an audience. From singing to clapping without the bullcrapping in between.

My second song was "The Greatest Love Of All", and it meant a lot to me. I knew it from George Benson, and the lyrics about teaching children well was a powerful message and I was singing from my heart. The audience took the roof off. I was massively relieved because I had to concentrate on the breathing and we had toyed with taking it down a semitone. My back was also still killing me after injuring myself at the gym, and the big notes were difficult. Thankfully, it all came together perfectly.

'Very nice. Really, really well done, I loved the suit you wore tonight.'

That was all Sharon had to say as she sat there looking ridiculous with her dog on her lap, stroking it like a Bond villain.

Kate even pushed her for further comments but she had nothing. Louis was equally reticent.

'Both songs were very pleasant and nice.' He wasn't exactly gushing. 'And he's got this great confidence which I wish I had.'

It was a bizarre thing to say and Simon picked up on it, pulling faces back at Louis.

Then he said what he really meant.

'Simon, you're a very confident guy and some of your acts are getting as confident as you and sometimes it's not very nice.'

There it was – a personal attack. He had managed to rein himself in only for a moment before he was off again.

'I think you're both overconfident,' Louis rounded.

I had to set him straight.

'At my first audition I was accused of having a defeatist attitude so I just think I've come a long way.'

He couldn't have it both ways and the audience loved it. Even Annie and Sinitta were laughing and applauding.

'The whole purpose of this competition, particularly with the older category, is to give someone with talent whose been kicked in the teeth by the industry and give somebody confidence,' Simon announced.

I was thinking, Simon please don't make this a sob story. The fact is that competitions with an upper age limit are ageist. Not all music genres are dominated by teens. Music doesn't stop when you reach 25. I was really not happy about the things people were saying.

I couldn't know the irony of these words at the time. In the moment all it did was set Sharon off mumbling something off-mic about looking for sympathy.

Once again I felt forced to defend myself and specifically pointed out my good friend Alan Glass who was sitting next to Lloyd in the audience. We had often written songs together over the years and he knew how hard I had been working. He got the real me. And I let everybody know.

I think this was the point where enough was enough with those two. In seconds, I had gone from standing there nodding at Louis and Sharon's pretty bland opening remarks thinking 'Is that all they have?' but once again they did have more and, once again, they attacked my character. They couldn't say anything about my vocal because the crowd were on their feet and they would have been aware of the voting, so they went for *me*. It's this narrative which, unfortunately, has stood the test of time and I have been fighting ever since.

Thankfully, come the results show, their words counted for little. Kate called for silence in the studio then absolutely screamed my name out. I loved that and knew whatever happened from here, I had made it. Tabby had not.

He was comforted by a mothering Sharon Osbourne who was also out. She expressed her love for Tabby and promised him support and management. I would like to say he had started a positive adventure after the show like Cassie did, but I can't. I have kept in touch with Tabby and after long consideration I've decided to say little about what happened next for him. That's his story.

Friday 10 December 2004

Early Evening

'Hi, Steve, how are you?'

An unknown number had flashed up.

I knew that voice as one of the many members of the production team on the show. At times there had been too many faces and too many voices. I was and am still bad with names, but I'm great at pretending to know people.

'I'm fine, yeah.'

I was done for the day after the mother of all exhausting weeks. I hadn't had time to even consider what might happen 24 hours from now.

'Steve, listen, I'm really sorry,' she said.

All I wanted was a meal with Eileen, a night in, and a chance to go over the song I didn't want to sing.

'I meant to tell you,' she continued. 'You've got to be at Simon's tonight for dinner in half an hour.'

'You're joking, yeah?' I replied.

Nobody had mentioned it – and now of all the moments to pick – I was wanted in Holland Park.

'I'm so sorry,' she begged. 'Please don't tell anyone I forgot, they'll kill me for not telling you.'

And she was gone.

I've looked back on this phone call so many times over the years. Was this part of the cynicism of the show, manipulating me one last time, or did she genuinely forget?

I just don't know because I had an excellent relationship

with the crew but then again, if orders were orders, anybody would be capable of forgetting to ring.

And when I recall what was to follow in a show where everything was choreographed to the second, it's hard to believe that this wasn't the first test of the night.

'If I had you booked around Europe, you wouldn't get to Cologne or Berlin, you'd be in the pub drinking.'

Louis had said that to me at my very first audition. Did they really still believe after all this time that I didn't want it enough?

I was due at Simon's in half an hour and I had December London traffic to deal with. I couldn't possibly get there in time from Wimbledon at this time of night.

I called up to Eileen.

'I can't believe it,' I explained. 'I've gotta go to Simon's.'

'You've got to do what you've got to do.' She understood.

Mild panic set in as I was at her house with no clean clothes.

'You'll have to wear this.' She held up to her nose a maroon shirt I had left there and just gave me a look.

The shirt wasn't clean but I had no choice, and I was annoyed. I didn't imagine I would be spending the eve of the *X Factor* final like this. A quick wash, quick iron of a whiffy shirt and we were off to Simon Cowell's £10m mansion in Holland Park. Nice.

I began to calm down in the car, convincing myself that it might actually be a fun night. I buttoned up my shirt and we started to look on the bright side. Everything that needed to be in the can had been filmed – it was just the live final left.

Yet, part of me was still fuming. Why now? Almost all of my time with Simon had been spent in 'show mode' and yet Tabby and Cassie would tell me every week how they had stayed over at Sharon's and had a great night. It made me a little envious that I had no real relationship with my mentor. Simon was always off doing other stuff, leaving me to Sinitta and Annie, the singing coach.

I let it pass for now and began to relax by turning on the camera they had left us. I turned it on Eileen and threw in a couple of my normal nags about her driving. It was her I wanted to be with tonight discussing everything and nothing.

Yet, when we pulled up at the house, I had to say goodbye. Nobody invited her in – a producer opened the door.

Alarm bells were ringing. It began to feel like work.

This was not what I expected. I don't know why. There was no sign of Simon for a start.

As nice as his house is, I wasn't in a good place physically or mentally. TV always seemed to come before performing music. There was always one more thing to do and now I was increasingly uncomfortable. The notion of a nice night came and went the moment the front door closed behind me.

Still in the hall with the researcher, I was conscious of my shirt. Annie and Sinitta appeared, and Annie handed me a crisp, cold glass of wine. I was starving but I needed this.

I get invited to dinner with Simon Cowell and I was left to chat to a runner and make small talk once more with Sinitta and Annie. Not that it wasn't nice being with them, but my future could be with his label. I needed to get to know Simon.

If this wasn't going to be about music, what was the point? The final was the next day and I still had to learn lyrics. I told Annie this and she reassured me I'd be fine. I didn't feel fine at all.

To think I had just been out to buy food especially, to cook up at home, only to be summoned at a moment's notice. I couldn't even smell any food on the go.

If the wine was meant to relax me, it only served to underline that I was drinking on an empty stomach.

The producer Tabitha called me over for a chat off-camera. Now they began to work me.

It was the same questioning as it had been all week and all series. The same, over and over again. And they weren't even filming. What did this mean to me? How badly did I want it? Was this everything I had ever dreamed of?

Well, right now I would trade it for a clean shirt and a plate of food.

She was dressing it up as a chat but I knew what was coming because I had had a stomach full of it. This, in TV, is known as the pre-interview, so that by the time you do it for real, you give them exactly what they want, even though I had been doing that since June.

I wondered for a moment if G4 had got the call at the last minute, or if they had it in their diary all week. Like Sharon with her acts, Louis was much closer to them than Simon was – and there were four of them to share the workload.

The fact of the matter is I never liked surprises and I was starting to want it all to be over. Roll on ten o'clock tomorrow night.

From the kitchen, I finally began to hear food being prepared. That at least was some comfort.

Then I heard Simon coming down from upstairs. You couldn't not recognise the sound of a man who likes to make an entrance. If I thought I was late when they rang me earlier, he was beyond overrunning.

Of course, there was no way he was going to come down until we were ready to go. Thankfully, now we were.

The food was all laid out immaculately; the cutlery set out for us. I needed this.

'Don't touch anything, we're filming,' came the call.

Inside I was seething.

And it got worse when I clocked what we were having. I could see the empty Marks & Spencer packets as our Chinese went ping in the microwave.

It's not as though he couldn't afford a cook.

It was all for show, and then we did it again. Ping it went and replacement dishes of the same were brought in.

The room went quiet and we took our places.

'A toast.' Simon raised his glass. 'To wish you luck and to thank you girls. It's been fantastic working with you. You're a good guy.'

Yet as Simon beamed and clinked glasses, I knew you could see the tension all over my face.

'Forget all that personal nonsense directed at you. That's just meant to wind you up,' he continued.

And in the moment I didn't see the irony of the very man behind the show laughing off all the abuse as akin to panto. It was a performance to him, but it was real to me. Only the cold light of day and the passage of time pieced that jigsaw together in its entirety.

'What does this mean to you, Steve?' he said.

It began again.

Three hours after I should have eaten with the only person I wanted to be with that night, I looked down at the M&S take-away going cold in front of me.

Annie and Sinitta glanced at me, looking like a couple of Stepford wives. Nobody was getting stuck in. This was all for show.

What have I become? I'm 35. I'm sitting in a mansion trying to impress a guy who turned up late to his own microwave dinner party. Why wasn't I saying 'What the fuck's this shit?'?

'*What does this mean to you, Steve?*' The question hung over me like a dark cloud.

What *have* I become? I came into this show confident of who I was, a soul singer. But I was now being branded something ugly. This show wasn't about my singing. It was about me as a person, and me as a person was something that I didn't like considering. I had spent weeks being insulted only to see those words repeated in the press and with a recent comparison to serial killer Fred West from Louis still fresh in my mind, the self-doubt of my teenage years rained down on me. I closed my eyes and covered them with the back of my hands with my fingers still locked. I don't think they knew that they were opening old wounds. I couldn't stop the tears.

They got the take and Simon intervened, taking me outside for a cigarette I would never normally smoke. I left the room, my hands still over my face.

That he held his hand up to the ensuing camera crew was as much television as it was compassion to me. They didn't need to be told to stop filming. They had the money shot.

That quiet moment with Simon was the weakest I had been. I will never know if he was sincere to me while we sat there talking. Future events make me believe it was just a chance for a cigarette and to reflect on what great footage he had in the can.

The dinner party was as good as over. The hell was just beginning.

Saturday 11 December 2004

Early Afternoon

'Who the fuck do you think you are?' Sharon screamed. 'I'm giving you a fucking compliment.'

But I was now well trained in the mind games that went on in rehearsal.

'I said it was a nice performance, Steve,' she came for me again.

I just didn't want to engage.

This was only a dummy run – albeit the final walk-through before the live show tonight.

The judges *were* in situ, not on this occasion replaced by some runner or assistant producer, but their words were only for the purposes of microphone level. It wasn't meant to mean anything.

That's why I wasn't engaging with Sharon and her initial compliment had brushed over me after a dry run of one of my songs for the night.

I was focussing on the lighting guy, the camera angles and where I needed to be in relation to Kate Thornton.

It was the performances later that counted and everybody knew that. It was the same for the judges as it was for the artistes.

Then she let rip.

Even though she had begun by saying it was a nice performance, it was hardly the latest earth-shattering compliment. The fact that I ignored it revealed her true colours and weeks of pent-up frustration.

It brought back the comment she had thrown at Eileen backstage a couple of weeks previously when Sharon asked her why it didn't bother her if her boyfriend called her a Volvo. Eileen just laughed it off as I had already told her.

Sharon was referring to a conversation I had with the other contestants. We had all just met and were meeting lawyers to go through the legal. There was time to kill and the conversation went on to partners. Somehow we were comparing them to cars and to be different, I replied Volvo. It's obvious to describe your partner as a Porsche or Ferrari, but a Volvo is solid, safe and reliable. I think these traits are important. I got a laugh in the room and the day continued. I didn't expect weeks later it would get back to Sharon and be used against me.

'Who do you think you are? I'm giving you a fucking compliment, you fucking cunt.'

Kate didn't know where to look.

I just looked at her smiling, as I knew it would annoy her. Bring it on, Sharon, I thought. I wasn't in the mood. The greatest moment of my life stood before me, but the last few days had been ruined by Louis Walsh's comments comparing me to serial killer Fred West on *This Morning* and Simon's farcical meal.

And it was just beginning.

'You shouldn't even be onstage,' she ranted.

You could hear a pin drop in the studio. The scurry of activity and constant murmur of background noise fell silent. The last-chance rehearsal had come to a screeching halt.

'You're nothing but a cab driver. You're shit. You shouldn't even be on the stage.'

Now, I *did* want to say something. Instead, I just looked at her again and smiled and the more I did so, the angrier she got. I knew my expression irritated her.

I could feel sympathetic warmth from Kate – caught in the middle. Only Simon could really intervene.

'Not now,' he urged, only for them to continue to fight it out in an ongoing war of words.

I felt Simon was genuine when he urged her to stop – a contrast to the manipulative filming of the dinner. Now, despite the exchanges that we had all witnessed over the previous few weeks, this was him being real.

Simon once again got firm with Sharon, and Kate led me away. Showtime was around five hours away.

I couldn't get off that stage quick enough. I didn't see Sharon again until we went live.

I found out after that my friend Alan, who had been amongst the rehearsal audience, had gone to see Sharon in her dressing room to tell her she had me all wrong and that I was a nice guy with a credible track record. He left short-changed. There was no moving her. 'He's an arrogant fucking prick,' she told him.

By mid-afternoon my manager Tim Byrne came to my dressing room to see me. His advice was to just keep being nice, and he reminded me that I was winning on two counts – because I had rattled her and because week after week, the numbers said so.

But that wasn't the essence of our conversation.

With my dressing room empty and open, whilst Sharon had been tearing into me, I had returned to find the newspaper open at an article slating me. It was a double-page spread. G4 were odds-on to win and I was nothing more than a slimy lounge room lizard.

Why were they doing this to me?

Tim implied it had come from Louis's camp. *He* was backing G4 all the way.

'What are they doing, coming into my dressing room?' I asked.

It didn't matter. What Tim was to tell me next shook me to the core.

If that wasn't bad enough, the *News of the World* were about to turn my life upside down.

Win or lose, tomorrow's front page should have been about tonight's result. The whole nation expected. We were box office.

'They're running a story,' I learned. 'You are adopted.'

I could take a mild tabloid insult or a full-on mouthful from Sharon, but this was something else.

It was one thing to label me a crooner or cheesy, but to attack innocent people who didn't ask to be under the spotlight was a new low.

'This is bollocks,' I replied, laughing.

But Tim was unmoved.

Only through his lack of reaction did I start to realise the severity of what was coming. In seconds I went from laughing it off to doubting myself and my whole existence.

I know this was a by-product of the whole make-believe world of the show.

They made telly, they held out dreams. It all looked so achievable and there were so many crew working on the show to a template of how to make that telly that some people had crossed a line into fantasy world. Your sense of reality can change when you are on the show. These are important people. People with power, people with money. I was from a working-class family. Anything *is* possible.

I had to ring Mum.

Questioning your whole identity was not where tonight was meant to begin and end. I was supposed to be running through a few drills with my vocal coach Annie Skates, well aware that I still hadn't learned the words to "Against All Odds".

My throat was drying with tension as the clock ticked towards the moment of no return, and yet here I was trying to work out if my whole life was a fake.

Mum had the same reaction as me.

She answered all bubbly and I could hear Dad in the background saying 'What's he want, what's he want?'

She laughed in the same way I had moments before.

Then she, too, fell silent as I batted it back to her as Tim had done to me.

'They're running a story that I am from Birmingham and my parents are ex-cons and crackheads.'

It was true that I didn't really look too much like my dark-skinned dad and more like my mum's side, but in my head I could replay all the family pictures from years gone by and I knew they were all of me and that was my family.

As Mum's smile dropped from her voice, I felt embarrassed even asking, putting them through this when this was their night as much as mine.

Those images of me as a baby that now came to mind definitely showed me with my sister, the same sister I have now! I know it's me deep down, I kept telling myself, but I had to hear it from Mum herself.

What was I even thinking? They couldn't have kept a secret like that from me for 35 years. It was rubbish. But I had had a wobble.

I told Mum I loved her and said goodbye then turned to Tim.

'These are the games,' I said, alluding to what had been brewing.

I didn't dislike Tim, though I never wholly warmed to him. After all, it was Simon's people who paired him with me during the competition, and Tim was very keen to be in with them long-term, too.

This time, I suspected Sharon's camp were to blame because of what had just happened at rehearsal.

I was now a far cry from that affable, blasé bloke who had sauntered through the competition. I had remained pretty relaxed throughout despite obvious moments and forged friendships which meant that I shared their emotions when new friends also left the show. Now it *was* just me versus G4. It had become this serious.

But these last few days and these final hours told me there was increasingly a third battle to overcome.

I ate tea and was trying to calm myself. I liked to remain in my casuals until as close to going live as possible. I was vaguely aware that the audience would be coming in by now and that the warm-up man would probably be doing his thing. I passed the odd celebrity in the ITV corridors, but all I really wanted to do was get it over.

I still couldn't be sure of nailing the lyrics to the Phil Collins track and I am sure the snail-like speed with which it was coming together was a huge indication that my gut feeling was right. I shouldn't even be touching that song.

I needed to find a zone – there were less than 90 minutes to go. I killed the time trying to make my vocal warm-ups count.

My phone was going into meltdown from friends at home and family who had arrived in the audience. I was beginning to calm myself for the first time since early afternoon.

Then I got the call.

'Simon wants to see you in his dressing room.'

I was quietly out of the way upstairs; Simon was beneath, just a stone's throw from the stage.

I had still to change properly and do make-up. Time was now running out for learning those lyrics.

I was expecting it was the usual drill about what I would be wearing. I had changed in his dressing room a few times while he would sit there with a stylist and pick from the three or four suits hanging up and decide on my outfit. For a 35-year-old man, I always found this humiliating. Perhaps it was something last-minute to do with the song or just the night in general. I wasn't even thinking it would be anything to do with Sharon from earlier.

None of these reasons were at the forefront of his mind as I knocked on his dressing room door.

'Come in,' he announced.

Simon was on the left, the former Page Three model and ex-girlfriend Jackie St Clair stood in the middle, and to her left as I saw it was another of Simon's former women – Sinitta completed the trio.

Simon just sat there smoking and grinning.

What happened next has caused me much reflection over the years. Was it harmless banter or was it manipulation?

Jackie St Clair opened her long coat. That left just a little thong and her high heels. It was impossible to avoid her breasts as she strutted towards me. Then Sinitta followed behind.

I admit it was a turn-on and I was tempted.

They really didn't know me. I was like a drug addict in rehab. This was taking me back to a period in my life that I had left behind.

Both had me up against the dressing room door. Sinitta undid her top and they began to touch me. I started to laugh. Simon just sat there beaming, puffing on his cigarette.

'I can't do this,' I laughed. It was a nervous laugh.

But still they continued.

They began to stroke my chest, reaching for my buttons, working their hands up my legs and touching me up full-on.

I guess for most single men this was just harmless adult fun that you either go with or laugh off, but for me this was more. Yes, Eileen was in the audience waiting to hear me sing, yes I considered the door wasn't locked and someone could walk in, but this was really about something that Simon could not have been aware of. This was about the fourteen-year-old me standing up to an unspoken incident I should have addressed 30 years ago. This to me was control and manipulation that was going to leave me carrying a dark secret that could stay with me for a long time.

'No, no, I can't do this,' I repeated.

It didn't stop them.

'I think you're beautiful and lovely but I can't do this,' I said again as finally Jackie backed away.

Simon was still smoking and still smiling. His ex-girlfriends began to do themselves up.

Then I tore into him.

'What are you doing?' I was firm.

It was the first time my tone had ever been disrespectful to him yet as he sat there and I towered above, I felt an equal, too.

'I thought it might relax you,' he grinned.

'This ain't gonna relax me,' I thundered back at him. 'I've gotta go onstage and sing "Against All Odds" and I don't even know the words.'

The girls left the room.

It had lasted no more than thirty seconds but left me fuming. It had been a crazy day with one thing after the other and the show hadn't even started.

'You've been stressed lately,' he replied.

'Look, I gotta go,' I stormed off. 'I've gotta get dressed.'

My heart was beating fast all the way back to the dressing room. Over and over in my mind were his words that he was trying to relax me, but for me this was the beginning of the end and I hadn't even won.

Ten years later, I weigh up whether I did take it the wrong way or not. Was Simon really trying to get me to unwind from the stress after my breakdown at dinner? Or was it anything to do with Sharon's outrageous attack that should have made major news but didn't?

One thing has played on my mind since.

I had come to watch Louis Theroux's documentary with Max Clifford in which Theroux interviewed Simon Cowell.

Clifford took them to Stringfellows, and despite Louis Theroux saying he didn't want to be filmed, Max Clifford was still able to farm out pictures trying to implicate the interviewer with strippers.

Max Clifford had been on the Simon Cowell payroll for some time.

I could see the element of control. With such control comes planning. As I opened Simon's dressing room door on the way in, his two girlfriends had been waiting for me and didn't hesitate.

Intended as innocent or not, this, too, bore the hallmarks of control.

***

'One leaves with a million-pound recording contract. The other gets nothing.'

My heart should have been racing because I was about to step onto the biggest stage of my life, but I couldn't even think about that at this point. I could hear the voice-over begin. Somehow I had to find focus and put daylight between what had gone on since the dinner last night and what lay ahead. The truth was that I had felt isolated all week.

Annie was very warm and supportive before the show, trying to keep it light. I wasn't really hearing her words. My head was like a boxing ring – two trains of thought fighting each other. Everything that had gone on today, this week and the whole series was against whatever was round the corner…and fundamentally I still hadn't locked in the lyrics to "Against All Odds".

'Hello and welcome,' Kate began. 'After 50,000 applicants and sixteen weeks of gruelling auditions, boot camps and live shows and millions of your votes, it's the final.'

We were off. This was it.

Jackie, the make-up lady, had been calming me down. The moisturiser she applied to my face had a comatosing effect. It blocked out the din of the angst dominating my brain. I didn't tell anyone about the dressing room incident. There was too much other stuff to stress over. I could feel myself drifting off. I just wanted to sleep.

I made my way to the backstage area, passing in a daze lots of people with headsets all bustling around. My hands were sweating, even though I knew the drill by now. I felt they wanted you to do well, even though they had a show to make. They were always very supportive. All I could think about were the words, the words and the words. I could take losing. I just didn't want to mess up. Then the other stuff would pop into my head. I was running my own VT in my mind. The journey alone to the stage area was the longest of all walks – right out of my dressing room, down the stairs, passing Simon's on the left, taking another right. It went on and on until finally someone had shone a light my way to point me to where I needed to be.

You sensed the whole world was watching. I could have peeked through the curtain and had a look. I didn't need to. You could feel it backstage. I was exhausted before we even began.

'We can go. Are you ready?'

I wasn't exactly marching like a soldier. When I thought about it, I should have been quietly confident. I knew that if I were singing "Dance With My Father" or "The Impossible Dream" I would be excited now.

Backstage I looked up to the big screen that the studio audience can see.

They cut straightaway to a tape of the press conference that we had held together – Simon and I with Louis and G4.

'There's no need for it to get ugly but you just never know with Louis,' Simon had begun.

The first question to me came from James Desborough at the *Sunday People*. Predictably, it was about Louis.

'He's a very aggravating little man. After Saturday, I won't have to deal with him again.' I meant every single word in my reply.

'I don't care if I never see Steve again,' Louis responded. 'I'll be working with G4.'

It sounded like that was going to happen whether they won or lost.

'G4 has an edge on Steve and he knows it.'

This was rubbish. They knew what the voting was each week and one week G4 had been in the bottom two. Besides, I wasn't really focussing on them. I was concentrating on my own performance.

It wasn't until five minutes into the show that I actually joined Kate onstage. They knew how to pad out half a dozen songs into a whole Saturday night.

Behind the curtain, I had waited patiently with Simon and a runner. Sharon was next to us. She was entering the stage from the same side. It was an awkward moment. So I complimented her on how she looked. She didn't say a word. I felt sad that I was about to walk out into the biggest night of my life and this woman hated me.

I had no choice but to put to one side all the issues of the last 24 hours. Simon and I got our cue and we walked out to cheers.

'I think they like you' were Kate's first words to me.

She looked amazing in her pale dress. I felt pretty good, too, next to her, all things considered. I had made it to the final. The nonsense would stop after tonight, and between now and then I had to hope that my singing would do the talking.

'I'm really nervous now. I'm really excited,' I told Kate.

I could spot Eileen beaming, but apart from that all I could see were the two hundred "STEVE" banners that my brother-in-law had made the week before. I spent the evening at their home signing each and every one of them. I didn't feel alone. I really could feel a lot of love from the audience.

'By the end of the evening, I will wipe the smug smile off Louis Walsh's face.'

Simon opened up for the evening.

Looking back, it seems madness that so much was made of the judges' competition. It never really reached those heights again. I don't believe they could have known it would have crossed the line as much as it did.

When G4 entered, Kate said the same to them as she had to me and any impact Louis hoped to make had been killed stone-dead by Simon.

'I've been the underdog since the start of this competition and tonight I'm going to take the smug smile of Simon Cowell's face.'

Simon just rolled his eyes.

Where had that underdog line come from? Just a week before, he had tried to join in when Sharon said that I was looking for sympathy. Now, he was playing that card himself. We had just heard him say 'G4 has an edge on Steve and he knows it' on the VT. Everything seemed a vacuous soundbite for the moment and *these* people were judging me.

The stage was set. They had made it abundantly clear that there were two competitions tonight. To prove it further, the next package was set to the tune of "War" and Louis opened up with 'Welcome to the world of Simon Cowell – population one' whilst reminding everyone that I was a 'cab driver who would sing karaoke at the weekend'.

All of this, of course, severely exposed Sharon. She had effectively been made redundant for the night. She cut a lonely figure after Tabby had exited the week before. For the sake of telly, they had to big her up.

'The show wouldn't be complete without her,' Kate announced as Sharon took to the stage doing a diva-esque dance to Aretha Franklin's "Respect".

It was about all she could really say without underlining the point further, insisting that Sharon was the only impartial judge tonight. Kate asked her if she had wiped the slate clean, only for Sharon to say there was no slate and none of it was personal.

Of course, those people watching at home hadn't known what had gone on that afternoon.

Finally, after welcoming back all the other finalists, it was time for Simon to introduce *me* through his VT.

I just wanted it over.

'I'd say that the ten seconds before Steve's name was announced were the longest ten seconds of my life,' Simon exaggerated about last week's results show.

I was grateful he addressed the overconfident line.

'The one week you are at your most nervous it gets levelled at you you're overconfident. He was literally shaking.'

'I cannot put into words how shocked I am it hasn't ended yet,' I replied for the tape, and I meant it.

And then came a massive thumbs-up from Simon. 'I see his career lined up for him.'

I finally got to sing some fifteen minutes into the show. Within seconds after the quiet vocal start on "Higher and Higher", the audience were up on their feet and I relaxed. It was a good reminder that performance was never part of the pressure. That had all come from other places. I had hit the ground running and I knew it was going well. The studio was electric and, even though I had barely rehearsed with them, I loved the gospel choir.

Not only did it give the show a rousing start, it put down a clear point of difference to G4 – plus Lloyd was in amongst the choir though I felt he deserved a place out front in his own right.

'I loved the song…having fun onstage.' I told Kate after. 'There's an atmosphere in the house tonight.'

All my backstage worries were forgotten. I was beginning to settle. In fact I felt fantastic. Jackie Wilson's classic had set me free. I knew, too, that whilst it was a major release of tension to get the first song out of the way, I was still part of that TV show. I had become very camera-conscious. It was always a juggling act engaging with the lens for people watching at home and connecting with the audience in the studio. So, as great as it felt, I was never lost in the moment. I was very much working. For now, I could relax and take a breather. It was G4's turn.

Louis introduced them as 'four of the nicest guys he had met in a long time'. This is a guy who goes around saying that contestants look like serial killers. I knew he was implying I was the opposite. He also stated they had the *X Factor*. It was a clever choice of words – so little had been made recently of the need for that something extra special. If he told the public his act had it, they might start using that phrase, too, and believe it.

G4 churned out all the clichés of the show in their VT – it meant everything, it meant so much, it was a dream come true, and it had been a roller coaster. They were drilled.

Then they tore the house down with "Nessun Dorma". It was a great performance.

As I sat watching it from the holding room I asked myself: Is this going to connect with more people than "Higher and Higher" on Saturday night ITV? I didn't think so.

Kate described it as a brave choice but actually it *was* right up their street. Afterwards, for anyone who was in any doubt, they reminded everyone it meant so much to them!

Kate was at pains to underline further the narrative of the show, re-emphasising that one of us would leave with nothing and we both needed your votes. Premium-rate phone numbers, of course, made them money, too, and the language they were using was pitching the show as the most aspirational and career-determining programme on telly. Not only were they after your money, they were also selling you a dream.

You couldn't not get sucked in, both as a viewer and as a performer.

Half an hour in and it was time for only my second song. Each judge had been asked to pick what they considered to have been their act's best choice from the series so far and Simon picked "Smile". I was really happy with the choice. I knew I had to make it count because it only left me "Against All Odds", which I didn't like at all.

You would have thought by now there was nothing left to say and that all anybody wanted were the performances, but on came another VT telling my story. Apparently, I was scruffy and nervous with a big smile at my first audition, and Simon had done something he had never done before by calling me back after Louis and Sharon had questioned my attitude.

'He found self-belief when we gave him a stage,' Simon announced.

But I knew that all along. I was a singer and not a TV prop. They simply loved telling me things about me.

'I hope he wins based on talent, being a nice person and being different,' he rounded off.

Then to remind us of the other agenda, Simon said he wanted me to win 100% and him 1000%.

Sometimes I would hear those tapes playing out and feel unrecognisable from the person they were portraying. Obviously, some of it was representative. You can't, for example, fake that moment when you find you have got through boot camp. That's why I was at my happiest when the first notes of the song would start. I knew, too, that after "Smile" they were going to the judges for their first comments of the night.

Again, I just wanted it done. It's very difficult for any performer to understand their own backstage tension yet be totally at one in the live environment. Little things made or broke you. When I went for my costume change I had found water splashed on the back of my shirt. It was soaked.

'How the hell is there water on the back of my shirt?' My confusion quickly turned to anger.

It was hanging on the back of the door and it didn't make sense. I knew Sharon's people didn't like me, but I couldn't let this get into my mind. These people were petty and I was starting to believe they could do anything.

Jackie told me not to worry and pulled out the ironing board.

'I enjoyed both songs. I preferred the first one. I liked "Smile", even though it is on the new Westlife album.' Louis just couldn't stop himself.

This had happened too many times now for it to be an accident.

'Very pleasant, very nice.' He had nothing constructive to say.

Then Sharon started in what seemed a premeditated choice of words and a continuation of rehearsal.

'Love, you know I love "Smile"…it's hard for me to put it in words so I am going to use one of your quotes. You to me are like a Volvo. Reliable.'

I was speechless. Kate asked me if I had really said this.

Jackie had done a good job but the back of my shirt was still damp and I could feel it.

'My girlfriend is here and I love her. I don't need to explain my relationship. It's perfect.' I was totally thrown by the question.

Sharon sounded ridiculous, and Simon agreed. But she showed her true colours, too.

When Kate pushed her on whether she liked the song, she had nothing to offer.

'What's not to like about Steve?' she replied.

A simple yes or no would have done. An inability to say either made her position clear. She couldn't answer the question in the negative for her own image. Nor could she say yes because that was her true feeling.

Simon tried to get the show back on track calling both

performances 'superb' and saying that there was 'no question he [me] could compete in today's market.'

The sooner that process could begin, the better.

I had to win yet, though. And there was still more theatre to come.

On his next VT, I cracked up backstage as Louis took his digs and self-promotion to a new level, spouting off about how 'every week G4 have shown they have the *X Factor*... in this world of manufactured fluffy pop music...' Accompanying the footage was Westlife's "Flying Without Wings".

He said G4 had never got cocky and were real singers. I think that was aimed at me. And then they delivered their version of "Bohemian Rhapsody". Simon was rightly generous towards them, saying both their songs were 10/10 and Louis had done a great job making them credible.

Sharon had a lot more to say than when judging me, calling Jonathan Ansell a 'superstar'.

'We've all grown into superstars in the competition,' he replied.

Ironically, that did appear cocky, but I knew he was just including the rest of the group in the compliment that was given.

With 45 minutes to go on the show, Kate called it 'neck and neck'. They loved that desperate, urgent language. Even Kate said she was bored of saying it. So far, there had been a million votes. Both G4 and I were blown away by that, but equally that just made me even more aware of how many people might have registered the unfair treatment I had been getting. I had to keep focussed on the fact that people were voting for me, despite what had been said.

Kate also announced that they knew some people were experiencing difficulties getting through, but added that they had 25,000 lines open. That was an awful lot of phone lines if true. Experiencing difficulties and urging people to keep calling were once again virtually in the handbook of lines Kate had to trot out.

Before our final songs, they ran a tape looking back at the auditions from June that began with Louis, Sharon and Simon trying to define what having the *X Factor* meant. This, of course, was a key selling point post *Pop Idol* and *Popstars*.

The irony that they then defined it in the compilation by showing so many of the shocking entrants was not lost on me.

Then, after another tape of the most memorable auditions and more reminders of the numbers to call, something strange happened.

Kate crossed to my dressing room. We were now at 2½ million votes.

'I know how close I am,' I told her.

She urged me to smile. I didn't hear her and I couldn't because I didn't know what was going on. All I could hear was banging. I was trying to concentrate on Kate, but this bashing on the wall from next door was distracting me.

Sharon Osbourne and her entourage lay behind that wall. What on earth was she or whoever playing at? They were banging and laughing and shouting for G4, knowing I was live on TV. I found it impossible to concentrate.

It was a relief when they cut to another package – this time showing my friends and family visiting the so-called *X Factor* pod to leave messages. Relief turned to emotion as I realised how much I missed these people. I had thrown everything at the show. Life had been on hold. Yet they came out to support me, and here they were again. Nephews, best friends, mates from Cranmer Middle School, even former babysitters! My parents offered down-to-earth parental advice, saying 'if it happens, it happens'…my sister Tanya reminded me to not be 'distracted by some of the comments'.

I had to turn away from the ever-present camera after Eileen's message. I didn't know any of this was coming and it was a lovely moment. Whatever happened in the next half-hour or so, these people would still be there. That was all that mattered.

By the time, G4 had gone through the same, Kate had plugged the tour, they had announced that one viewer had won a piece of Simon's lifestyle and they had showed a few more awful auditions. 3 million people had voted. It was going nuts.

Out on the set it was even madder. They had called back Robert Unwin.

And now he was performing live in the middle of the final.

Known for his crazy, high-pitched "I'm a Barbie Girl in a Barbie World..." audition, here I was on the biggest stage on UK television, watching him belt out "Tragedy". And then the judges rose to give him a standing ovation. The Chicken Man was back.

It was unbelievable.

'They clearly loved you,' Kate encouraged.

I thought they loved taking the piss. It's difficult to know if it was light relief at the highest point of tension or an undermining of the show.

'I don't know about coming back,' he told Kate.

It was decent of him to clear that up. He looked like a rabbit in the headlights – though, to be fair, that was his normal appearance.

'Can I just say hi to everyone at Pic a Chic?'

Priceless.

It was almost time to sing "Against All Odds". I still couldn't be totally sure of the song. That told me again it was the wrong choice. Throughout the live shows, the songs I had felt were not for me inevitably became the hardest to learn.

After the awful footage of the previous night's dinner, I was on.

I looked tired and drained on the tape. I couldn't watch it. It put me in the wrong place and I needed to focus. It just made me angry.

I remembered again when I was with Simon in his garden. 'Do you think you can win this?'

And then I recalled how he asked me again and again to just say 'I can win this', but I couldn't. Now I was thinking, did he want me to say 'I can win this', so that in isolation I could appear cocky? I no longer trusted what I was seeing. I didn't know what this show was all about. It was becoming soundbites and false portrayals, and the public were lapping it up.

'Somebody suggested this song after hearing it on the radio,' Simon began. 'He's had a tough time in life…this song sums up him. It's "Against All Odds".'

Though in previous shows that song was "Smile", of course.

And I am not entirely sure if someone did hear it on the radio, but if they did I doubt it was the Westlife version!

He loved that kind of narrative, and he had become obsessed with the line 'Take A Look At Me Now' as if it was a statement of the power of the show. From pub singer with his gear in his mum's garage to one million-pound recording contract. Take a look at me now.

It was a love song from a movie. It wasn't a rags-to-riches story. It was about a guy who lost everything emotionally now living in 'an empty space'. It wasn't about materialism. It couldn't have actually been further from the narrative just as "The Impossible Dream" met it head-on. Simon wasn't letting me near that song.

Time and time again, I told him. He just replied to me to keep focussed. We had been arguing about it all week. These were the earlier niggles becoming real cracks in our relationship.

At the back of my mind was just one thought – if I am a serious recording artist, is this the kind of song he wants to hear on the radio from me?

The intro started in free time and I felt sick. It wasn't to a set tempo and I had to recall my previous phrasing. I knew it would be a miracle to get through this song without one mistake. I hadn't done it yet. As a performer it's awful to sing when you are just thinking about remembering lyrics. It's even worse when you don't like the sentiment of the song and don't want to sing it. This was my big final and I knew I had "The Impossible Dream" and "Dance With My Father" sitting comfortably in my head.

As I struggled to keep my focus I could sense I was going to make it, it was actually going really well and then just as the song was building towards the climax with the big gospel choir, pyrotechnics went off and the audience started to scream and cheer. Here I am passionately singing about losing the love of my life and they made it look like the Super Bowl. Hot dogs, anyone?! It was then that I tripped up on a lyric and stumbled over the finishing line to rapturous applause. This was ridiculous. I looked to my left at the people clapping. I didn't deserve this adulation for that performance. I closed my eyes, my head fell to one side and I absorbed the clamour of the audience. At least it was over.

Kate and Simon joined me and I apologised to Simon that I had messed up.

'Good news. It's time for your final judges' verdict. The last one ever, Steve,' Kate said, holding my arm.

'The last one ever,' I repeated.

'The last judges' verdict *ever*, Steve.' Kate was making a point. Here we both were again but it wasn't the rehearsal. This was it.

Louis said it was a pretty good performance but he preferred the Westlife version. Right to the last, he just wouldn't let that go – his face radiating no warmth or sincerity in my direction. Then, when asked if he had anything else to add, he simply replied 'This was OK – that's all' and stared straight ahead smiling.

So it was either a pretty good performance or just OK?

That contradiction was nothing compared to what followed.

Kate asked for Sharon's thoughts and I heard my sister shout out 'Fabulous!'

I shook my head.

'No, not fabulous,' Sharon began.

'For me, he's not a superstar.' She was still brewing from earlier. 'I just have to say this...I am so fed up of Mr Humble... Mr 'Should I Sell My Volkswagen?'... He's been overconfident from Day One... he's not what he seems...all that BS he gives out ...he's even fooled Simon...he's full of crap and he's an average singer.'

Rehearsal was one thing – live TV was another all together. I knew how she felt about me, but I wasn't expecting that on the final.

Then came the line that nobody has ever picked up on.

'There's an awful lot that I could say,' Simon defended. 'But I won't.'

He was referring to earlier.

The phoney war that had been created to promote the show was now out of control. This really wasn't in the script. Sharon meant every word.

'I think it was inappropriate to be personal tonight,' Simon replied calmly, only for her to talk all over him cackling 'he's a fake' and shouting that Simon knew I was going to win. That was all about the weekly vote count, of which I had no idea, but they clearly had every.

Looking back, my slip-up wasn't a major deal but it would have been noteworthy on any other day. Sharon didn't even comment on my performance. It was as though she knew what she was going to say. I could have pointed at her and sung 'Take a look at that cow!' and she wouldn't have referenced it. She had her mind made up.

Some parts of TV are for the cameras. That I had experienced the same just a few hours before tells you this was for real. She meant every word of it.

But did Simon know I was going to win? And if so, was it because he knew the votes from previous weeks or was the whole thing manipulated, or was it both? Cassie had told me that Sharon believed it was. Maybe Sharon thought I knew this. This would explain why she loathed me.

People often ask me if I regret going on *The X Factor*. I always say no. Knowing what I know now, I do have one regret. I wish I turned to Simon, thanked him, walked off-stage into the audience and left the building with Eileen and my family. Whatever the result, my time on *The X Factor* had been ruined.

When Kate turned to me, I exhaled heavily and said something, anything just to fill the time. Inside I was relieved it was all finally over.

G4 had chosen the Radiohead track "Creep" as their last attempt to impress, and I thought it was a silly song choice. Even if they had put their distinctive stamp on it, it really was beyond the mainstream. If anything was a sympathy vote song, this was it.

I could do no more. My performances were over. I had to sit and wait. In 2004, there was just a short gap before the results show aired.

Simon was probably smoking like a chimney in his dressing room, celebrating what a success it had all been. My phone was in overdrive with texts from well-wishers. Beyond the simple fact of being in the live final of a TV talent show for the second time in my life, I had been on the end of an avalanche of abuse, circumstance and negativity. In isolation, any one of the day's events would have seemed extraordinary. Together, they were just madness.

My manager Tim had come to see me in my dressing room.

'I can't believe Louis is going on about Westlife.' He said what we were all thinking. 'Sharon was out of order. Don't let it worry you. Just ignore it.'

It was easier said than done.

'I knew I'd mess it up.' I told him how pissed I still was about the song.

It felt like a loser's song, not a winner's track. "The Impossible Dream" had a more appropriate message.

'Even if you don't win, you'll get a deal,' he reassured me.

I had to double take. What did that mean? Were G4 being told the same? What was the point of the whole shenanigans of the last few months if it didn't matter in the end?

I was amazed and it took the edge off everything. But I was still fuming about the fake thing. She did a lot of damage with that word. It was a narrative that was forever to be attached to me – and this from a woman who had spent thousands on plastic surgery. Maybe people should ask Tabby how truthful Sharon is. I knew in my head that the judges' competition made it a battle of egos but that didn't justify the comment.

When it was time to go again, all the usual recapping began. In the package, they included Sharon's Volvo comment and her rant. I had no idea what the voters made of it. I had always said I didn't want to look an idiot. I never imagined I would end up having my character destroyed.

All I knew was what I felt, and it hurt. There was more footage in the VT of the comments than there was my singing. That in itself tells a story.

'So have you had a chance to reflect?' Kate asked *Sharon*.

It was as though there had been words in the gap between the shows.

'Everybody did great,' she batted it back.

Then she was off again.

'People are mad at me. I can't apologise for people playing the victim.'

She couldn't let it go, even if someone *had* had a word.

'I won't put up with anyone who is fake,' Simon tried to counter.

'G4 have the *X Factor*, they deserve to win.' Louis was shameless in his plugs.

'By the way, Sharon, just enjoy the show,' Kate concluded the section somewhat lamely.

When she crossed to us on the backstage cam, G4 and I were in the same dressing room. There was one minute left to vote.

'I'm fine. Very nervous. I didn't do my best in the last song. I am sorry for the people who voted for me. I don't want to let anyone down,' I told her.

This theme rang true to the last.

And now she announced that 7 million votes had been cast. When we passed the million figure earlier, I was shocked. To multiply sevenfold was just extraordinary.

'To win it would be amazing,' I signed off.

It was time to re-enter the stage.

It all hung on this moment.

***

'After 50,000 applicants and sixteen weeks of fierce competition, this is it. Only two acts remain – Steve and G4.'

As Kate began the now familiar drone of padding out the results, I stood immediately to her right. On my shoulder stood Simon. Across the stage, G4 were to her left. Collectively, nobody knew where to look – ahead with a glazed vision towards the audience, trying to make out a family member or close friend amidst all the TV lights and crew…or simply down at our feet as our fates were called.

'One of them is about to become the winner of *The X Factor*. The other leaves with nothing.' Kate delivered the iconic soundbite, unaware that the future would show this to be a sham.

'The public have been voting all night and I'm about to

deliver their verdict. Good luck to you both. Can I ask the official adjudicator for the vote, please?'

This was it.

That music that plays on the TV at this point matched every raging heartbeat inside me. In the gap, the audience filled the void with equal cries of 'Steve' and 'G4'.

Kate announced that it was now 8 million votes.

'OK, you ready?' she asked. The pressure of those votes weighed heavily on me. This meant a lot to many more people than those on the stage.

'The winner of *The X Factor* is...'

Then...nothing...twenty seconds of silence interspersed with a crowd holding their breath before bursting into a frenzy.

I looked skywards, closing my eyes. Louis was smiling, shaking his head. The G4 boys were all linked – their arms around each other's shoulders. Simon looked calmly into the distance, whilst Sharon was chatting to her vocal coach in the audience.

I found it all so funny. Virtually everyone in the audience had their hands over their mouths. I can see it now. I had made the final. I wanted to win but I was happy. I didn't visualise winning; I was there taking in the moment. Then Kate called it.

'Steve', she shouted, after looking left to G4 and closing her eyes herself.

Simon jumped on me, almost punching me. I couldn't react because my back was still aching. I was happy but I know I didn't look it. I shook my head in disbelief. I just had never thought about *this* moment and here it was. I hadn't planned how I would celebrate. I distinctly remember thinking *'Now this deal can't go wrong.'*

In the audience, I could see my family and friends jumping around. My mum and dad were hugging and everyone was congratulating Eileen. Onstage, I made my way across to shake hands with G4. They were more than gracious in defeat. I shook hands with Louis, though I was tempted to remove my hand and put it up to my nose with my tongue out. I wish I had.

The camera panned to Sharon. She was clapping politely.

'Congratulations, you are the winner of *The X Factor* and a million-pound contract,' Kate shoved the microphone in my direction.

'I don't believe it' was all I could muster, smiling back at her, but shaking.

'I am shocked. I cannot believe this is happening,' I uttered as she raised my hand like a boxing champ.

Seconds later, they wanted me to perform.

'I'm shocked. I can't sing,' I told her, but before I knew it she was announcing my debut single would be released on 20 December and I was on. I still didn't know the words. This was totally unexpected.

This time it didn't seem to matter. The lyric seemed even more ludicrous now I had won. Simon was right: 'Take a look at me now' was the line everyone was singing along to. It was crazy. I couldn't help but laugh about the whole situation.

If I forgot a line now who cared? I would just cover it with laughter and a thank you. But Simon did care. He was standing with Annie trying to get me to keep it together. They weren't smiling. I was unaware that I was in the middle of making my one and only music video.

With ticker tape falling all around me, I turned to see all the finalists behind me. Without a doubt, it was my favourite performance of the series but it was chaos on the stage.

'Thank you, thank you so much, oh man. Oh my God.' I was talking nothing but gibberish as the song ended. I had won *The X Factor*.

'You got what you always wanted. You are a recording artist.' Kate told me, but that was for later.

I wasn't really taking in anything at all.

'I'm always amazed. I don't want to wake up. This is so funny. You've changed my life beyond belief,' I announced.

'It's what this competition is all about,' Simon announced.

Then he promptly snogged Kate.

Even the main man needed his release of tension.

As the credits rolled, it turned out that 22 million votes had been cast all series. That was a phenomenal amount of revenue and support. It had been massive. I was truly ecstatic to have won and to finally have some sort of indication as to how much good feeling there was through the numbers of voters, but I was also relieved.

Straightaway after, I had to do *The Xtra Factor* – the world and his wife seemed to be on the show. It's a blur. I have little recollection of it except that nobody else seemed to really know what lay ahead.

Ben: "How does this work, Simon. Is Steve a millionaire now?"

Simon: "He will be by the end of the year, probably yeah."

Ben: "Tell us what a million-pound contract means: is that the amount of money you are investing?"

Simon: "Well, the money is important obviously but whoever won the competition it's such a show of public support, so as long as we make a good record – and we will make a good record – then he's got a chance of what we've always promised the winner."

Ben: "So that's the amount of money you are willing to invest in Steve to make it work?"

Simon: "The minimum amount."

Ben: "The minimum amount! So it could be more than that?"

Simon: "It could be more, yeah."

Ben to Steve: "How do you feel now that Simon's going to be your boss for the rest of your life?"

Simon: "It's the other way round now – he's my boss. That's how it works in the music industry."

In my head, I was struggling to take in the achievement whilst all around me trying to weigh up what was fake and what was real. Even in the moment of victory, and in fact especially in the moment of victory, there was so much already to mistrust, as amazing as it was to win.

No longer would I have to stand there and take the weekly character assassination from Louis and Sharon and finally at the age of 36, I might now get a genuine shot at the music business. My original expectations to just get more gigs had been a genuine motivation. Now I understood what lay before me.

That was to come. I still had some unfinished business to deal with.

Feeling much more relaxed, I stood in the corridor by the stairs to my dressing room having a chat with some of the production crew. The show had been a great success and pretty much everyone was celebrating. This wasn't all about me. I genuinely felt happy for all the people who made it work so well. I suddenly felt a hand slap across the back of my head. I looked around and saw Sharon's assistant walking off down the hall on the way to her dressing room. I exited the conversation and ran after her. I tapped her on the shoulder and she turned round.

'Hey, guess what? – I won.' I held up my index finger, smiled and walked away.

A moment later Sharon stormed out of her dressing room.

'Don't hit my staff,' she yelled at me and began to walk back off.

'Whoa whoa whoa.' I followed her back into her dressing room. I was thinking about that nonsense story that I was told was going in *The News of the World.*

'Excuse me, your assistant hit me on the head. Now you're accusing me of hitting her. I've got witnesses, so don't even think about going to the press with this.'

***

'Just fuck off, get the fuck out of my dressing room,' she screamed.

I looked at her and thought: what am I doing here? Why am I getting into this?

I changed my tone.

'Sharon, *The X Factor* is over. I don't know why you hate me. I can only wish you all the best. I really do.' I replied and I meant it. I didn't want to make enemies, especially with people like Sharon.

'Don't give me that,' she replied. 'I hope you fucking fail. You've got your deal and good luck to you, but I hope you fucking fail.'

We were done. I wasn't angry. I just felt sad.

Louis had also blanked me after doing *The Xtra Factor* walking past, muttering, 'I'm so glad this show is over.' And I felt that way, too. I genuinely enjoyed all the decent, hard-working people on the crew. More or less without exception, they worked long hours under pressure and were still great to be around.

But when it came to it, I wanted to withdraw. It was made worse that, even though I was the winner, the after-show party was limited to me plus two! I had a choice to take Eileen and my mum *or* dad. It was a no-brainer. I wasn't going to be spending my evening there.

I had a few formalities to complete but I was determined to get the hell out as soon as I could.

For the benefit of the press, I found myself signing a contract at the judges' table once the audience had left. I've no idea what I was putting my name to. Ironically, the man doing the honours was a guy called Tim Bowen whom I had met before the competition through bizarre circumstances by chance in the sauna at my gym.

In one of those forced moments of conversation, I had found myself discussing New York, music and what we both did. He told me he was in the record industry. He asked my name politely and said he would keep an eye out for me. Now, he was signing me up and offering me champagne.

After briefly showing our faces at the party, I told Tim Byrne that I was going to leave. Eileen had managed to organise a little get-together for all my friends and family in the Italian restaurant across the road from the studio. Tim didn't seem too bothered that the winner of *The X Factor* was leaving so early. Nobody did. I was acutely aware that the show was the real winner.

In an instant it had all changed. I was now fair game to the world at large. Sharon and Louis might have gone but everyone else wanted a piece. Paps had followed us to the restaurant and were snapping continuously.

Despite having been told not to go to bed too late because I had a full day ahead, that was never going to happen. I needed that moment with my loved ones, the people I trusted. I had to be around those who hadn't changed throughout the process when everything was going on around me. People were coming into my life thick and fast and many wouldn't stay the course.

It might have looked odd to not stay at the TV studios long into the evening, but I knew it was the right thing to do. I needed the right people around me before it all started again.

12 December 2004

At 6 am my alarm went off and I crawled out of my Pimlico bed for the last time. I wasn't happy. I couldn't imagine a footballer doing *GMTV* the morning after winning the FA Cup. I wasn't in any state to tackle the long list of commitments already inked in. I had my prize, it was a record deal, but this was TV. I could see that I owed ITV and the people who voted, but it didn't stop me from being in a foul mood and Eileen was the one on the receiving end.

Over the month our relationship had become strained. It was all my fault. Eileen was there to support but I couldn't be held up. I had too many things to deal with and *X Factor* had taken me back to a dark place and a horrible me that I hadn't seen in years. Neither of us can remember why I barked at her that morning, but I stormed out and she made her own way home.

The one thing I had always said I didn't want out of the show was to make a fool of myself, and here I was the morning after winning *The X Factor* feeling humiliated. The games of the night before were fresh in my mind and had taken the gloss off my victory. Now I was having to do media not knowing what else could come my way.

By 7.00 in the morning, I was already at breakfast TV; magazines and papers followed for the rest of the day. I was no longer on a talent show. I was in the media circus. This was a whole new scrap altogether. The only good thing was I was due to record *Top Of The Pops* that night at Shepherd's Bush. I can't talk for other singers but for me this was a dream come true. Even though I was worried about my lines and the song, doing the show outweighed those concerns. I would be given a break and there was an afternoon rehearsal: I had time to correct the mistake I had made last night.

Tim was with me for much of the day, feeding me lines to say. His main advice was to just keep being positive. Being the first winner was massive, but just half a day later was way too soon to evaluate what had gone on and which bits I would share publicly. Sometimes it was hard to know what the journalists had actually seen for themselves or just what they had heard on the grapevine.

Equally I couldn't always be sure what had gone out on air and which bits *felt* like they were part of the circus. It wasn't the time to mention the dressing room incident or the adoption. They were just markers that there was another agenda at play. Besides, this was my first day in the new job, so to speak. It really should have been about me and the future.

I knew very little of this so-called mapped-out career that Simon had promised on one of the tapes. I had spoken to him briefly after the show and he had assured me that my album wouldn't be one of just covers. I don't know why this even came up at this stage. It had to be my discomfort at the winner's song.

He would have plenty of time to think about it as he headed to Barbados. He promised he would see me in the new year!

Many of the journalists wanted to ask me about Sharon.

'If it helped me win, that's great,' I trotted out my standard response.

In reality, I didn't mean that at all. Tim had told me to be positive and this was one of his lines.

At the back of my mind, I wasn't sure if the slate was clean. Almost her last words to me were that she hoped I failed. I didn't believe she just hoped that. I thought she would be actively making that a reality.

But so what? I had the might of Syco and Simon Cowell behind me. She hadn't managed to stop me yet.

But *they* had stopped me smiling. That natural joy you are given and encouraged to radiate from cradle to grave had been stripped from me. I had never been photographed this much in all my life and I was very conscious of my face. They had spent so much of the narrative talking about me smiling; Sharon's first words to me in June were 'Hello, Smiley'; I had sung a song called "Smile"; and then just last week Louis had been on ITV comparing me to the serial killer Fred West. You don't forget a comment like that.

This was the territory I was now immersed in. You couldn't know how you would get written up or what the journalists would cling to. Much of their minds would have been made up before they met me.

By the evening, my suspicions were confounded when I was at Shepherd's Bush Empire for the pre-record of *Top of the Pops*. I had so many interviews that the break I was promised and the afternoon soundcheck and rehearsal had been cancelled. I no longer wanted to do it. I was tired, my voice was knackered from the show and the media guff that I had done all day, and I felt now that I knew the lyrics even less than the night before.

I went out onstage. The place was packed and I looked down at the first few rows. It was a mix of cheers, screams and indifference.

I was introduced and the song began. I hadn't had a chance to get a feel of the venue, and I had no idea what my mic would sound like. It didn't matter because I went blank and I didn't sing. I just couldn't remember a thing. But hey, this isn't live TV like *X Factor*… it's a pre-record. So you can do it again. I gathered my thoughts and this time I delivered. The crowd were cheering and my day was finally over. Well, almost…

'Did you hear them booing you?' A female journalist who had been allowed backstage approached me afterwards.

I was taken back. Was this a joke?

'No, I didn't hear that.' I was shocked by both the question and that she might be there waiting for me.

'Who are you? What paper are you from? The only negativity I am hearing is from you.' I confronted her.

'You know you'll be doing an album of covers, don't you?' she continued.

How did these people know so much more than me – or were they just being provocative?

'I'll be amazed,' I replied. 'Simon Cowell said I would do an album of original material.'

A new narrative had begun.

Boxing Day 2004

Asia and Indonesia were being ripped apart by a devastating tsunami. The whole world quickly sobered up from its Christmas Day celebrations. You could not fail to be moved by the blanket coverage on the news.

It was a stark reminder that even if you had everything in life, it could be gone in a flash, and to many at this point it looked like I had the world at my feet.

The run-up to Christmas as newly crowned *X Factor* champ gave no indication that the big day was coming. There was so much to do, though the truth was that the real work would start in the new year.

One photo shoot followed another, and meetings merged into more of the same. Whereas my sole motivation for entering the show had been to get more and better gigs, Tim was now talking about putting me out there for £25-£30 grand a time which was far higher than I had expected and I questioned it. That potentially was life-changing because albums and recording careers can come and go, but I knew I would always sing. More importantly, I thought it was nonsense. How can you justify £30k for a show unless you are a star?

I was keeping an eye on the press, too. The same journalist – Neil Wilkes – who wrote up the 'Sharon says Simon is a wanker' story in October had run the 'Booed at *Top of The Pops*' line, lifting some quotes from an interview I had given to Radio 1.

This made me very suspicious of how stuff was ending up

in certain places. I didn't recall speaking to the guy, though it is possible I did. I certainly messed up the vocal for the TV show and had tried to explain how disappointing this was to Radio 1. I made no attempt to hide it, but to deal with it honestly. I hadn't heard any boos, but I concede that of the 2,000 people there may have been pockets of people leaning that way. But what did that mean? Was my performance poor? Were they G4 fans? They don't like *X Factor*? I know so many people were cheering that I didn't hear these supposed boos, but that is what made the press.

When so many people had been so warm towards my winning, negativity in some of the press was already setting in.

Tim had told me that Sharon had apologised on Christmas Eve to Simon for calling me fake and full of crap. At no point did she say sorry to me. And I told him this. I was itching to say something but did my best to toe the line. It smacked of an end-of-show debrief and their attempt to defuse the lingering tension. It was already too late.

Heat magazine had me down as a sex symbol – this agenda was starting to be the norm. The more I read it the more I felt it positioned me as seedy, and that was not something I had fed them. They asked me if I had expected to do so well and I was quoted as replying that I had played in a pub of 30 with nobody listening. I was making the point that I was just happy singing, but now I see that it looked like I wasn't grateful.

I do know that when people tried to attach the words "Michelle McManus effect" to articles about me, it didn't really bother me. She had been the last winner of *Pop Idol* and was perceived to have done little since. I knew I would be disappointed if it went that way for me, but I felt it was something I could accept – much of the business was like that.

Woman's Own were also calling me a 'hunk' and the 'housewives' favourite'. The narrative was set.

By the time I came to do *OK! magazine*, I was getting asked questions like 'So are you fake?' The first question was always about Sharon, the second about sincerity.

Ironically, I pointed out to the magazine that they had dressed me up in Marks & Spencer suits and put Eileen and I in a hotel as though it were our house. I told them this wasn't anything like our lifestyle and yet they still asked the question, having created that environment themselves!

I found it strange, too, that just because I had won a singing contest, I was now getting asked if Eileen and I were getting married. I was unaware that, on the day of the final, newspapers in Scotland were running front-page stories that if I were to win I would propose to Eileen.

Eileen also pointed out that some papers had suggested we were splitting up. Both lines were nonsense.

OK! dubbed me sexy. I just didn't get that all.

Then they quizzed me about the actress Tina Hobley as though I was hiding something. I had just explained that Eileen meant the world to me and now I have to defend the fact I had bumped into Tina in a bar, she supported me on *The X Factor*, gave me some sound advice, kissed me on the cheek and left. It was a complete non-story until they made it one.

They continued the tone, citing a pop gossip website which had described me as "Will Young's randy old uncle".

I just replied that I thought that was fantastic, even though I had never heard so much rubbish in my life. I suppose much of this was about coercing something sensational. If they prod me a couple of times with a few gentle lobs like Tina and Will Young, I might eventually open up about something. And I half-did.

I knew where this had all come from and it was something I needed to address, but I wasn't ready to say more just yet.

'People realise I've done some naughty stuff. I was told not to knock it until you tried it.'

There – I put it out there. That could have meant everything and nothing. I had a past: who hasn't?

There was nothing nasty about it – not at all. It was more cheeky than anything else. That final quote about naughty stuff got highlighted in the article and I was conscious that we might be here again at some point in the future.

Either way it confirmed the truth – the narrative of the show ruled. People were still asking the fake question (even the public would come up to me to see if it was true) and whatever I gave out in an interview, they would pretty much take it where they wanted.

I started to question myself again, especially as I was giving an interview alongside Eileen who knew me best. Why were they pursuing this line?

There was almost nothing about my music. To be balanced, they weren't that kind of publication. There was just a little footnote at the bottom saying that "Against All Odds" was out now. The gossip was the story, not the music.

And that's why Simon rang me from Barbados.

'You're going to be number one,' he said. 'I would like to give the proceeds from your song to the victims of the tsunami.'

It was an impossible thing to refuse. In fact, it was very easy to accept. My life was great. These people had nothing. I was giving something I hadn't even received yet. This was simple.

'Don't worry, I'll look after you,' he said.

That was the big deal for me. I was so pleased that he said this. It's a line I have said to myself many times since.

'I'm sure I'll have other singles.' I gave him my blessing.

What he didn't know was that I didn't care about the song anyway. It wasn't that the tsunami had left me cold and heartless. I didn't really give a toss about the track. Yes – it was massive to have a number one song, but I didn't want it to be that one. And if it turned out for some reason that it was my only single and there was some truth in the 'album of covers' line then that was how I would potentially be remembered. That would be the only credit against my name.

No disrespect to Phil Collins, but I didn't want that to be any kind of musical legacy. I had hated the Mariah Carey and Westlife version. I didn't want this track damaging me, and when I heard it on the radio, despite what I might have said to all the DJs up and down the country in promotion, it made me churn.

I didn't see it as any great achievement at all. It also brought back all the bad stuff from the show.

The single had also been released unfashionably late. In the years since, it has become the norm to see the CD of the winner's song available immediately, and in later years you could virtually download any track as the show went along, but in 2004 this was not the case.

Simon had allowed a week to pass before my song came out. The much-talked-about race to Christmas number one in subsequent years was not an issue then. Simon stood aside. The reason was that Band Aid 20 was out with a remake of "Do They Know It's Christmas?" and he knew that, especially with so many current artists, management and labels having a chance at claiming a number one, he was on a hiding to nothing if he stood in their way. Neither the public nor the industry would thank him for pushing his wares in the face of famine.

I learned that "Against All Odds" was going to number one on New Year's Eve. I was having a quiet one with my family as I was conscious that next year could be a very big year for me. My dad had a friend who was going away for the holidays and we were offered his mansion to see the new year in.

An ecstatic Tim Byrne rang me with news. He was very excited. I had a glass of champagne in my hand as if I was expecting the call.

'Ah great,' I said. He could tell that I wasn't sharing his enthusiasm.

'Steve, you're number one. You'll look back and remember

this moment. It's a big thing.' I think he was disappointed that I wasn't jumping up and down with joy.

I was upset that he was blissfully unaware that the public humiliation over the last few weeks was sending me down into what I would later refer to as "Lazy Sadness".

2005

"My job is a combination of promotion and protection but each year it's more about protection than promotion".
Max Clifford

At the start of the year, I can only remember two dates in the diary: a meeting with Simon, and another with Max. I felt there was a lot to discuss with the former and slightly less with the latter.

Word had got back to me that a couple of interviews I had done had upset Simon. I really didn't see that this was my fault. The only slightly contentious line I had given was to *OK!* when I said I had tried a few things in my love life in the past.

So, if it wasn't that, it must have been the whole Sharon saga. It looked like people kept asking me, and I wouldn't let it go. The truth is I had to do the PR for the single, and it was all anyone wanted to talk about.

So, even though Tim had warned me to be positive and to play it down, I was unable to stop that juggernaut.

How could any of that have been my fault? The show only had itself to blame. Sharon had attacked Simon in the press last October; Louis and Sharon had torn into me on a regular basis which Simon acknowledged several times; and one of the USPs of the show was that it was a scrap to the death between the three judges.

It had achieved what it had intended to. You can't reverse that process with hindsight. I *did* want to move on but I guess he had plenty of time in Barbados to think about it. My only concern was that I was pretty sure he couldn't have read every single word written about me, him or the show, so that meant someone was briefing him or providing a cuttings service. If all he was hearing was the bad stuff, then there had to be an enemy within.

By now, I had answered the same questions so many times that none of this was anything new. What I really wanted to meet him about was my album.

I had the dubious distinction of knocking Band Aid 20 off the top spot only to be replaced by Elvis who in turn became the 1000th number one ever with the remake of "Jailhouse Rock". Nobody would ever remember that except me, but I felt it was a good place to sit regardless of what the song was.

None of that was real. I needed to crack on.

I put some feelers out to Evan Lamberg at EMI about looking for a possible duet for the album. I knew he would help me. It was in his interests. He owned the publishing on a number of my songs that I had written in the late-90s as part of our big deal then, and would be able to recoup and possibly make money if my work was on my album.

I contacted Ian Levine, too. He had been behind some of the early Take That stuff and had spotted me on *The Big Big Talent Show* in '97. Simon had known Ian for many years. Ian had great delight in telling me about the time he was a DJ and Simon kept asking him to play Sinitta's "So Macho". So Ian took the record and smashed it over Simon's head. I loved that.

We began writing in earnest with Clive Scott, former keyboard player from 1970s band Jigsaw, and within no time had managed to lay down the rawest of raw demos to play to Simon.

And they were just that. We knew there were two to three good songs on there, but we weren't stupid enough to think it was anywhere near polished. I just wanted to show Simon some ideas for style.

By the time the meeting took place, his mind seemed already made up. In front of Sonny Takhar, the label boss, and my manager Tim, I began to air the demos.

He skipped through each track, stopped the CD and announced.

'I've decided you're doing an album of covers.'

I didn't even realise this was going to be a meeting as blunt as this. I thought it was a general 'which kind of direction are we going in' conversation with a view to putting something out there later in the year.

'I thought we weren't doing an album of covers,' I protested.

The press had been right. I looked to Tim for support and continued.

'Are you sure? These are just demos. I think people are expecting original...'

'Look, I know what I'm doing.' His tone had changed to that of a man I had not previously known. His face was stern and his word was final.

'We're doing an album of covers.'

I gave a half-smile and said OK.

Darius from the TV show *Pop Idol,* like the press, had also proved to be astute when he warned me at a record company do at Cocoon restaurant in London:

'In the world of Simon Cowell, only Simon Cowell matters. Don't think you are that important to him.'

Simon was almost unrecognisable from the man who had mostly supported me all autumn. I didn't feel I could argue for my creative input, though, ironically, this could have been my greatest moment of power.

If I played along and had a hit album, I could come back second time around with more say. At the back of my mind I knew Simon's track record in the business and there were a significant number of acts like those Teletubbies or actors Robson and Jerome where he had taken an existing product and added to their fame with music. After being on the TV all of the autumn, I, too, was now existing product. I wanted to make music. He wanted to sell units.

From here on, I was losing all the time.

I could have tolerated an album of soulful covers – perhaps nine classics with the odd duet and maybe three new songs but no, I was told.

There was no point arguing with him. I just kept thinking I had one shot at this and if he fucked it up, we were falling out.

The reality was that the opposite was also true. I did have one shot at it, but if *I* fucked it up, we were done, too.

It was an unhealthy start. By the time *The X Factor* gigs started, I was staring at a list of songs to narrow down into just a few. I was keen to make the best of a bad situation and embrace this album.

When the tour began, I learned more…but before that happened, on Simon's recommendation, I was to meet his PR guru, on a rumoured salary of £250,000 a year. I didn't want to meet Max Clifford, I wanted to meet producers.

'If there's anything we need managed in the press, he can sort it,' Simon had told me of Max, and then asked me if there is anything he should know. I assured him that there wasn't but agreed to see him anyway.

I didn't see any point in meeting him and I couldn't warm to him from the moment I walked into his New Bond Street office. Three or four women sitting at desks on phones smiled at me, and almost immediately Max came through and ushered me into his office. I was on my guard knowing what he did, but he was very relaxed and confident.

The conversation started lightly enough but he was making me fully aware from the off of who he was and what he had done. It didn't take long before he was name-dropping stars from The Beatles to David Beckham and this was his currency.

The phone rang and Max took the call. It was brief but he

told me what it was about. A football manager was being outed for having an affair by the tabloids and he was going to make it go away. He said he wasn't sure he could because the manager had left it so late to tell him. I wondered if he was trying to make a point.

I asked him how he could help the manager. To watch him, he was very good, but he was also stupid. He loved the trade and I was watching his indiscretion first-hand. He told me the manager's name and someone else's secret that he would trade with the newspaper to protect the manager.

He behaved as untouchable but I took that as a warning. If he could spill the beans on who was ringing, then he could certainly do that to me, and Simon Cowell was probably in the news more than most of his clients who came and went as the tabloids chewed them up and spat them out.

I could see the potential that I might be part of that process. I viewed him as nothing but a heartless assassin. None of it was ever personal. He was paid to bury things and people.

He even opened up on Simon, telling me that *X Factor USA* was the big one, and that by 2007 he expected it to launch there. This told me where Simon's focus was and it was what I had suspected: the TV show.

'If you do something wrong but say sorry the public will forgive you. If you are caught out lying, they won't.'

He then proceeded to single out Gareth Gates and his relationship with Jordan. He blamed the demise of Gareth Gates on this one affair. I personally put it down to Simon Cowell for making him sing "Any One Of Us". But anyway...

I knew why I was there in that meeting and it was to tell Max everything or to convince him there was nothing. Max had said many times over the years that so much of his work was keeping stories out of the news, rather than putting them in there. And he was telling me he could look after things.

My mind was now racing. I was reliving my entire life from shoplifting as a nine-year-old to the things I had buried so deep that digging them up just sent me down into the hole from where they came. My life was complicated and not for family viewing or for the ears of Simon's PR man. How could I trust him? I didn't even trust Simon and anyway I wasn't the one paying Max Clifford bundles, Simon was. Max worked for Simon: I wasn't there for my benefit.

'Don't ever lie to the press,' he reminded me.

From then on, every time I read an item by a star saying sorry, I remembered his technique.

Max Clifford wasn't trying to look after my secrets, he wanted to own them.

I don't know if I convinced him that I had no real baggage, but I left the meeting telling Max nothing and learning a lot. I was now swimming with the sharks and sooner or later I would need to deal with my past, I just hoped it would be on my own terms.

Just before *The X Factor* tour started, Max took me to a Tsunami fundraiser at David Lloyd in Raynes Park. He drove a Bentley with his then girlfriend and now ex-wife Jo by his side, and I sat in the back. The ride was uncomfortably smooth. The wealthy control freak was driving me insane with worry and he didn't even know it. I didn't want to go but I felt I had to. We arrived and I was introduced to many people, some of whom I remember, some I don't. I spoke with Rodney Marsh who told me about some celebrity WAG who had made it her aim to sleep with me. That was a bit scary. Max would love that. Sir Trevor McDonald didn't have such gossip, and anyway I was too busy thinking about Lenny Henry's impression of him to take in anything he was saying. I felt bad about that considering how iconic he was. I could see, though, how Max Clifford's influence cut across everywhere: he was off talking to everyone, and in return people appeared to like Max or at least respect him. I spent a bit of time talking with Jo but it was small talk. She told me how they met and it seemed quite romantic. She had helped him after the loss of his wife. Maybe he wasn't that bad after all.

I left the fundraiser a bit confused. I didn't really know why I was there – unless it was specifically to feel his power.

The tour was a nightmare.

It started in Newcastle on 15 February and would trawl the country for the best part of a couple of weeks, visiting Glasgow, Aberdeen, Sheffield, Brighton, Manchester and London.

I was pleased to see some of the gang again, especially Verity and Cassie, but it was very difficult to see the end of the series and 2004 as anything other than a cut-off point in all our lives.

For some, they had been out of the competition back in October. Then for G4, Tabby and myself there were new commitments and a shot at the business.

Tabby was often being filmed, G4 seemed to be having lots of secret chats, and I needed to wrestle some sort of control back in the making of my album.

It was when I opened the tour programme in Newcastle that I feared the worst. Simon's other operatic act Il Divo were on the back; Westlife were on the inside front cover, and G4's album was out on the Monday.

What? G4's album was out on Monday?

I was '*currently in the studio putting the finishing touches to my album*' and you could win a date with me.

I was livid on so many fronts. I wanted this sexy Steve nonsense to stop, for one thing, and for another, much more importantly, why was the G4 album about to be released?

The rule was that no act could put an album out within three months of the final. Yet here we were within two and they were ready to go. I felt cheated – a piece of rubbish and totally unsupported.

My manager Tim was powerless to intervene or didn't want to. I don't know which.

It was all done – the recordings, the art and now the publicity machine had just rolled into town exposing me to ridicule, really leaving it unexplained why I was seemingly missing in action.

Once the shows started, it went from bad to worse. Tim was also heavily involved with the tour. He had managed Steps and they had huge success on the road. He was not only my manager, he was the producer of the show. From the outset the gimmicks that they had for me began to fall down and Tim had a great idea that I would come onstage by standing on a platform that would lift me higher and higher while I sang "Higher and Higher". Genius – for a five-year-old. Every night my heart sank as I went higher and higher on this ridiculous little stage that slowly wobbled up 20 feet above the crowd.

Just three days in and I kicked off.

I couldn't help thinking that the white ribbons that looked like giant toilet paper unrolling from above the stage were symbolic.

'This shit is not working,' I told Tim, only to be reassured to try again and that would be the last of it. By the time I got to Wembley, it was a far cry from the pyrotechnics and live choir in *The X Factor* final. As I sang my finale "Against All Odds", I eagerly anticipated what the "ribbons" had in store.

One fell straight to the floor; another was left dangling halfway. Two did as they were required. Well done.

I had always imagined what singing at Wembley would be like. The 10,000 people and my performance were as expected. I just never thought it would be accompanied by backing tracks and oversized bog roll. It was a huge disappointment.

But it was the Sheffield leg on 19th where I had really lost it.

Robert Unwin, the Chicken Man was on the road with us. Tim wanted him to join the finalists at the end of the show. I was not happy. Any credibility we thought we had was gone having Chicken Man touring, and now was he to share the bows with us? It was a disgrace. We had all worked so hard to make it to the live finals and this guy had fallen at the first audition. He was only there to be laughed at.

Each night I would sing five songs, G4 would do one less, and Tabby had three.

He had been booked as the novelty act to sing "Barbie Girl", but suddenly Tim was telling me he would join all of us onstage for our rousing finale of the Dionne Warwick song, "That's What Friends Are For".

One by one all the acts would enter the stage singing a line before we all joined in for the song's climax.

Chicken Man wanted to join us as we started to wave our goodbyes – or he was threatening to walk!

It was simply an absurd situation.

'It's about being good, not failure. It's about musical integrity. Let him fucking walk,' I told Tim after he approached me to see if it was OK.

I should have realised that if Tim couldn't even stand up to Chicken Man, I was going to have no hope with Simon.

'You've asked my opinion. Now do what you want,' I told him.

It's this sort of thing that gets you a reputation for being difficult.

That night the final song started, and one by one each finalist came onstage to sing a line. First Roberta, then Verity, then 2 to Go, then Voices With Soul, then Cassie, then Rowetta, then Tabby then G4, and then the audience started to laugh.

I came out to sing my line to be greeted with laughter and Chicken Man walking across the stage waving at the crowd. All the finalists without exception looked around at me.

Afterwards, I let rip at Tim backstage. 'It's a fucking joke.'

He was the show's producer and around him you have crew at the side of the stage to give people like Chicken Man their cue. I just couldn't believe that the timing of his entrance, straight after G4 had sung their line, was an accident. Tim took me to one side and said that, even though it was bad I must never lose my temper in public. I just couldn't help it. It was one embarrassment after another and I wasn't putting up with it anymore.

It was one thing for those who really were having their final moments of public exposure but I had been given a chance at a career I had dreamed of and it was flying off-track. This episode did nothing but tarnish it. It was now too late to go back and support Lionel Richie. I was supporting Chicken Man.

The end of the tour couldn't come soon enough. Some of the reviews were scathing: "Brookstein says he feels blessed, we've all been cursed", said one paper.

***

"It's the other way round now – he's my boss. That's how it works in the music industry" – Simon Cowell

I decided that now was the time for me to have an operation on my sinuses. I knew the day was coming but it seemed a perfect foil to explain why the act who came second were now at the forefront of the show's plans and I was nowhere to be seen. I took eight days' rest, though in fact I was meant to be off for two weeks.

Behind the scenes we continued to work on the album. G4 had sold 245,000 copies in their first week. Not surprising, considering it was straight after a sell-out tour and just in time for Mother's Day. I felt like I was now racing against time.

On 5 March an email arrived from Tim with the track listings.

From: Tim Byrne
Subject: Your album (well Simon's album really...)
To: Steve Brookstein
(edited)

I think that things are more set in stone than you realise. Because you are due to record in a few days' time and because the album has to be delivered early in April, the above fourteen tracks will have been commissioned so that studios are booked, producers booked, mixers booked and backing tracks can be prepared in time for you to record (the finer details about budgets are being argued about and I promise you I've been playing hardball).

If the album bombs (and it wont!) then the argument about costs is irrelevant. If the album exceeds all expectations (and it will!) then the arguments about costs become irrelevant as we'll be making so much money it won't matter. The only time it has real impact is if we land somewhere in the middle and the decision about a second album is borderline (and we know that that isn't going to happen for 2 reasons: 1) you are fantastic and 2) you have a massive momentum from The *X Factor*, more than G4 and look at them!)

Your biggest point to make right now is about the type of songs you are recording — too many negative ballads maybe...

Glad you are feeling better, have a nice day! And send my love to Eileen.

Tim x

My friends, who were also the people who knew my music best, could not understand the album I was making. They knew me as a songwriter not an artist, so understandably they expected me to have written the songs. They encouraged me to be true to myself and saw no point in an album of covers. Equally, they knew that it was still an opportunity. It just wasn't going to be an album they would rate.

The album was coming in under budget. That, at least, was a pressure off. Nobody in the music business liked the conversations with the bean counters.

I had been trying to get my friend and long-term writing partner Livingstone Brown in to work on some of the tracks. This was clearly out of the question. The power and the control were with Simon.

And when BeBe Winans flew over from the States to duet with me, I was left in no doubt as we tried to play with the arrangement on James Ingram's "Yah Mo Be There". This was to be a major selling point of the album.

BeBe had won four Grammys and worked with everyone from Whitney Houston to Al Green. You name them, he's worked with them, and despite Simon promising me big names to sing with on the album, it came down to my contact in New York. That's how we got BeBe on the album.

In the studio, the engineer Graham Stack pressed Record and the gospel legend hit the notes perfectly. Suddenly BeBe stopped, saying that he couldn't hear anything.

'You're singing the wrong lines,' the engineer objected.

BeBe told him to stick with it – he was just trying something out and changing the chorus. It sounded awesome.

They started once more only for the same to happen.

'That's not the chorus,' the engineer repeated.

Stop and start – it happened a couple more times. The tension was rising a notch. BeBe went back through the glass and told the sound guy that he knew James Ingram and Michael McDonald and that they were all fine with it.

I began to lose it now – we were in the presence of a legend. The producer, Brian Rawlings, who wasn't even at the session, was called in.

'I know Simon Cowell,' he said. 'He's not going to want you to mess with it.'

BeBe was so annoyed he was on the point of walking out and flying home.

'The only reason I'm not going home is because I like Steve,' he said.

I was honoured but gutted. Yet another great moment in my life ruined by outside influences.

My pleas fell on deaf ears. The next thing that happened – the producer, the engineer and the A & R guy were ringing Simon at the label. Word came back to us that it had to be like the original. I apologised to BeBe.

And like a professional he laid down his vocal. He was brilliant. Each take was great. A different league to me: it was a reality check. Then I stepped up.

'Heavenly Father, watching us fall. We take from each other and give nothing at all.'

They stopped me dead. I hadn't sung it that badly.

'You're singing the line wrong. The first line is Heavenly Father watching us all.' I sensed the engineer was on a power trip.

'What?' I questioned.

'Just sing the line on the sheet,' he said.

'It's wrong! Where did you get these lyrics?' I asked.

He told me he got the lyrics off the net and reiterated just to sing what was on the sheet. I was exasperated. Off the Internet? Is that how it worked these days?

I had no choice other than to fall into line. The result is set in stone – I am singing the wrong words to one of my favourite songs from two of my favourite artists, just to satisfy their level of control.

Ironically, BeBe and I went back to Livingstone's studio and recorded it our way. That track never saw the light of the day. I had already lost heart with my new album. Simon wasn't exactly hands-on. He was in America and not responding.

After the BeBe incident I had washed my hands of the album. There was nothing I could do to change the course of events. I had fought for my musical integrity both at the original meeting and in the studio, and my mentor was on the other side of the world. A corporate gig for Thomas Cook took my mind off things and was well received, but when I woke up the morning after, it only served to remind me just how unbusy I was. I don't recall doing any other paid gigs since the show ended. That wasn't right because I had always gigged and it was my bread and butter, and if I won the competition as I did, surely I had more commercial worth.

That was a fight for another day.

When Simon did call me from Los Angeles, I felt it was all part of a game.

'The sun is shining, I've got the roof down on the Bentley. I am playing your album and it's amazing.'

I didn't share his joy. In fact, I was barely able to listen to it and that has continued to this day. It was weak and watery and some tracks like "How Can You Mend A Broken Heart?" broke mine. I actually used to sing this all the time at my gigs, with a backing track that I had bought for £3 that was better than this production. The arrangement on my version was wrong and it had this crackle like an old record stuck on it, even though it was a CD.

Equally, to show Simon's way on thinking, my version of "Hang On In There, Baby" was based on the production and feel of the later version by Curiosity Killed The Cat, and not the original classic by Johnny Bristol. It was a cover of a cover, and not a very good one.

I felt short-changed – a frontman for a product I didn't believe in.

If they had trusted the changes BeBe had made to the duet it could have been a single. It was authentic for radio play and he was a star, often remembered for his collaboration with Eternal.

There was to be no single.

In the face of changing technology, nobody really quite knew the value of it as a product anymore.

Simon was kind and enthusiastic but the fact remains he was a long way away. I knew the press would ask me if I had spoken to him, and now I couldn't say I hadn't and I would reset the scene of how he called me from his car with the roof down and the sun shining, and everything would look rosy and the stuff dreams were made of. The truth was it had been a nightmare for me but, like it or not, my album was coming and once again, I would have to face the media.

I began a three-day radio tour in Cardiff mid-April, fitting in the written press in the middle before returning to the TV studios for pretty much the first time since the show.

Little had changed – which is understandable since, apart from the tour, I had seemingly been in hiding. So many of the questions and themes were the same. I couldn't shake it off.

A journalist called Rebecca Hardy ran a piece in the *Daily Mail* called "The Fake's Progress". She might not have given the story that headline herself, of course, but it wasn't going away. I reminded her that firstly it was a TV show, and secondly I had spent about five minutes in total with Sharon during the whole series.

It seemed almost impossible to give an interview without talking about somebody else on the show. I wondered how much longer I would have to fend these questions off. I was most amused to read that I could make £10 million in my six-record deal. I had seen little money bar the monthly retainer from the label up to this point, and I was starting to have severe concerns that "Heart And Soul" might be my only album under Simon. That article appeared on 24 April. The very next day I replied to Tim's email below with some ideas:

From: Tim Byrne
To: Steve Brookstein
Subject: Press

Hi, Steve

Sonny and I are putting pressure on Stuart and Alan to be spinning positive stories about you in the press.

To help them place stories we need to feed them stuff – both about you presently but also stories from your past. Please could you email me about four pages of notes of stories that have ever happened to you in your life – it can be seemingly trivial stuff like bumping your head in the playground as a kid, to holidays as a kid to being knocked out in a game of football – how you and Eileen met – how you lost your virginity... etc We only need one line on each story at this stage.

I will edit any stories I don't think that we should pass on – before I send them to Stu.

As soon as you have the time to do this would be great.

Thanks
Tim

Even at ITV where I wouldn't have expected such a grilling I still was being asked to set the record straight. On *This Morning* they asked me if I was doing a Volvo ad – I wasn't. Also was it true that I had been turned away from a VIP area at a Mariah Carey do? – that was untrue, too, though I *had* actually attended.

It wasn't even a story. It just underlined the truth that someone was feeding nonsense about me and other people wanted me to fail.

The more promo I did, the further I felt pushed away from

the truth. I began to feel a fraud. I had become fake! I was selling something I didn't believe in and often I was doing so on the network that made me. It was a complex circle of fate where you eventually became what they told you that you were.

When the album went to number one, somebody at the label sent me a magnum of champagne, but the chart position papered over the cracks. I had shifted a fifth of what G4 had in my first week.

I had still to release a single other than one for the tsunami. I had made no video, and my album was all covers. By now, I was severely doubting everything about who I was dealing with and the decisions they were making. One point nagged me more than any other. I was the housewives' favourite.

That was obvious by my age, and through the way they had positioned me all along. Yet, it was G4 whose album came out for Mother's Day. Mine was closer to Father's Day and I knew my market. Not many dads wanted to wake up to the gift of a Steve Brookstein CD.

I should have acted on Tim's email about getting press sooner but equally you would think that we would all have had the conversation by now. Another 'fake' story had already just landed.

Yet at the same time, the label didn't stop the fake bandwagon running out of control. Eileen and I were asked to stage an engagement shot for the press at a jewellers.

We met Stuart from Outside Organisation PR in a coffee shop and he told us we had to wait for the photographer to take the pap shot. This was no normal paparazzo. He was one of the best. He was also two hours late.

Eileen was getting anxious because she was now running late for a gig. I had drunk four cups of coffee and was hungry and grumpy. This was meant to be a snap of Eileen and me looking through a window at jewellery. It could have been anything. If a paper wanted to speculate, well that's down to them.

The photographer and his ego finally arrived and briskly led us to the jewellers. We walked in to see two glasses, champagne and diamond rings. Eileen stepped back and her face couldn't disguise her displeasure.

'This isn't what we agreed,' I said to Stuart.

The pap interrupted. 'It will be great, I can make this look like a pap shot.'

This wasn't the point. We had no intention of getting married. This was too important to us.

Then the badgering began. I felt like a teenage model getting encouraged to show a little more shoulder and cleavage. I was fuming. Eileen looked at me and I felt so bad.

'I'm going to be late for work,' she whispered.

I turned to Stuart and told him we had to get going.

I hurried him along, we made our excuses and Stuart put us in a cab and I called the label immediately.

'Don't fucking ask me how it went…' I screamed down the line at Dan Parker, the A & R man and one of those who had infuriated BeBe Winans.

'You make me do stupid things all the time,' I thundered. 'And this was not what we agreed.'

Sonny Takhar grabbed the phone.

'You can't speak to Dan like that.'

I was furious.

'You guys are responsible for this. This was not meant to happen. There is no way this is going in the paper. It will look bad for Eileen's mum and dad and my relationship is far too important.'

'OK it won't go in the paper, but you can't talk to Dan like that,' Sonny replied.

Eileen said nothing as I ended the call. The cracks were appearing between us as well. As for the label, our relationship was severely on the rocks. I was in danger of losing everything.

The pap shot was a bad idea, wasn't me and went wrong on

the day. I looked at Tim's email again. 'Anything would do'– it said – from the trivial to life-changing.

It was after this that I spoke to *Closer* magazine.

I don't remember the name of the journalist at *Closer*, except that she was tall, slim and very attractive. I had just finished a photo shoot and we sat down in a quiet corner.

Max Clifford's advice never to lie to the press was always with me and I was prepared that any day I could be asked that question. Today was to be that day.

After a few standard lines about the new album and how things where going she hit me with it.

'You're a big hit with the ladies, are you a big hit with the guys?'

Many of my previous interviews had been sex-led but it wasn't a conversation that I had instigated.

It had all begun when I had a phone call from my ex-girlfriend Katie Jackson during *X Factor*. She had been offered around £10,000 to do a kiss-and-tell on me. The fact she called me told me that, despite the bumpy relationship that we had, she still cared for me. Some people are just not good for each other but both can be good people apart. We brought out the dark side in each other. She had issues and so did I, and we entered a world of debauchery. Two consenting adults had a good time together but it wasn't good. We knew it was wrong and it eventually broke us up.

I told her that, even though I would rather she didn't speak to the *News of the World* about it, I could understand why she would do it. It was a lot of money and she was going through a tough time. I assured her that I wouldn't hold it against her. She still was very special to me.

I had no idea what she was going to talk about and I told her that I would rather she didn't speak about certain things.

She went ahead and it was probably the best kiss-and-tell you would ever read. Usually, the ex is saying how bad the person is in bed and how small their appendage was. Katie had apparently said she "liked the way I swung my mic" but it was seedy and, with a poor photo of her, it made her look bad, not me. I couldn't believe some of the things she had come out with and some of things she didn't say. I was sad for her, but relieved for myself and I was left confused. Now, I understand that this was during *The X Factor* at a time when I was part of the solution, not the problem. It was probably this that started all the interest in my sex life.

I had met Katie at a karaoke in Morden in 1996. She was beautiful and had one of the best voices I had ever heard. Within three short years we had virtually every major record label in America wanting to sign her.

After I appeared on *The Big Big Talent Show* in 1997 and failed to get much interest from the TV exposure, I began to focus on getting Katie a deal. Together with Livingstone Brown we wrote a song called "Platform Paradise" in September that year. I remember this well because Natalie Imbruglia's "Torn" was a hit weeks after we wrote it. Both songs had a similar feel but totally different. We instantly knew how good it was. We kept it to ourselves but we became excited by what we had stumbled upon. For months we locked ourselves in the studio and wrote songs and things just got better. The only thing was that Katie was shy, and neither she nor we felt she would have the confidence or persona to carry it off so we formed a studio band called "Maker". It was basically Katie but it protected her from all the pressure that could come her way if things went big.

Our first interest came from a young A and R man from Telstar called Simon Banks, who would go on to manage KT Tunstall, Cloud Control and The Wombats. He was very keen to do a deal, and meetings were put in place. Suddenly, a manager friend of Livingstone's called David Christensen in the USA, who had received the demo, informed us that labels were going crazy for the music. Before we knew it we were being flown out to LA and New York to have meetings with all the top players. Co-founder of Interscope and Beats by Dr. Dre, Jimmy Iovine, had the most amazing house. He gave us the full tour, swimming pool, indoor cinema, games room. It blew me away. But to top all that he also loved our songs. We went to see the heads of Motown, Capitol and Atlantic. When we went to DreamWorks we met with Mo Ostin and David Geffen, and they invited along Robbie Robertson from The Band which was equally impressive. We really were getting the star treatment.

Back in New York, the head of Epic Records, the late Polly Anthony, invited us to her apartment overlooking Central Park for a small drinks party. That was a lovely evening. Both Katie and I felt real warmth from Ms Anthony and took her very well. I'll never forget she played us a track from an artist she said would be massive. The song was "I Try" by Macy Gray.

Sadly, when Donnie Ienner at Columbia Records showed interest in signing *Maker,* Epic had to pull out. We were told they wouldn't compete against each other. Joanna Ifrah, an A and R executive at Columbia who was also a friend of David Christensen's, was desperate to do the deal. We even met with Doug Morris, the CEO of the world's largest label, Universal.

We flew back to the UK having met the biggest names in the music industry, with all but one making an offer. As the bidding went up it was down to just Columbia and Elektra Records. Columbia had Katie doing an a cappella audition in the office of label President Donnie Ienner, whereas the team at Elektra made us feel extra special. Whilst in LA they took us to see Alanis Morissette and Garbage and went to the after-show party mixing with the stars like Nicolas Cage, Val Kilmer and Gwen Stefani. Just two years after *The Big Big Talent Show*, I was in Hollywood. But it didn't stop there. They took us to lunch at The Beverly Hills Hotel and I managed to meet James Caan and Paul Michael Glaser. Obviously we discussed music with Elektra, but getting a sense of how much they wanted to work with us meant a lot, too. For our manager, money was everything. The more they wanted to spend meant the more they had to lose and they would make it happen. For me it was who could help us make the right record. This was to be one of my big regrets.

Both labels had upped their offers to well over half a million dollars, but the best offer was from Joanna Ifrah at Columbia. However, Sylvia Rhone, the CEO at Elektra was keen to talk to us directly. David insisted that we didn't. He kept on saying that things were starting to drag and that we were in danger of losing everything. He was friends with Joanna and said that the deal was great, which it was. Both Katie and I were disappointed, as we had wanted to go with Elektra but accepted his advice and didn't take the call from Sylvia Rhone.

We had been naïve and trusting of our manager, but this wasn't the subject *Closer* were interested in and Katie was equally open with the *News of the World* as she told all this to their journalist. It was all ignored. She phoned me to say that all the quotes attributed to her were not true. She went on to explain how they pressured her into what to wear at the photo shoot and how to pose. This I could relate to. She had really been stitched up and was devastated.

'Have you ever been with a guy?' the *Closer* journalist prodded.

'I've done things.' I didn't want to go into too much detail but it was clear. Katie and I had done lots of things. I'm not boasting and I'm not proud. But this wasn't a secret. It was just a question that nobody had asked me. I didn't think I was or am at liberty to share everything, but this was a doorway to discuss a topic that I was passionate about.

'I've questioned my sexuality,' I continued.

I could tell she was excited about getting this exclusive. She happened to ask me the right question on the right day. I was happy to talk openly about my past, I was ready and it felt easy.

I was no longer going to have something that I worried about coming out from a third party.

'I questioned my sexuality, it wasn't for me, but if young people question themselves that's OK,' I added.

I had a new album coming out and I was the housewives' favourite. This was nothing about selling records. This was about helping myself get over something and helping others find peace if they were going through the same.

I had said enough, for now.

I left with Stephanie Faber, the PR girl who had been listening in.

'That'll be interesting,' I smiled, but she didn't smile back. She raised her eyebrows and just said, 'Well, it's your choice'. Disapprovingly.

I was breaking ranks and talking to the press without the say-so of the record label or Max Clifford and, more importantly, I hadn't shared my 'secret' with them. I had told the world.

Within thirty minutes my phone rang. It was Tim.

'Steve, what are you doing? You can't say these sorts of things.' He was disappointed with me again.

I couldn't understand his reaction. What was the problem? It was 2004 not 1984.

'I said that I had questioned my sexuality. What's the big deal? Tim, you're gay. *You* understand.'

Yes, I had been candid in the interview, but there were good reasons and I honestly believed I was doing the right thing. I had won *The X Factor*, had a hit record and was sharing something very personal that I knew wasn't exclusive to me. I was angry that I wasn't getting his support. I don't know why I was surprised. I was already starting to sense who he really worked for.

'We should have talked about it first,' he lectured me.

He may have had good intentions but I had long lost my

ability to trust him or anyone else on issues like this. I backed myself. I had to come clean and explain my motives.

'Tim, when I was young, a friend of the family abused me.' I paused. 'Don't worry, I'm OK about it now, but I know who I am and I have nothing to be ashamed of. You are making me feel bad.'

I had put my cards on the table and I hoped Tim was hearing me.

'I'm sorry to hear that. We really need to talk,' he said.

But we were done for now.

It turned out that *we* didn't need to talk, *I* needed to talk to Sue Evison from *The Sun*. Tim phoned back shortly after to inform me of this and that the *Closer* article wouldn't be going ahead. It had obviously gone to higher authority and Max's fingerprints were all over it.

This was ridiculous. I had no idea who knew what now, but this story was being managed. What hadn't been a big deal for me was huge for the record label. So big that they were seemingly pulling favours from two publications.

Within a day I was meeting Sue at a restaurant off Tottenham Court Road. Like many female journalists in the tabloids, she appeared to be a nice woman but had some sort of long-standing understanding with Simon. I instantly took to her. It may have been because I needed to. I was finally putting the wheels in motion to address something that I had carried for over twenty years and this was the most important meeting of my life. I admitted that in my two-and-half-year relationship with my ex we had done many things, including one that had made me question my sexuality. I also alluded that this was due to something that had happened in my past. I didn't expand on the details.

I was certain this was going to be big so I had to tell my immediate family. Eileen already knew about it, but my sister and my parents didn't. They took it how I expected, giving 100% support, much to my relief.

On our next meeting, Sue pulled out the double-page spread that she had been working on and it was extraordinary. I didn't recognise any of the comments attributed to me, and the tone set a new narrative. It was all about my shame – as though I had done something wrong in the past. Sue led me through the article and the quotes whilst trying to convince me that it all made sense. It didn't. I was horrified. It looked like Max Clifford had managed to take control. They had buried the *Closer* article and now *The Sun* was going to run this pathetic story.

The truth was that I had done nothing wrong. I was a young adolescent and the wrong had been done to me. My actions as a consenting adult were as a result of these wrongdoings and I knew it.

I know people are born gay, but I also know people are influenced sexually by experiences. Until the age of fourteen, I was a normal, slightly shy boy, who would take the Freemans catalogue and look at the swimwear and underwear pages.

A family friend abused their trust and introduced me to a seedy world of hardcore porn and cruising for hookers around Bedford Hill in a car smelling of sex with stains on the seats.

My openness and liberal attitude were because of my past. I had let go of my shame and now they were trying to hand it back to me. It was a further manipulation, another form of control, and more emotional abuse.

Once more I was phoning Tim and complaining about something again.

Within half an hour he called me back.

'It's OK. They are not going to run the story. It's gone away,' Tim said, like it was a disease, a problem, something another generation brushed under the carpet.

He sounded relieved. Was *I* meant to be thankful? I had told *Closer* because I wanted to share this. I asked him how this could happen? It could only have been Max having to trade secrets.

'Sonny wants a meeting,' Tim added. I didn't think it was to discuss music.

When I arrived at Syco, Sonny Takhar thought he knew which buttons to press, saying I should record "The Glow Of Love" by Luther Vandross. So much for Simon not wanting to do songs where people would draw comparisons as he had said on the show.

People always feel they need to make small talk. He was just trying to put me in my comfort zone but I had no time for chit-chat. I was going through a major transition so I got him to get to the point.

'I don't think you should do any more interviews,' he began.

This had gone right to the head of the label.

'I don't see what the fuss is about,' I replied.

But I heard his words and his measured tone. At this point, I was still the only *X Factor* winner they had. Neither party really wanted to fall out for good. I was a few months into a dream that had barely got going and they needed me (presumably) to go back on the show and endorse the next series.

The meeting was a gentle reminder that it was their way or no way at all but I couldn't see how this could ever be resolved. They had given me a dark dirty secret that I was meant to be ashamed of. I was not prepared to go down that road again. This wasn't *my* indiscretion, it was theirs.

When I spoke to Eileen later I told her this was not going to end well.

I had no regrets, though. I wasn't going to have Max Clifford controlling it. He had a lot of power but this was one secret he couldn't trade.

The last time I ever saw Simon Cowell was 11 June 2004. *X Factor* musical director and producer Nigel Wright was celebrating his birthday. I liked Nigel. He had produced on my

"Heart and Soul" album and, even though he delivered what Simon wanted, I respected him immensely. It was an honour to be invited to his party.

It was a big bash. He had the most amazing marquee in his garden. There was a stage, a large dance floor, the works and a buffet and I was on a table with some friends and Martine McCutcheon, who had also worked with Nigel. The night was drifting by and I still hadn't managed to have a word with Simon.

He was sitting elsewhere and people were going over to talk to him all the time before finally I saw my opportunity.

'Hi, Simon,' I said not having seen him since him for months.

He briefly looked at me and returned to scanning the room. Hypocritically, I began the conversation with small talk instead of getting to the point.

I commented on how lovely his girlfriend Terri (Seymour) looked that night.

'You're welcome to her,' he replied, puffing on his cigarette and looking straight ahead. Mr Nasty very much in the building.

He took another big puff from his cigarette, blew it out to the side of his mouth and lent over to me.

'You're so lucky you entered last year,' he continued. 'The standard this year is so much better.'

This was no way to talk to your artist who just three weeks previously had a number one album – and now he was already thinking about the likes of the new Justin Timberlake in Shayne Ward and soul singer Andy "the binman" Abraham.

It was clear where I stood.

Simon didn't want to talk about the album. He barely wanted to converse at all.

I had to assume that word was getting back to him about the engagement shoot, BeBe Winans and *Closer* magazine.

I had to find my company elsewhere and it was a friend of

Simon's who asked me if I had thought about TV presenting. It hadn't even been on my radar. Was that where they saw me heading – as a celebrity, as a cheeky chappie judge, or as host of one of the ITV shows? I had no desire to go down that route. Was that what he really meant when he said he mapped out my career on the final the previous December? Or was he subtly telling me I was no longer on the label?

He certainly didn't want to talk about a second album. My career was in serious trouble.

The rest of June was pretty quiet considering my new *Number One Recording Artist* status, and what Simon had said to me had begun to sink in. It was time to look at what my contract said. Was I going to be able to save this relationship or was I going to have to leave the label?

Then something totally random happened. Eileen was in the kitchen when she saw two teenagers leaving the communal entrance to our apartment with three bikes, two of which were ours.

'Steve, someone's stealing our bikes!' Eileen shouted to me and I ran out.

I was within feet of grabbing them and then did that stupid thing they do in the movies. I shouted at them to stop. They looked back and dropped Eileen's bike and fled. I was barefoot and topless but I was no Tom Cruise. I was knackered after 50 metres of chasing them. I have no idea why I didn't get on Eileen's bike!

"STOP THEM! THEY'RE NICKING MY BIKE!" I shouted as they rode past a guy. I couldn't believe my luck. He was just about to get onto his motorbike and responded to my pleas.

The boys disappeared around the corner with this complete stranger hot on their heels. By the time I caught up with them I was jogging so slowly and my feet were sore. The police had the thieves face-down on the ground outside Colliers Wood bus station. My bike was lying on the floor and the guy who had saved the day was standing next to his motorbike. I couldn't thank him enough.

'I owe you a drink, fella. What's your name?'

'Simon,' he replied. What were the chances of that?

From a business who tried to invent stories or manage the tone of them, I handed the label on a plate exactly what they had asked for in their earlier email. Any British tabloid would have run a "Have a go hero" story about someone who had won a reality TV show watched by so many people. It was what they did, day in, day out. It was funny, it had a sense of justice and it involved somebody very recognisable and the hero was called 'Simon'.

But this time, there was nothing. I was being neutralised. I couldn't even get that in the paper.

Just six months after winning *The X Factor,* my mentor was hardly speaking to me, and his PR guru was killing stories. July left me with a lot to think about.

1 July 2005

I was in Ireland for the Daniel O'Donnell TV show. It was one of the best experiences I ever had on television, but it also fell on a sad day.

Daniel is a legend in Ireland and there seemed no expense spared on the show – production values were intense and I was invited to sing "Dance With My Father" (finally) with a huge band. It was amazing.

It was just what I had dreamed of every week. I told Simon I wanted to do it. I so loved the song and felt so relaxed performing it that I gave one of my best performances of it ever.

But I had to retake it – off-camera someone was moving away the steps I had to walk up to enter the stage, and as I sang the mics picked it all up. I didn't mind and it was a joy to replicate my first attempt. A song I had begged to sing on television, I was now asked to sing twice!

During that show, we learned that one of my biggest influences and writer of the song, Luther Vandross, had passed away. A shining beacon of light had just been extinguished. It was he as much as anyone who prompted me to take up singing and now he was gone. He was just 54.

I was not alone in mourning him. On the programme with me were the legendary Drifters, one of whom, Patrick Alan, I had known for years. To be on the same bill was a wonderful moment. I took it as a massive confidence boost at a time when interest in me was all but dead, and I really didn't know what I would be doing by the time this show aired in September. It gave me heart and hope that I could move in new circles and be respected within them away from the circus of the previous few months.

I had never had the chance to meet Luther, let alone work with him, though I saw him at Wembley three times. On one occasion he walked around the crowd. I reached out and we shook hands. That was as close as we got and I still hold onto it with love.

That night, we decided to celebrate Luther's life, hitting a piano bar in Dublin, and together spontaneously working our way through some of his back catalogue. I hadn't envisaged the night ending like this when I boarded the flight to Ireland. Even in death, he still brought me some of my finest memories.

Back at home, however, I knew what needed to be done.

This was the first of a few emails I sent to the only man left who could really salvage the situation.

To: Tim Byrne
From: Steve Brookstein

Dear Tim,

I hope you are well and haven't been affected too much by the hurricane. Just a quick note to suggest we meet up on your return to discuss where we go from here.

I realised the other day that since winning *X Factor* in Dec 2004, I have only done two paid gigs totalling 35 minutes and we are now in mid-July. Last year in the same period I had sung over 200 HOURS! Maybe the band should be put together to play venues like Ronnie Scott's? I also understand Syco have to decide on the option by 9th November. I would like to decide on the song I perform on *X Factor* sooner rather than later.

I would like your thoughts as to what we intend to do.

Best wishes Steve

I was back to where I started – just wanting more gigs. It had taken me a long time to put down in writing how I felt after the Thomas Cook corporate gig, but I had been busy working on the album.

Tim was away and not back until 18 July, but he will have noticed the two key points in my correspondence.

I was putting it out there in writing for the first time, the only two cards I had to play recalling both the conversations with Sonny and Simon.

Without saying so directly, I was forcing the issue on a second album and the trigger clauses in the contract, whilst floating it gently that appearing on the new series was not clear-cut.

The *X Factor* tour – all the gang with the exception of "real winners" G4 who were off promoting their album.

My nephews Sam and Harry at the judges' table after the *X Factor* Final.

The support of my family and friends helped me make it through the night.

My bizarre Robert Palmer photoshoot. Funny, Simon said that he never wanted me to be compared to anyone.

The man who talked me into having singing lessons, Ryan Lee. He had released "Broken Wings" with Tim Laws under the name *Network* in 1992. In 1996 we recorded the Teddy Pendergrass classic "Only You" under the name *The Funk Essentials*.

After MCA closed and the release was abandoned we never recorded together again. I think this photo was taken in 1998.

At the after-show party of *The Big Big Talent Show* Final in 1997 with Jonathan Ross.

One place I have played more than any other over the last ten years is the wonderful 606 Club in Chelsea.

Tabloids prefer to mention the one ferry gig I did in 2006.

As a big fan of Shalamar, it was a dream come true to tour with Jeffrey Daniel (left), Howard Hewett (right) and Carolyn Griffey.

I've been lucky to do some great things over the years, but supporting Dionne Warwick in 2004 is still one of the highlights of my career.

One of the few people in the media who have supported me from day one and after it all went wrong. Thank you, Fiona Phillips.

2005, over at Livi's studio with the amazing BeBe Winans to rerecord "Yah Mo Be There".

Below: dear friend, producer and songwriter, Clive Scott. We miss you, fella.

Above: Alan Glass has worked with so many greats. Friends for over 25 years. Still writing great songs.

Left: 1999, David Christensen with Katie Jackson in New York with the world at our feet.

Great times recording Eileen's album.

At the Oxo Tower 2005.

Above: Photos by our good friend Morag Livingstone.

Left: In 2008, Eileen and Hamish came with me on the Our House tour.

I took this photo of David Bradford at Price Studios as he took photos of the band. He also took the photos for this book, my album and Eileen's album. I love his work.

Below: Luca Boscagin on guitar. Emmanuel Waldron on keys.

28 July 2005

I was one of the last people to arrive on the red carpet for the premiere of *Herbie: Fully Loaded*. I had had a couple of beers, was running late and in a very bad mood.

In my head this was the night I left the label.

I finally had the confidence to do it ethically, but I had no confidence left at all.

The formalities were far from done but you know in your mind when it's over. Tim had been true to his word and after returning from holiday had met with me to discuss the situation. At Costa Coffee in Wimbledon I put all my frustrations on the table from the lack of gigs to the absence of singles. Even though singles were selling poorly across the board, the release of an individual track got you radio play and media coverage. I, at least, could see that was still important, but for different reasons. Tim's only solution was a lame repackaging of the album for the Christmas market and suggesting an additional two songs. One of the songs he suggested was "Buy Me A Rose" by Luther Vandross. The thought of covering a Luther track so soon after his death seemed inappropriate and I was having none of it. And once again, didn't Simon stop me singing "Dance With My Father" on *X Factor* because it would draw comparisons?

It had been six weeks since I saw Simon at that party.

I didn't really want to talk to anybody at the premiere but I was still going through motions of running my diary. Small issues were becoming big demons – and it wasn't just the press. The tide seemed to be turning against me with the public.

Outside the cinema, I caught sight of Matty – a long-term G4 fan and big devotee of most things *X Factor*. As usual, he wanted a photo. I had always obliged in the past.

Life should have been fantastic, just over six months from winning, but I had that sinking feeling that it had all gone wrong and was going to get worse before it got better.

I waved at Matty, saying I would catch him later. He overhead me saying 'Can we just go in?'

It must have upset him because soon after he took to the forums, slagging me off, saying I had changed.

I was encouraged to explain why I seemed to be behaving differently, but I was reluctant. At that stage, I didn't want to air dirty linen about the relationship with the label simply because I knew the next month would be key.

In 2004, I had occasionally infiltrated the odd forum or two under a fake username just when I thought a topic about me was going off the rails. I had to call myself 'Muggy' after the website *Digital Spy* had banned me from using my real name when I simply tried to set the record straight on a few previous digs. How I had become fair game so quickly was beyond me. Now, I did decide to engage in the end, regrettably suggesting he might like to take a long walk off a short pier.

The *Mirror* picked it up.

Either somebody helped it on its way to them or their journos were trawling my timeline and threads about me, waiting to pounce. I could draw no other conclusion.

By 1 August, I was now emailing Simon. The silence out of BMG was deafening. The new series would air in just nineteen days.

From: Steve Brookstein
To: Simon Cowell
Cc: Sonny Takhar, Tim Byrne, Dan Parker.

Hi Simon,

As discussed with Tim, I'd like to set up a meeting with you and Sonny to go over where we are at.

Hope all is well and I look forward to seeing you soon.

Best wishes Steve

I was ready to force the discussion. *X Factor* was about to start and I wanted this resolved one way or another. Privately I was telling my friend Livingstone and those people close to me it was all coming to a head. The only person who was replying to me was Tim. I do not know if he was party to a bigger picture but he had to be the middleman – his income would depend on both Simon and me, so it was in his interest to keep dialogue open.

I was becoming a recluse, snappy and tetchy at home. Not playing their game had taken its toll. With the second series imminent and trails running all the time on ITV, none of those who already half-knew their fate – because they would have probably filmed boot camp – could imagine what was about to happen behind the scenes to the show and its very first winner. And despite previous reports in the aftermath of last year that Sharon might lose her job, she was returning alongside Louis for a second series. For Shayne and Andy plus Journey South, Brenda Edwards, The Conway Sisters, Maria Lawson, and well, Chico, an autumn of hope was just beginning. For me, the sun was setting on my *X Factor* life.

Thursday 11 August 2005

When I woke that morning I could not have foreseen in my wildest dreams what these next ten days would bring – far from it, in fact.

I was relaxed and quite excited. Today was the day.

I had let Simon have his say the last time we had a big showdown in February. Now, my voice was the only one that was going to be heard.

A lot of water had passed under the bridge since then.

Now, more or less six months on and with a number one album behind me that was still pretty much panned, and with word coming to me again that album number two would be the same, I couldn't wait to look him in the eye and say to his face everything that had been brewing for some time.

One of the things that I wanted to have out with him was that, apart from the winner's song "Against All Odds", they had never released a single. I won the competition and yet I couldn't get the radio play because there was no track out there in May to lead into the album, and when they did talk about a single they then wanted to put out my version of "Dance With My Father" – in the same couple of months when Luther Vandross had died!

Despite Simon always giving me the line that singles were on the way out so there was no point, G4 managed to release three and an EP in 2005 alone! Oh, and two albums in nine months.

And then there was the timing, too – the housewives'

choice who won the competition releases his album for Father's Day. You know who had been number one on Mother's Day – G4.

Even Ged Doherty, President of the Music Division at Sony BMG said Simon should have released my album earlier. When they did there were so many issues it's no surprise that all I saw was negativity towards me alongside glowing reviews for G4.

Yet, I had done everything they had asked despite my frustration. I remembered too, that they asked me to go to that party with Mariah Carey. Then I got slagged off for going. This wasn't an isolated incident. I didn't understand how simple things like that could get so spun out of perspective, particularly when the most connected record industry man in Europe had hired the most connected PR man in the same continent.

Now was exactly the right time to put all this on the table.

I felt in an excellent position to deal.

My contract stated that on 9 November, my next advance would kick in for a minimum of £125,000. I felt sure Simon was regretting that. By the same day, they had to decide whether to pick up a second album from me or let me go. That was my hand.

To counter, Simon was desperate for me to appear on the new series of *The X Factor*. We now know this as the norm a decade later, but back then the embarrassment would have been colossal if I was nowhere to be seen at the start of the second series. To add insult to injury, not only did they want me on at the start of the live shows, they were inking me in for the final.

This wasn't about showcasing new product from me. This was about endorsing the credibility of the show. I needed to know what they thought of me artistically before I was going to go back anywhere near that stage. Things had been in the balance for too long.

So, I had cards to play and that's why I was bringing up the options now.

I was hoping it would be amicable and pleasant. I didn't see any reason for bad blood, I just wanted them to know how I felt and to show them professionally that on this occasion Simon hadn't known what he was doing.

Either way, I knew one thing, and so did Tim when I met him just before 11 am that morning.

I *was* leaving the label.

Tim wanted a quiet word before we went in just to be sure of what I was going to say. Deep down, he knew. Distance had been growing between us, too. When I really needed to talk in July he was caught in a hurricane on holiday. He had been decent but hadn't exactly been hands-on. Nor was I entirely sure that he hadn't given them a whiff of my mindset. Remember, they appointed him to me and *he* wasn't my manager until I won the show. He was almost in the uncanny position of representing both sides.

It didn't matter. This was about what I was going to say. Tim's job would be to pick up the pieces, and if that meant brokering some sort of confidentiality agreement then so be it.

I was ready. I had rehearsed this so many times in my head. It was time to make a start towards the journey's end.

I knocked and entered the room.

'Sorry, Simon can't make it. He's got to do some work on the show.' Sonny Takhar knocked me dead in one fell swoop.

I looked at Tim in surprise. He didn't seem shocked. Then I looked back at the MD of the label.

Those words that were so ready, moments before, went walkabout.

'Let's see where we are up to,' he said calmly from in front of his desk.

That phrase in itself meant that he was ahead of me. They had a deal in their head, too.

I somehow found my composure at Simon's no-show and began to find the words.

'It's good to get together to talk about the next album,' I set my position out.

'When the option period comes up, I don't want to be stuck with an album of covers and a load of negative press.'

I told him, too, that I just wasn't gigging anymore, and I had always done so. It's what I did.

And then, after about twenty minutes of chit-chat and pointers to where I was going, I told him the consequences for the second album looking like it was going to be a dud.

'If that's a case, I'm leaving the label.'

The lack of reaction told me everything. I felt sure that Tim had tipped them off.

'We'll put things in motion for you to leave the label in the New Year.'

Sonny had moved behind his desk to put distance between us now that we were coming to the business end of the conversation.

I was stunned how ready and matter-of-fact he was about the time span and the money on the table.

'You'll have to sign something, of course,' he continued. 'We did it with Gareth Gates, too.'

Gates had been runner-up on *The X Factor's* predecessor, *Pop Idol,* and it was the best part of a year before anyone knew he had left the record company. The difference is that I could see what they were trying to do.

They still wanted me on Series Two and they assumed that would buy my silence. If they could just get through the autumn, there would be another winner by Christmas and I would have fallen off the radar. If I was still under contract, I wouldn't be shooting off in the press.

The stupid thing is that I would have signed that confidentiality clause and agreed to it. But then Sonny blew it.

'OK, as it was £1 million record deal, how much are you offering me to go away?' I asked.

'£12,500,' he said sheepishly. I can't believe it was he who had decided on this figure.

It was like chess but without seeing any of the moves.

'Right, oh,' I replied.

This was not how I thought the meeting was going to go.

My mind propelled into overdrive.

That's an insult, I thought. That is not going to happen. They're trying to bury me.

I could feel myself about to explode but I wasn't there yet.

'No, that's a joke,' was my first attempt at knocking him back.

Tim was saying nothing when really he should have been doing all the talking. Tim knew that I had mentioned £100,000 or even £50,000, but £12,500?

By now I was fuming.

They hadn't even spent half of the supposed million-pound deal, and they were offering me twelve and a half k to go. I couldn't hold back any longer.

'You can stick it up your arse, you're taking the piss.'

I lost my cool.

'You want me to perform on *The X Factor* and I could sell my story for more than that.'

I had been well and truly hung out to dry. I stupidly hadn't considered that Simon's ego would actually allow him to send me packing when the talk was they wanted me on that show.

They were trying to bury me, and, worse, they were one step ahead of me.

The meeting had nowhere else to go.

'I'm going, I gotta go, thanks for the meeting,' I uttered, shaking my head in disbelief as Tim followed me out as far as the lift.

'That's a joke, mate,' I told him.

'I'll try and go for more,' he replied.

But I hadn't felt that he had supported me in there. His tone was generally non-committal.

As I pressed to go down and Tim turned to go back towards the Sony BMG office, I realised I had made a mistake. I had shared far too much with him. It had to be the only way they knew. They should have thought that meeting was about the second album and how many original tracks were going to be on it. That was my smokescreen for engineering my departure if it didn't go my way. That they already had an offer ready was based on information they shouldn't have been party to. I had been a fool. I should have kept my mouth shut until the credits began to roll on Series Two.

Friday 12 August 2005

It was Eileen's birthday. Today of all days.

I had rung her on the way home from the meeting and replayed the entire conversation as I could remember it. I was still seething so I was jumping about from one bit to the next, not necessarily in the order it happened.

Then I would remember a bit more and let rip once again. She mostly listened as she had done so many times before. It was only in the years that followed that I realised I had been talking at her and not to her.

'Guess how much they've offered,' I had said. 'Go on, guess.'

She had known, of course, how much I had already in my mind.

When I told her the figure and she asked me what I was going to do, I had simply said 'I dunno'.

I had let it all out at such pace in the car that when I had no steam left to come off and paused for her opinion, my entire tone changed on that question.

I wanted things to be amicable.

'One of you will leave with a million-pound recording contract and the other will leave with nothing,' Kate Thornton had said on the night.

Eight months later, I had never envisaged that it was possible to leave with both.

I didn't want to go to the press despite what I had said to Sonny. That wasn't my style and I wanted things to be amicable.

Also, at the back of the mind was the *Closer* article that got pulled and I really wasn't sure if they would now dig that up out of context. Nor could I know how any of it would play out full stop. Could I be absolutely 100% certain that the waters wouldn't get muddied and I could do my story justice in the 2000 words or so that I would get in a paper?

By the time I had got home, I was quiet. I had nothing else to say. The expectation of the meeting and the gut-wrenching outcome left me shattered. I had spent many hours of that previous night just contemplating.

One moment, I thought they had just made me a low offer to call my bluff so I would come running back and agree to everything and do the live shows. Then, I thought I had genuinely stunned them – surely nobody knocks back an opportunity to return to *The X Factor*. But that's exactly what I had done to get out of the deal.

Then my head was telling me it couldn't be true. I had six million votes and just twelve weeks before my album had been number one. Now I was dead in the water.

By the time I went to bed, I was starting to see some daylight between today's events and where I had to get to.

Immediately, I had to make sure that Eileen had a good day. Things had been tough and this was a chance to try and switch off a bit, but I still had legal moves to make.

When I awoke that morning, one phrase more than any other loomed large in my head.

'Log everything,' I had been told.

And then I wished Eileen a happy birthday.

In the cold light of day, I wasn't feeling overly negative. I had been here before a couple of times. Artists left record labels. It happened. It was just another record deal gone wrong. Now I needed to be practical. Negotiations started here. Emotion and disgust at their offer counted no more.

Although subdued for large parts of the day, there was no

way we weren't still going out to The Comedy Store in London that evening. It had always been a favourite of ours, and sometimes when the chips are down it's not the best place to go because you can't find anything funny. On other nights it's the perfect tonic. We really needed a good laugh.

But even before we headed out, I was back on the phone to Tim.

He couldn't see that I was serious about not going back on *The X Factor*.

'I'll tell you what, I'll go on and I'll show my arse. That's what I will do, Tim.'

And I meant every single word. I could even visualise it there and then on the big stage. They couldn't legislate for what I might do on a live TV show if they virtually dragged me there against my wishes.

'I understand your frustration,' Tim sympathised. 'I'll get it sorted, and get you off the label and then you can do your own thing.'

Since the meeting at Syco. I wasn't even convinced that he called to resolve the issues. Part of my thought-process now was that all he was interested in was my state of mind so he could report back. I didn't let on at this point that he would be next to go. I was happy for them to know that offer was an insult and performing on the show wasn't going to happen without a reasonable pay-off. I then made my excuses to hang up.

As I put the phone down, only two things were resolved in my head. I needed to meet with the lawyer fast and I had left Tim uncertain of what I might be capable of doing next.

Purely out of self-protection and not through any malice, I had begun to play Tim. What I didn't realise was that it was a massive mistake. From this conversation onwards, I had become a risk no longer worth taking.

Saturday 13 August 2005

Tomorrow is another day, as they say, and yet whilst I got up calm and with clarity, despite being picked on at The Comedy Store for being 'that *X Factor* bloke', this Saturday became representative of much of what would follow in the next seven days.

A charity match versus *Hollyoaks* left me with a dead leg, sore arm and pulled calf. Even though I was one of our better players and the only minor celeb in our team, they still wanted to sub me in a 9-1 defeat! Either way, it proved a minor distraction from the crisis at hand.

My focus had moved to the future I was trying not to dwell. Instead, my priority was to get as much money as I could to record Eileen's new album and, after that, my own. I could see a glimpse of that even if I wasn't able to get there yet.

After the football, I was stiff but energised. That high that you can get from physical exercise transferred itself to my brain and by 4 pm I was heading to the spare bedroom to finally spell out to Simon what I couldn't say at the meeting because he didn't show.

From: Steve Brookstein
To: Simon Cowell; Sonny Takhar
CC: Tim Byrne
Subject: re: meeting Thursday 11th at 11 am

Hi Simon,

Firstly I'd like to convey my disappointment that on my arrival at Sony BMG on Thursday 11th August for such an important meeting I was informed that you would be absent due to something cropping up concerning the new series of *X Factor*. I found that quite amusing.

However, I'd like to say it was good having the discussions with Sonny and Tim, and I think we are all on the same page. I understand that you are not interested in my original material and would only consider an album of covers if we were to proceed to the next option.

I did everything asked of me during and after *The X Factor*, whilst enduring a bitter and evil torrent of abuse from Louis and Sharon in the name of entertainment. I am still grateful for the opportunity the show has given me. I also appreciate that, although we don't see eye-to-eye on my future direction, you have no interest in holding me back from pursuing my goals.

The delay in the release of the album was instrumental in its underachievement, which Sonny acknowledged, and that meant the tour was delayed indefinitely. Also, with my only release becoming a charity record, the offer of letting me go with immediate effect and a £12,500 handshake wasn't what I was hoping for and told Sonny that. I requested £50,000, which I consider generous but fair.

I do not wish to dwell on what could have been. Can we resolve this on Monday morning?

Best Wishes

Steve

The cursor hovered over the 'Send' button. There was so much I wanted to say.

I was still annoyed that he didn't have the balls to meet me and look me in the face. He could barely look me in the eye at Nigel's party, but he could get away with that at a big function. In his own office, there should have been no hiding.

Reading the email back now, it doesn't reflect how I felt or represent the tone I would have taken if he had been at the meeting.

Yes – I did want to leave amicably. I saw no point in anything else. But I see the early stages of me setting out my legal position here.

Not only had I been advised to log everything, but it had been highly recommended that I convey in an email their mistakes (especially where they had admitted them) and a reminder that I had done what they asked and it hadn't worked.

I typed it out a couple of times. Eileen had a quick look at it. I didn't really want to ramble in it. I recognised that to be concise was to my advantage. The most important point, though, was that I knew I had done the right thing.

I had no doubt that I had to press 'Send', despite its potentially devastating consequences. It could only go one of two ways. They would pay me up and buy my silence until the New Year, or they would bury me.

I felt confident that they were unlikely to turn me over whilst exit negotiations were still ongoing.

I had made my second mistake in 24 hours and, even though I couldn't be sure that Tim would relay my mood rather than my expectations back to the label, either could condemn me.

Now I had showed Simon my hand, too. At the time I felt it was polite and professional. Clearly, when I refer to his absence from the meeting due to filming commitments as 'quite amusing', I have undoubtedly wound him up.

Even though I sent it on a Saturday encouraging a Monday deadline, I knew that he wouldn't come back within that timescale but I hoped it would focus his mind and force the issue. I did not realise that, with or without my email, he had already moved on.

Simon had other plans for Monday.

Sunday 14 August 2005

I checked my email as soon as I woke. There was nothing. Then I checked it again regularly until we went out for lunch.

We had spent much of the previous night with Martine McCutcheon and a photographer friend of hers at a live music venue in Putney as Eileen's birthday celebrations continued across the weekend.

As the evening drew to a close, Martine asked us what we were doing for lunch today, saying she knew a place in Fulham that did the best Sunday roasts going and before we knew it, the four of us were out again with Martine's mum, relaxing the afternoon away.

Again, it was a welcome distraction and I was able to switch off. In fact, if I *had* talked about everything, I would have only got more stressed rather than offloading the tension. Plus, Eileen and I had been through a lot. The last year had put our relationship through the wringer because of all the external pressures. I owed it to her that we just stepped out of the moment at least for an afternoon.

And it was wonderful, talking about the industry and talking about life. Martine had experienced a dalliance with pop on the Virgin label under the guidance of someone of whom I had never thought highly.

Hugh Goldsmith ran a label called Innocent Records, which was a subsidiary of Virgin Records. He had many well-known acts including Martine, Atomic Kitten, Blue and Billie Piper. In 2000, after the success of signing Katie to Columbia, Livingstone

Brown and I made our second major signing, this time to Hugh Goldsmith's label. The contract counted for nothing. No sooner had we put pen to paper than we were told to walk away from the artist (Laura), and let them take over. We were the production company, and the money was in the songwriting and production. It was clear to us that we were not going to get any part of the pie. Reluctantly and furiously, we took a small pay-off and walked away. We didn't want to stand in the way of the artist as she was a talented singer and superb dancer, but the label didn't share our vision and ultimately they let us all down. Her album never came out and they dropped her. It broke my heart. We had worked so hard on developing her album.

Martine was no longer with the label either and was now focussed on her acting career. She was looking at scripts for later on in the year. I remember her saying how the intelligence drama *Spooks* was potentially on the table which we all agreed would be a massive coup for her.

She had also recently been party to some of the abuse I would get in public after the two of us were queuing to get into Vingt-Quatre restaurant in the early hours just a week before. The doorman would normally let us in, and after a bit of sarcasm in the queue from one or two unsavoury individuals, we asked if we could go in only to be knocked back. It wasn't a problem and there wasn't a scene. The *Telegraph,* however, of all papers, took great delight in writing this up with some reference to *Breakfast at Tiffany's,* alluding to the character she had played in the soap opera *EastEnders.*

Today, thankfully, there was no such rubbish. It was only when we got back that the nonsense began.

***

Tim had emailed at just after 11 am. I hated it when an afternoon of total pleasure and peace is ruined by the knowledge that throughout that time a ticking time bomb had been sitting in my inbox waiting for me.

I read it twice. And then broke down.

When a relationship comes to an end it is sad and when you part on good terms you start to question what you could have done more. How did it all come to this?

I was angry and upset. I knew my gut feeling to break from Tim when he was away in July was correct – and now he was on holiday again. He hadn't even mentioned it.

Here I was at the lowest professional moment of my career in the middle of a game of cat and mouse and the man who is representing me, but actually had got me just two gigs since I won *The X Factor*, emails me to say he is in Venice. I couldn't believe it.

I read it again. He didn't want any commission. What? For a deal he didn't do when he was assigned to me as I won the show? How very decent.

It made me absolutely focussed that he wasn't getting a penny.

There he was telling me I was a nice guy again. How many times had I heard this? 'Nice guys don't win' rung very, very true.

He hated seeing what I had had to endure over the past months? Did he not think to stop it? Or did he really have no voice at all?

Then he turned the email onto himself saying that he was reassessing his own game and losing faith in the business.

The truth of the matter is that he went on to work for Simon in various capacities almost uninterrupted for the next decade!

'I will benefit from a fresh person taking over my affairs and he has been putting this dialogue off'. Well, it's a good job one of us brought it up rather than drifting any further.

I can see the relief in his language when he says it is a weird email to write. I read it simply as his gratitude that I had forced the issue because he didn't have the spine to do the same.

But then he wants to talk to me before I do anything. Is this to help me or to protect him? I am in no doubt, as kind as he appears to be towards Eileen and me, that business is business and information is power, and that as long as he was in the know, he still had his hands on the control.

I took just one thing from the email. At least he said he was going to talk to Sonny.

Then I scrolled down in my inbox. There was a much shorter correspondence waiting but this was the one I needed to focus on:

From: Rhian Williams, Firstmarch
To: Steve Brookstein
Subject: Chink before you drink...

Hi, Steve

Good to meet you the other night.

In light of what you told me, if you are looking to leave your agent – and you don't believe he'd stand in your way, you should ideally get something in writing from him. I haven't seen your contract so I don't know the key clauses (termination and notice periods etc) but if, like you say, he's willing to let you go immediately, I suggest something along the following lines:

Tim,

Just a quick email to sort out our management situation.

You know my preference is to move on and explore new opportunities and from what you have told me, you are looking seriously at a move back into television.

Our contract aside, my understanding is that we

are both happy to walk away now and wish each other all the best for the future. Let me know if I've got this wrong so that we can meet soon and sort this matter out.

All the Best
Steve

As for the record label – again I can't really advise until I've seen the contract but initially you have indicated that they would be willing to release you and pay the remainder of your advance (plus £12k). Having given the matter further thought I think it is probably wise not to put into writing any indication that you are terminating – or perceived to be terminating. There may be something in the contract which penalises you for doing so.

Let's revise this when I see the contract.

Look forward to seeing you on Wednesday – let me know if you cant make it, but in the meantime, I'll have a think where we can get salmon and eggs at 11 am in Soho!

See if you can bring the management and recording contracts along.

Similarly, let me know if you want me to invite Stuart Higgins (agent, ex *The Sun* editor) along for a chat too...

See you then
Rhian

It had been Martine who had put me in touch with Rhian. I was grateful that she took the time to email on a Sunday afternoon. Her counsel continued to be the most rational voice in my head.

It became hard to focus. My inbox showed quite clearly

both sides of the problem. Calm, considered practicalities going forward from the lawyer, and a bundle of debatable, well-meaning nonsense from my manager.

One made me resolute; the other made me question myself. When I spoke to Rhian on the phone I knew what had to be done and was very systematic about it. But if I tried to reply to Tim on email, it just took so long. I was gutted.

One by one the wheels were coming off and, even though I had forced the situation and it was what I wanted, the dismantling of the dream in a little over 72 hours was hard to take. Simon, the label and the manager were all, in effect, gone and I was starting to feel like I had no control in this at all.

By the time Eileen and I made our way to the spare bedroom to compose a reply, it was well into the early hours of Monday morning. As we knelt down at the computer, we reread Tim's words.

Now, all we could see was spin and some of the tears in shock from earlier became outright anger. Relief, emotion and uncertainty had torn my soul apart all evening. I had said little all night. Some hours on, and I found Tim saying he didn't want any money to be a disgrace. That topped the lot. I just didn't feel he merited it – perhaps he knew that. There hadn't been any other big bucks or lucrative deals, and, most importantly to me, where were my gigs? On one of the few deals he did with Thomas Cook, Tim managed to get himself a freebie holiday to the Seychelles!

Eileen was more disappointed than me. In fact, it was bigger than that. I was risking everything if I stayed. Eileen told me she wouldn't stick with me through another album and that I had been awful to live with. Moody and short-tempered had been the norm. I wasn't happy. She wasn't happy. Leaving was for the best. Tim was always so pleasant to her in the emails, but it was Eileen who reminded me again that I was sitting here doing nothing, and so, after a momentary wobble, I began to compose a reply. It's thanks to her that I finally saw the light of day.

From: Steve Brookstein
To: Tim Byrne
Subject: Re: (no subject)

Dear Tim,

I have a lot of respect for you. Your email was touching and confirmed what I already knew. You are a gentleman with integrity, thank you for your generosity it REALLY will help me out and I won't forget it. Though I also have lost faith in this business on numerous occasions, music is all I know.

You have always been more than a manager. I know our friendship will long continue and Eileen is fond of you, too!!! Dinner or lunch whenever you want. We've been thinking of you on your birthday, but guess you've been trying to separate business from pleasure. Yes I am sad, but hey...take a look at me now! Same words, right sentiment.

Talk very soon.

Steve

It would be incorrect to say I didn't mean a word of it, but that wasn't far from the truth. Sincere or not, I had my game head-on. This was all about following the legal advice. Don't get emotional, keep it polite and remind them of the facts. It would be rude to just ignore Tim's original email but I had nothing to give in response. Pleasantries were the order of the day.

I didn't get much sleep. I was never to see Tim again.

Now And Then

With the glow of the sun, and the birds sing their song
It was here, and it was gone
Holding hands with the moon, a sunny soft afternoon
I don't know where it went wrong
Now and then, I remember when... you loved me.
Now and then, I'm there again.
Spending years in one day, Wasting time on the way
I was weak and you were strong
Watching stars falling from your eyes, watching truth turn to lies
I don't know where it went wrong
Now and then, I remember when... you loved me.
Now and then, I'm there again.

Monday 15 August 2005

There was nothing in my inbox from Simon. I don't know what I was expecting. If he couldn't be bothered to show for a meeting and hadn't apologised up to this point, I was foolish to think replying to me was the first thing on his radar when he stepped back into the office.

I was grateful for the distraction that Eileen, Livingstone and myself were in the studio working on a track for her new album.

It was a fantastic leveller, too – a great reminder of why I had even entered the competition in the first place. What a contrast, as well, to be with my girlfriend and one of my two long-term confidantes, cut off from the outside world on this of all days.

I had wonderful memories of Livi's studio. It wasn't big but it had a calmness that brought out the best in me. It was in Kensal Road just off Ladbroke Grove, and was in a building, Canalot Studios, that was a hub for creatives. You would always see big names coming in and out. It was inspiring. We had written many of the songs there that got us so near in the US, a deal with Hugh Goldsmith and my publishing contract with EMI.

Today was different, and there was no way I wouldn't make the session even with everything going on with the label. Whether it had been Eileen or not, when it came to music I was 100% committed.

On the way into the studio Eileen talked about Tim's email

and how sad things had turned out. I was going to speak to him again today and get him to push Simon to respond to my email to him. I was determined to get it sorted and hoped my 'Can we resolve this on Monday morning line' focussed his mind.

I knew I had a fan base. It was a no-brainer that I could have made a great album for Simon. Eileen had been in the audience every week and had seen their reaction first-hand. Livi was of the same opinion. But it was over and my hopes from here were about re-creating more of these studio sessions with my £50,000 pay-off so that we could pick up the pieces and start again, again! My plan was to take a timeout whilst carrying on working with Eileen and then maybe go to a small independent label some time in the future. I was fed up of being burned by the big boys. I was back in an environment where I felt happy.

We were starting out on a song called "Now and Then". This was to be the title for Eileen's album, which was a mix of old jazz standards and some new songs written specifically for the album. We wanted a title track.

We would always start a session with coffee and a long chat about things and we had lots to talk about. Livingstone had a good perspective because I trusted him and he had known me for so long. We were all in agreement. It wasn't who I was or what I was meant to be doing, and it was right to force their hand. I would finally find out how badly or how little they wanted to work with me, though I had long since questioned their desire to do anything meaningful at all.

When it came to the song, Livi and Eileen wanted it to be an uptempo number but I was adamant it was to be a ballad. Though I felt I was focussed, I was clearly leaning towards melancholy. It is only years after that Eileen told me just how sad I was on that day. I didn't realise until she told me.

"Now and then, I remember when you loved me. Now and then I'm there again."

I was clear that was the chorus and in the hours that followed we had written one of my favourite songs. I can see how subconsciously I was penning my current mood.

In between writing and takes we would all stop and chat about the situation.

Then I received the first of many calls. It was Clemmie Moodie from the *Daily Mail.*

I stepped out into the hall. 'Simon has just done a press conference,' she began. 'He says G4 are the real winners of *The X Factor.*'

This was it.

'And Louis says you are being dropped from the label.'

We were on for a few minutes only and she did most of the talking. I wasn't ready to share with her what I knew. I had to find out for myself exactly what they were doing. Where they pressuring me into accepting their offer?

Of all the press I had dealt with I had felt that Clemmie was one I could come close to trusting. I also had a call from a PR called Amie Scott who had been working with Max Clifford previously. Both wanted my story.

Amie was talking about selling it to *Heat* magazine and Clemmie wanted lunch the next day. I really was not making the best decisions at this point – understandably – but for the moment held them off.

'I'm in the studio, let me think about it,' I stalled.

But I couldn't think straight at all.

I headed back into the studio to apologise for the delay and to relay the news.

Eileen shook her head as if to say 'enough is enough'. She felt this had started to go wrong when I shouted at the A and R guy Dan Parker after refusing to go along with the set-up pap shots of our 'engagement'. I had felt it coming since that party in June.

A long day just got longer. Clemmie rang again, and I

spoke to my lawyer. Rhian was now my only counsel. Tim was for small talk.

We tried to carry on working late into the night but the phone didn't stop.

'This is what we do, make music. This is our power.' Livingstone offered his perspective. 'You're better off out.'

I knew he was right but it didn't stop that sinking feeling. One by one, the nails were going in and the Syco machine was ramming the coffin lid shut.

And why? Because I said I wanted to leave the label? Because I had done an embarrassing interview? Because someone had told Simon I had been difficult?

I do not see sticking up for what you believe in musically as difficult.

Livingstone then suggested I read "The Art Of War" by Sun Tzu. Sun Tzu was a Chinese military general, but the advice he gave for fighting foes in conflict has been interpreted for business.

We had a good chat about the terrible position I was in and considered all my options. I felt I was on the verge of a humiliating defeat, and I saw no way out. This book would become my bible.

By the time I got home, I picked up an earlier email from Tim:

From: Tim Byrne
Subject: Re: (no subject)
To: Steve Brookstein

Your talent will always find a way of expressing itself Steve. Life's journey is a complex road but I know you will search for the positive in every scenario.

I will telephone Sonny and then report straight to you and look forward to speaking soon today.

Let's go out and get trashed!

Tim x

The email didn't merit a reply this time. It was brief but by saying 'search for positive' it was saying 'don't do anything stupid', so I just hit delete. This was no time for turning crucial, life-changing decisions into poetry. Tim was now officially out of the game.

And when I learned that there had been a new offer, it was this that tipped me over the edge and persuaded me to meet Clemmie. Under the new deal, I really was going to bare my arse on *The X Factor*.

Stressed as I was, I spotted their cunning. Now there was a split offer on the table. I could have 20k. They were making it look like they had upped the deal – as though my valid points had got to them. There was a catch, though.

I could have ten now and ten when the series was over. They were attempting to buy my silence. Meanwhile they were setting their new narrative. You couldn't have a confidentiality agreement that only went one way.

I also clocked the parallel lives that they were running. Here they were fronting up to the media in what I do believe was a scheduled conference with the new series starting on the Saturday, but laying into me at the same time. The negotiations were purely to keep me from going to the press before they did. They had got the jump on me and the new narrative was set.

Tuesday 16 August 2005

In the early hours of this morning, I wrote it all down in my diary:

"Can't sleep. One of the worst days of my life. I feel totally let down. The phone hasn't stopped ringing all day. It started with a call from a friend at the *Daily Mail*. Apparently Simon did a press conference today. Both he and Louis are trying to bury me. I fear they will succeed.

Louis announced I had been dropped, and Simon said G4 and Louis had won *The X Factor* on account that they have sold more than I have. Thanks, Simon. I can't begin to say how that makes me feel. Simon has undermined my achievement; he is now saying that this year will be bigger and better. Last year's finals were like a freak show. Thanks again, Simon. You, Louis and Sharon chose those acts from 50,000 and those freaks were the best you could find.

Simon also said at the press conference that we are still in touch and that he is considering what to do with me. The thing he did not mention was that he had just agreed with my manager that I could go and was willing to give me a £12,500 handshake so I went quietly like Gareth and Michelle (McManus from *Pop Idol*)! £12,500?! Nearly 6 million votes and that's it, huh? Oh well. I guess I shouldn't be surprised. I kept the email in case I need to prove it. He has now upped it to £20,000. Half now and the rest after *The X Factor* is finished. Funny that! Oh, and as for seeing me, I've not seen Simon since Nigel Wright's birthday party where he said to me, 'Steve you are so lucky you didn't enter this year!' Thanks again, Simon.

What should I do? Sod the money and tell all? Very romantic. Not practical, though. I could be better at keeping my diary and one day once I've made it big as a singer/writer I can tell all in a book!!! Hee hee!"

The giddiness of 4 am was a mask hiding tired and emotional eyes. I had learned hard from my mistake that trying to be civil and respectful only backfired.

By this morning, though, I was under no illusions. I had to act quickly to save myself. This was it. Negotiations could continue or conclude behind the scenes, but he had put down a marker. Now it was my turn to fire off some rockets.

That lunchtime Eileen and I met Clemmie in Wimbledon Village.

I stopped on the way to see the fallout in the papers from the press conference from the previous day.

Simon was bigging up Il Divo.

'They've done 5 million albums against 250,000 with Steve. Sometimes you win because you're popular. G4 came second and they sold more records.'

That made me sick and didn't sound like the man from last December who said I deserved to win.

Then he crushed me.

'He would still be singing in pubs.'

'No, I would have supported Lionel Richie!' I thought. Ironically, that show was at Wembley across the road form Fountain Studios on that very night I won *X Factor*. It was my *Sliding Doors* moment.

This pub singer label had stuck. That label was ultimately going to be used as a tool to embarrass me and reduce my worth over the years.

Then to top it all, the judges had vowed to be nicer to each other in the new series, saying last year had 'ended badly' to put it mildly.

All the rumours that Sharon was getting sacked because of the way she spoke to me turned out to be nonsense. And when Simon decided early in 2005 to take Sharon back, I knew she had a good chance of getting her wish.

'Last year the final was all about the talent; I thought it was all about me,' she was quoted as saying.

Her arrogance was breathtaking.

It fired me up for the meeting with Clemmie.

I couldn't bring myself to tell her the whole story. I was very concerned about how her copy could fall into the hands of a sub and, before I knew it, a headline was misrepresenting me. I also didn't know how many of the press knew about the *Closer* story and if that was going to appear on the agenda after Max Clifford had worked so hard to remove it. I was now worried that Max could find a way of twisting that story to ridicule me further.

I did my best to make sure Clemmie was in full possession of the facts that mattered. I hoped she would be true to what I was saying.

'Who gets dropped twelve weeks after having a number one album?' I asked her.

I wanted to remind people that the claim that I couldn't sell records so soon after a number 1-selling album was absurd.

I felt neither relaxed nor relieved at the whole interview. But I was calculating. I had worked out in my head that I needed to do two things. The first was to leave stuff out. I made sure she didn't know about the Sinitta story or Sharon's personal attack at rehearsal.

I could have easily put it out there, given what had been said yesterday re the judges' behaviour but it didn't need to play now. Even in my dazed state, I could see that both those stories had weight, and that the time and place for them was not now.

I was also conscious that, even though Simon had gone on the attack, we were still in negotiations and I should pace myself.

My second strategy was very much predetermined. I was absolutely sure I would leave them with the words 'cheesy' and 'karaoke'. They had damaged my reputation and I was going to give them some back.

And that's exactly what I did.

Wednesday 17 August 2005

"*The X Factor* Is Killing Music" read the headline.

'Oh God,' I thought.

What have I done? One day's decision is another day's consequence. I felt good but naughty. It seemed the correct thing at the time and I had the right to say it.

I was desperate. I kept thinking if they had just given me fifty fucking grand none of this would have happened, but I now see they could never have been able to offer me a figure that might help me get back on my feet.

I had been batted into a corner and had nowhere to turn. It wasn't about slagging off the show at that point. It was simply about exuding muscle – to tell Simon I wouldn't go quietly if he was playing by those parameters. There was no need for him to be so dismissive of me at the press conference particularly as he knew I was the one who wanted to leave the label. They wanted me there, subservient but quiet; they wanted me on the new show and were happy doing a new album as long as it was their album.

I would have respected him if he said we were parting because we had different ideas musically, but he had clearly moved on and done so at speed.

I no longer saw his lack of replies to my emails as rude. I just understood where it put me in the priority list and, foolishly, at the time I was 'negotiating' with him on Saturday in a one-way dialogue, he already knew he was having a press conference on the Monday. That was the game I was losing that I had turned up two days late for.

'*The X Factor* is all about one big theatre. It's turning music into WWF,' I had told Clemmie.

Again I was referred to as a former pub singer. In an article that was supposed to be pro me, I was still singing down the boozer.

As I read it, I remembered Max Clifford giving me a lesson in PR in his office, telling me that you sometimes had to put a soundbite out there at the start of the week and then bang its drum again a couple of days later. By the Friday, if you had done your job properly they were repeating your words ad infinitum.

Suddenly, one of the Sharon and Louis phrases from last autumn was becoming my epitaph. It smacked of Max.

Sure enough, as the years rolled by, this was where it started, and from here it became unstoppable. I was forever the former pub singer from this moment on.

I read on:

'I've now got to break away from *The X Factor*, which is fundamentally cheese and regarded as so by anyone and everyone in the industry.'

I was happy with this line from Clemmie but also felt short-changed.

'Brookstein, 36, spoke out after it was revealed that he had been dropped by his label, Sony.'

I specifically told her the truth about the sequence of events and she knew that it was me who wanted to leave and that they had spun it to save face. Somehow, a subeditor had quashed any balance she might have included and I was no better off than when I started.

It was a waste of time. Whether external forces were applying pressure or it was just sloppy editing, the key detail was omitted. Nowhere in the article did it confirm the truth that it was I who was parting company with Simon.

I felt as well that the voters needed to know this. Many

people forget the huge numbers that were cast and, of those, countless came up to me to tell me of the £600 they had run up in phone bills. I was stunned at the time and felt guilt on their behalf. Nobody should shell out that much only to be spun a lie later.

Clemmie did mention that the million-pound deal wasn't that at all, but it didn't leap off the page in the way that such an outrageous lie should.

Instead I was left feeling hollow and ridiculed when once again the same old *X Factor* speak reappeared at the foot of the article.

'Although he has replaced his Volvo, he has exchanged it for a Mini – not a Porsche.'

This is what journalists did. It was a harmless phrase, but it was a piss-take, harking back to Sharon's belittling of me on the night. One innocent, out of context, barely on camera comment and it becomes the language of the show prominent in beginning the process of mocking me.

Clemmie rang to say it was a good piece. I wasn't that happy but she insisted that she did her best but higher powers interfered.

Amie Scott was pushing me about doing the *Heat* magazine piece. I knew it was time to withdraw for now. Even though she was no longer working for Max Clifford I just couldn't trust her, and having seen what happened with *Closer*, I just couldn't count on the editorial process anymore.

I had to get in front of a TV camera and say the words myself to anyone who wanted to hear it from the horse's mouth. I would bide my time and refocus on the exit deal.

Written press were now off the agenda and next week's *The Dukes of Hazzard* premiere would be my moment. I knew, too, that I had said the wrong things to Clemmie. I was angry and didn't mean to attack the show that so many good people were working on. My issue was with Simon and the record label.

The only quotes she should have walked away with were 'Simon is lying. I requested to leave the label. There's more that I can say, but I won't.'

Only after the event did I understand this. As I said, I wasn't making great decisions and they had upped the ante.

With just two days to go until the new series and almost a week on from the non-meeting with Simon and Sonny, I had a word with myself.

I took a step back and sought clarity. Rhian got me back on track. Rattled by my own article and feeling an inner lack of self-worth that I had brought on by doing it, I decided to have one final crack at Simon. I really didn't want to take on Max Clifford and *The X Factor* machine. They had gone public and I had responded. I was hoping they would call a truce. This was my last card and, knowing that he wouldn't reply, I was simply engaging for the legal trail:

From: Steve Brookstein
To: Simon Cowell, Sonny Takhar
CC: Tim Byrne

Dear Simon

I understand from Tim that the offer of £12,500 and immediate termination of the contract has been changed to £10,000 now and a further £10,000 in December still with immediate termination of the contract. Obviously this is on top of the outstanding advances due to me.

Please can you contact me by email by the end of play this Friday 19 August with confirmation that the improved offer is correct. I would like to conclude this matter in a manner that shows mutual respect.

Best Wishes Steve

I wasn't expecting a further offer to reach me via Tim. I had pretty much given up on any concept of 50k.

I just wanted to show him we could both play the game. It was a far cry from when he released "Against All Odds" and assured me 'Don't worry, Steve, I'll look after you'.

He was *definitely* taking care of me!

The lack of respect shown by not turning up to the meeting told you that he had already decided how to play the game and, looking back, unless he was offering me a new album with some originality, he had no choice.

Even if we could agree on a figure, once I had done *Closer* and *The Sun* interviews, any confidentiality agreement could not include these confessions. It could only cover *X Factor*.

Rhian emailed to support me to say I had done the right thing.

From: Rhian Williams (FirstMarch)
To: Steve Brookstein

Thanks, just received this.
    Looks good – let me know as soon as you hear anything.

Best
Rhian

I knew I had as well. The only problem was letting her know as soon as I heard anything. That was going to be a long wait.

Thursday 18 August 2005

Today felt insignificant. It was the calmest day of the week by a long way and, of course, before every storm comes that calm.

There was no reply from Simon. Tim had almost gone to ground, and Rhian was just checking in keeping me on track.

I was forming a plan about the Duke premiere next week and generally ignoring Amie's calls. Part of me sensed she had learned from Clifford and was trying to make a name for herself, and I was the obvious first port of call. Overriding, though, was the belief that I just couldn't get it out there in the printed word.

I was keen to get money from Simon on moral grounds, but Amy's offer of 5k for *Heat* was neither here nor there and there was no ethical yardstick to measure that against.

I knew on this day that my motivation for talking to the press was taking me nowhere. I couldn't persuade any journalist to write the truth that Simon was lying.

Instead they kept churning that line that I couldn't sell records. I sold them a TV show and some 6 million votes!

I was surprised that nobody questioned that I had been "dropped" weeks after a number one album with no single support. The blame for the lack of success was being put firmly at my door.

To be suddenly on the outside of spin was a very harsh place to me. Even though I don't feel that I had done well in the press that year, there's a massive difference between that and it turning full-on against you.

I sensed foul play when I got a tip-off that the tabloids were about to run a story about one of Westlife being gay – as if that was a surprise to anyone. Westlife, of course, were very much part of the Simon-Louis stable and the press must have known for ages that Mark Feehily was not straight.

Why, on today of all days, was this story about to run? I am convinced it is related to the *Closer* article that Max Clifford pulled in which I questioned my own formative sexual experiences and the notion of choosing your own sexuality. If I had gone to the press or even done a blog, it would have made it awkward having an artist in the closet, especially if it was the label's decision. This told me that they were concerned I was putting everything on the table before the new series started on Saturday.

As it happened, I wasn't.

I had the entire day to lick my wounds. I just wanted it over. The negative press had gone from casual digs in the last half a year to approaching a now full-on assault.

I was determined to fight but I couldn't take much more right now.

Within 24 hours, I didn't have to.

Friday 19 August 2005

'Yeah, of course I've seen it!'

The credits were still rolling when the phone rang.

I assumed it was one of my friends asking if I'd watched it. They would have known I would, of course. It was not unusual to get the call after something *X Factor*-related had been on TV. I couldn't have got it further wrong.

Just an hour before, Eileen and I had turned on ITV2 in our kitchen to watch an *Xtra Factor* special – *The Joy of X*.

In reality, nobody remembers this show and probably hardly anybody saw it on the night, but media types would be watching. It was to be Simon's big curtain-raiser for the much-anticipated Series Two – a look back at Series One.

Of course, being closer to the show than most, I had heard whispers of what the second series would be. In fact, they were more than whispers because they had come from the horse's mouth.

At that party for Nigel Wright in June, Simon told me himself.

'The standard this year is so high.'

In particular he was alluding to the likes of Andy Abraham, and the eventual winner, Shayne Ward. By this point, word had also got back to me that they were going to be tighter than ever on the contracts and that acts like Andy were being quietly advised not to mess up or end up like Steve Brookstein.

Clearly my emails to Simon had upset him.

So I didn't know what to expect when *The Joy of X* aired.

Initially, it was the same old same old – compilations and recaps of last year's competition featuring the best and the worst. It felt a good, light-hearted watch and they just wouldn't let that chicken thing go! And then, a short while in, it dawned on me how little I was in the show. I had enjoyed seeing all the old clips and all the old faces, many of whom I hadn't seen since they left the contest, but once that bit was over I stopped laughing about it in the kitchen and withdrew into myself.

'G4 are the real winners,' Louis announced with glee.

There was that soundbite again from earlier in the week.

Then Simon said it, too.

Where was the narrative supporting me as the winner? Where was the carrot to those watching 'that you could be the next Steve'? Why were they bigging up G4 and their platinum album and their forthcoming tour when I had never released a single to their three and I had barely gigged outside of *The X Factor* tour?

'I feel like I've been erased from history,' I turned to Eileen.

I began pacing up and down. I thought about the tour, the adverts in the programme, G4's release date. *Were* they the real winners all along?

Or maybe I was just too much like hard work? My experiences of the record deals taught me about options in the contracts, and that had caught him on the blind side. Most artists he had ever worked with would have waited for the manager to bring it up and mine hadn't even thought about raising the question. He knew I was looking to bring originality to my work. It wasn't like I was greedy either. I would have happily done another album half-full of covers if I could have put three or four original tracks of mine on there. I was first and foremost a singer/songwriter. I had no intentions of being his latest Robson and Jerome squeaky clean bubble gum pop.

And yet, they weren't slaughtering me on the *Joy Of X* itself. They couldn't. I had 6 million votes. You can't alienate all those viewers. It wasn't Sharon tearing into me all over again – Simon admitted to 'mistakes' in that press conference earlier in the week. This, though, was character assassination by what they didn't say.

'Can you believe it?' I turned to Eileen.

Eileen just soaked it up. She had seen enough at first hand of what the last year had done to me.

Even Tabby who had come third had a show made about him called *What Tabby Did Next*, and that was scheduled for the next night. The guy who wasn't even runner-up got a TV show made about him when the answer to the question in the title was nothing. Here I was – the winner – all but airbrushed from the story before my very eyes as the narrative turned into a piece all about Simon wanting to win next time. Who actually even cares which judge wins? They didn't even care which winner won.

I can tolerate an edit for functional reasons like time. I just about understand a manipulative cut to position acts or judges accordingly. But the fact that it was all about G4 being the real winners told me I was gone and there was no way back.

I had been saying for a month I had wanted to leave the label and if negotiations had stalled as either side jostled for position, I was now in no doubt of what was coming.

Staring at the TV as the show wound up, my heart sank. I was finished.

And that's when Max rang.

'What's that about?' I was in shock that Max was calling me at home on the eve of the new *X Factor* straight after this hatchet job on me. This was moving too fast. I never expected that they were willing to go this far.

When Simon had said 'We let him go' and hearing about it second-hand was one thing, but when Max rang and coldly delivered his threat, it impacted on me directly.

'Talk to the press and we'll bury you.' He didn't beat around the bush.

'I'm sorry?' I questioned as though I just hadn't heard him.

The truth is I had. I just didn't believe what he was saying.

'Look, Steve, I would love to see you about at the charity balls and that in three years' time, but all these things aren't going to happen if you talk to the press. We'll bury you.'

I looked at Eileen. 'Who is it?' she mouthed.

'Max, this is out of order,' I told him, facing out at my kitchen window.

He knew I would be watching and there was no coincidence in the timing of the call.

'They've already admitted they took too long to release my album.' I threw everything back at him.

'You're a nice guy, Steve. These things happen.'

That was his lame response.

'Why do I have to take this?' I never thought I would be raising my voice to Max Clifford.

'Why am I the bad guy? I did everything asked of me.'

He was calm just like Tim. I was sick of this passive-aggressive 'I'm sorry but...' bollocks.

I was now furious. I had not spent my twenties coming to terms with my demons to have a bunch of power-crazed, money-grabbing freaks do this to me. It was not right.

He listened without trying to calm me down or interrupt. It was like he expected it and was waiting for me to run out of things to say.

'Don't make life hard, Steve, It doesn't have to be this way,' he uttered as he had probably a million times before.

He had an ice-like tone of condemning me whilst radiating a 'don't shoot the messenger' stance.

I couldn't stand to be cheated or patronised anymore.

'Oh right, I understand.'

I could not believe I was even having this conversation.

Then he repeated the threat again.

Eileen could hear every word but by now I had nothing left.

'No hard feelings.' And Max signed off, knowing full well that those three words meant nothing to him.

I said goodbye and hung up.

I wasn't done at all. I had plenty left in the tank. I just didn't want him to know it. I knew he would put the phone down thinking 'Job done. That's Brookstein taken care of. We won't hear from him again.'

But, like Louis Walsh, he didn't know me.

'This is it now,' I told Eileen.

I fell short of calling it all-out war but I knew what I had to do. That *The Dukes of Hazzard* premiere next week suddenly assumed more importance than ever. That was my moment to look into a TV camera and say my piece and those red carpet shots were so brief that they wouldn't be able to edit anything out because there would be nothing left.

I categorically ruled out doing the *Heat* magazine piece. I couldn't know the headline they would make and I wouldn't get copy approval. One thing I didn't want at this time was anyone saying I had done it for money. People needed to know about Max and they needed to know the lies and the spin – a control which went all the way back to last autumn when they started positioning me as a pub singer, a Volvo lover and a guy desperate for fame who kept his speakers in his mum's garage.

Could they spin the *Closer* article? I had done it just before I was 'dropped', and the links to child abuse and the fact that it never came out at the time caused them a problem. I was worried, but I sensed it was more their secret than mine. I was willing to speak about it all, but now I had to keep it back. I didn't trust the press.

I no longer cared about the 50k, the 12½ grand or the split offer. I didn't want blood money anymore to gag me forever. It was immoral that a million-pound record contract had come to this, but all that mattered now was getting my story out there – not for cash but for integrity.

And yet, when I looked back on the last seven days, of course I now realised they had been screwing me all week. It's one thing knowing something is coming but when it does it blows you out of the water.

As I pieced it together, it all made sense.

'Simon can't make it. He's got to do some work on the show,' Sonny had said last Thursday.

I now understood what that work was. He was back in the studio and the edit suite rewriting the history of Series One.

'G4 were the real winners.'

It kept playing in my head.

If only I had waited and not played my hand the week before Series Two. I thought that was the time to deal. I was so annoyed with myself but how was I to know?

Tonight, for the first time, I realised that there was going to be no deal at all and that in fact they had already long since begun to bury me.

Saturday 20 August 2005

ITV2 aired *What Tabby Did Next*. Today it has been reported that he has been dropped by Sharon. I had worked with an artist for two years before we finally got her signed to a major label, but just eight months after all Sharon Osbourne's big promises to Tabby she was letting him go. Not exactly artist development. On camera she had made out they were close and she mothered him so much you would think she was considering adoption. He did get one major gig and that was supporting Rod Stewart... a gig he got himself!

Tabby told me just weeks before that Sharon had said he would be releasing a single.

On next to no sleep, he had flown off from Ireland for a meeting and driven with Sharon to the label headquarters in Putney. He said to me it was like old times and everything was going to be great.

He waited outside whilst Sharon went in for a meeting. When she came out, it was all over – different expression on her voice and her tone had changed in a matter of minutes. She had cut him dry, or been told to, accusing him of going to the press, and saying Louis had told her this.

There was no obvious reason to the timing. Perhaps it saved Sharon. I had been virtually erased overnight from the show's interest and now Tabby was gone, too. Perhaps Simon couldn't be seen to be the only mentor who had burned his star?

Was the only way for Sharon to survive or for the show to

proceed incident-free to pretend like none of it had ever happened? It looked that way.

The next day it was all over the *Mail on Sunday*.

Monday 22 August 2005

One by one, they were letting me know that the wheels were off. They had moved on and their new show was on the air. Senior executives were no longer replying to me and gently they were stripping me bare. One of the few emails I did receive simply told me not to contact Simon again.

I hadn't foreseen that the burial was instant and this petty.

I was due to attend *The Dukes of Hazzard* premiere in London. Eileen was travelling back down from Scotland especially. I didn't care for the movie, nor the supposed red carpet trappings, but sometimes you had to move in these circles to meet people, pick up advice and let people know you were still out there.

I had always thought the red carpet was for stars. I was realistic, I had won a talent show, but I wasn't a star and ironically felt like a fake. But after the war of words of the previous week and the untruths being cast about me, I needed to set foot on it this time. Twitter was still a year away (though for me five years), so this was my best chance to speak to one of the many cameras. Simon had stolen a march on me by addressing the entire tabloid press and recording his propaganda TV show. I had to do the same.

Half an hour before we were due to leave, the phone rang. We were already dressed for the night. It was Dan from the label telling us that our invitation had been withdrawn. Overnight we had become persona non grata.

Eileen didn't deserve any of this but it was a clear message that the machine was brutal and that Max wasn't joking. Obviously, I was fuming.

It was like *Closer* all over again but this time over a damn movie. They had pulled that article because they perceived it as dangerous to the kind of pop acts they were selling, or for some other darker reason, and now, free from those constraints, I was silenced again.

They obviously took one look at it and knew it was a risk. The soundbites on the red carpet are often just that – short and inane. Occasionally a Tom Cruise will take your phone and pretend to call a friend, but for the most part it was just a show of Hollywood glitter. There was absolutely no doubt that the showbiz journalists, many of whom I had already met in the previous six months, *wouldn't* come to me for a word.

They were turning off my oxygen and leaving nothing to chance. They couldn't have me contaminating the clean air of the new series.

The one positive from this mess was that the more they knocked me down, the more they built us up. My relationship with Eileen had been crumbling since the stresses of the show but now she was seeing first-hand what I had been going through. She understood my anger and I understood she was still with me despite my terrible moods. We hugged. We were dressed up with nowhere to go and my career was going down the toilet, but somehow it didn't matter. This was the closest we had been in months.

It was clear I had been played. When I was sending those emails, they had the power and the patience to sit it out. They would deal with me in time. They had to air their new series.

I had nothing but the woman I was holding in my arms.

I had to get free from the deal and find a way of salvaging what I could. I had to finalise the exit. I couldn't move on contractually without getting what was owed to me, and that included incidental detail like my fan base from www.stevebrookstein.com.

Naturally, I could barely bring myself to catch any of the new series but I was curious as to how much better the standard really was. The theme tune even made my stomach churn. It was like catching the scent of an ex who had gone with my best friend.

The confidence I had before I entered *X Factor* was gone and, despite Sharon's accusations, I had never felt so vulnerable.

I would fulfil any other arrangements that hadn't been taken from my diary, but now it was time to give something back whilst protecting myself from further ridicule and humiliation. I wanted to work on Eileen's album. It was where I felt safe. I would be back to being the man I was before *X Factor*, writing for an artist with the hope of getting them signed. And I had total faith in Eileen's ability.

You should never spend money you don't have, but I had plans for that £50k. Instead I was left with nothing, not a single piece of paperwork telling me I was free.

That's not entirely true – my release from contract with Tim was handwritten on a comp slip in which he simply relinquished all rights. That was it. It was unbelievably nonchalant. I suppose as he wasn't getting another penny from me, he wasn't willing to spend another minute on me.

I finally got my database to my website, back but they dragged that out, too. I lost a lot of fans in this time and, going forward, they were all I had professionally.

They wanted it over and they wanted it done quickly, with no real legal nous for anything in the future.

That's why I, more than any others, can tell my story.

I was still in touch with a few contestants from our year and a few staff from the show in general. Several things got back to me. One, in particular, seemed to ring loud and true – that they *had* tightened up the contracts in the second year and *were* putting it out to the likes of Andy Abraham and Shayne Ward that 'they didn't want to end up like Steve Brookstein'.

It was hard to put that year above all years behind me, but every autumn that followed, when the trails and the music would start up again, it all just came flooding back. You could try to get on with your life for eight months or so but then, come the autumn and you saw the same themes, techniques and positioning, you wondered how many more would end like me, knowing it was not a good place to be.

I would find myself questioning all the decisions I had made. Should I have pursued the options in the contract? Was another album of covers that bad? Was I a fool not to go back on the show as the previous winner and to fall out with Simon publicly?

It became a matter of principle to walk away. I was prepared to sacrifice everything so that I wasn't seen to endorse the product. I was well aware even at that point that, by reappearing, I was opening myself to that criticism in the future.

I didn't really know what I would end up saying as time went on, but I was clear that whatever I would say would be undermined if I had emerged on the first live show saying I had a fabulous time and it had all gone brilliantly.

It hadn't, and that would have been playing the game to enable me to slip away from the label quietly in the new year. I couldn't stand the thought of Cowell blaming me for his mistakes, and if it was his agenda to support G4 ahead of me from Day One, then that was also unforgivable. 'It's a winner's show – only the winner will get signed.' It was crock.

Instead, I looked for funding for Eileen, a massive talent in her own right but, by channelling my emotions, my fear of rejection and my anger into her work, I was in denial.

I should have been out there talking to other labels who just wanted me as an act rather than a controlled product. It was still early enough in my story that my TV exposure counted.

People knew who I was. It wouldn't even be a risk for another record company to sit down with me and manage a career plan and a two- or three-album deal.

But I missed the moment because I was too scared to put myself out there and, before I knew it, Series Two was coming towards its conclusion and I was becoming the forgotten man.

I had been voted off the Sky One reality show *The Match*, which was a huge disappointment and I missed out on the game at St. James' Park that October. Tim had warned me not to do it when it had originally come up, but I thought it was football and would be a good laugh hanging out with the likes of Philip Olivier from *Brookside*, the cricketer Phil Tufnell, Ralf Little, Will Mellor, Jonathan Wilkes and a host of ex-pros. The chance to play in front of the crowd at Newcastle was as good as it was going to get for me in terms of football!

I *had* been a decent player at school – the former Charlton and England full back Chris Powell and I were in the same side.

'You'll have plenty of opportunities to do things like this,' Tim had said but I didn't believe him.

G4 were doing cookery shows and I love football. It was just a bit of fun and shouldn't make a big impact on my music.

As bad luck would have it, I had pulled my hamstring with a third-degree tear during a friendly match for my Saturday team. It was three weeks before the trials but I was told I would need 4-6 weeks to recover. I was desperate to play so I strapped up and went anyway. I just wanted to do something to make me feel better. But I didn't make the team and got a lot of stick from within that show about falling out with Simon. Ben Shephard, still working on The *Xtra Factor* made it clear just how stupid I was for doing the *Daily Mail* interview slamming the show.

Albeit in different disciplines of sport and music, in half a year I was both reality TV show winner and loser, and even ITV presenter Fiona Phillips was noticing my absence, writing in her column in November: "Last year's *X Factor* winner Steve Brookstein knows all about what it's like to give it all, have it all and end up with bugger all. He had a number one single and album after which he was cruelly dumped by his record company. Since then he's been mocked and branded a loser."

I was touched by this. It was just a few lines in a national paper and not enough to rock anyone's boat, but here was an individual – working for the same TV network as the show – who seemingly had seen through its narrative in her column.

She appeared to have a clear idea of the whole story and not just a selective memory of the bits the show wanted you to remember. She had followed my journey through the show and had voted for me, and was backing me now she could see that I had been chewed up and spat out.

It was notable, too, because the show had a very decent, at times, cosy relationship with the showbiz journalists who wrote about it. If they were in with Simon or Max, then they had half their year sorted in terms of stories. In 2004 or 2005, none of them were likely to break from the pack.

On 29 September Ally Ross of *The Sun* had run the headline "*X Factor*...just don't mention Steve, you know, Steve Brookstein". He saw what was going on. After writing my name six times, he went on to say that *X Factor* had managed to go six weeks without saying my name. Little did he know that it would take over six years before I would be mentioned again.

It was 22 November that really marked a line in the sand as to where I now stood.

'Steve Brookstein is back singing in pubs,' cried the papers.

It was my first real gig since leaving the label. It was an easy win for the tabloid scum to readopt the pub singer narrative. If only they had been there or checked out the story.

The Bedford Arms in Balham is a credible music venue. The likes of Paolo Nutini have appeared on their bill. I was not in a karaoke bar.

In fact, I had top musicians playing the gig, including strings and horns. It was three times the size of the band that did *The X Factor* tour and the show was 100% live!

Even though I had been inactive as a live act for much of 2005, I had still done a tour and recorded an album. Making music is a blessing that only goes from unproductive frustration to wonderful elation. It was the stress of *Closer,* exiting the deal and my early burial that had destroyed me. It had been the most challenging period of my professional career of fifteen years – this gig was meant as a thank you to my family, friends and the people who voted. I didn't charge an entrance fee and didn't invite the press. I was also thinking of making it even more special.

In 1983 I had bought Jeffrey Osborne's album "Stay With Me Tonight" and I fell in love with a track called "Forever Mine". It was a proposal song and, even though I was still three years from even meeting my first girlfriend, the idea of singing "Will you marry me?" in a song seemed the ultimate in an unreserved expression of devotion for this shy fifteen-year-old boy. I had never kissed a girl and I had visions of marrying my first love, whoever that may be.

Twenty-two years later I was putting the finishing touches to the song, I had a pianist with a string section but more importantly I had the woman I wanted to make my bride.

The Bedford was packed and, despite the negativity in what I perceived as the outside world, I felt safe. Eileen had done her set and I was moving through mine. Eventually it came to "Take My Hand, Be Mine" and I called out to Eileen.

'Babe, I want you to listen to this song, because I mean it.' I was a wreck. This was it. Just piano, strings and vocals. I didn't sing it well but I sang it right.

I went out to Eileen and took her to one side. The most important thing in my life was coming together. It was a magical night.

Some weeks after, I opened the paper to find a hatchet job. When I saw the reporter's name, I was dumbfounded. It was Clemmie Moodie, to whom I had spoken at length back in August when I left the label.

I had been so high that night, and now once again they dragged me back down. The story which they had all chased about 'when I would propose to Eileen' wasn't the story. It was 'Steve's back in pubs'.

I rang Clemmie to ask what was going on and was all but told there were certain things that had to go in the article.

"In the sort of London pub usually described as a 'proper boozer', the head barman announced an impromptu gig. At that point, a somewhat nervous man wearing a dishevelled T-shirt and jeans and with stubble on his chin appeared on the stage.

Judging by their underwhelmed response, the punters assumed this hopeful was using the pub to gain some performing experience.

It was only when his face broke out into his trademark ear-to-ear grin that the assembled punters finally recognised him as Steve Brookstein – the man who performed to ten million viewers every week on last year's *X Factor* TV show, and who went on to win a lucrative six-album deal with promoter Simon Cowell's label, Sony BMG, exactly a year ago.

Brookstein's two-hour repertoire of self-penned songs certainly made for an entertaining set. Especially when it culminated in a tearful proposal to his girlfriend of two years, singer Eileen Hunter, who was in the crowd. (Luckily, she accepted.) But wait a minute. After beating 50,000 singing hopefuls to win one of the most popular television competitions in the country, isn't Steve Brookstein supposed to be strolling up red carpets to perform in front of packed auditoriums by now?

Didn't he win the hearts of housewives everywhere with his mix of cheesy vocals and self-effacing humour? Six million people had voted for the hard-up pub singer from South London to win the competition. They were bowled over by a man who had stubbornly refused to give up his dream even as the years – and opportunities – went by.

SURELY he was going on to bigger and better things? He should have been making millions as part of his prize. Apparently, not. Back where he started 15 years ago in a South London pub…"

And on it went. All the usual language was there from 'cheesy' to 'pub singer' accompanied in the stereotypical tone – the brackets around Eileen's acceptance almost an expression of surprise.

She signed off by seeing my career mapped out ahead of me. It didn't look like the map Simon had the previous December:

"One suspects, however, that for Brookstein there will be many pub gigs to face yet."

The power of her paper meant that those words would be read by more than those of 'Moogster' who posted the following on a forum:

"Having read the *Mail* article and being present at the Bedford gig, the number of downright lies in the article is astounding.

1. The Bedford gig was nearly a month ago, not 'a few days ago'.

2. The 'proper boozer' is a large pub with two largish separate venues on the site.

3. The 'impromptu gig' was advertised and fully booked weeks before it took place. Steve was also backed by a full band, with at least ten instrumentalists and three backing singers. The way the Mail have written it is as if he jumped on the stage and grabbed the mic.

4. The 'young customers' could not enter from the pub as the gig was fully booked.

5. The assembled 'punters' had travelled (some from a long way) to attend the gig.

6. The 'two-hour repertoire' lasted less than an hour, although the audience would have loved it to have been two hours."

Clemmie hadn't even been there.

Not only did I feel like I was back to square one, but the joy of that night was taken from me. I had to talk to the press again, and this time it couldn't be her.

On the actual show, there was a new storm brewing. Louis was accused by Sharon of running an Irish mafia after the elimination of Maria Lawson. He was backing The Conway Sisters from his home country.

Lawson, a survivor from boot camp of 2004, finished 8th in 2005. I saw her at a premiere on 28 November only for her to refuse to be photographed with me. As the show headed towards its December conclusion, Journey South, Andy Abraham and Shayne Ward were the front-runners, and this year they had a novelty act. Chico Slimani seemed to be surviving week after week. For the second year running, it looked like Sharon was throwing her toys out of the pram.

Ofcom later cleared Sharon of her remark, but Louis was back speaking out to the press. Rumours were circulating he had quit after being humiliated and 'bullied' by Osbourne. She had also thrown water over him live on air.

Dismissed as a publicity stunt, the show did state that he *had* quit – he couldn't take the pressure anymore. Miraculously, he reappeared the following week.

It was against this backdrop that I chose to speak to James Desborough, now Showbiz Reporter at the *News of the World*. It was he who had opened the press conference before the final last year. Ian Levine knew James and assured me he wouldn't stitch me up.

I sat with James for two hours, and told him the whole

story. I left out the episode with *Closer* magazine. That's not to say he might not already know it, but I couldn't take that chance of unearthing all those emotions to a stranger who wanted a story.

My suspicions were permanently at fever pitch with everything to do with the press now and a combination of Max's phone call and the bandwagon of the new series told me I was going to work very hard to turn things around. The Bedford Arms piece, as it turned out, was the first of many.

I made sure James was in full possession of the facts – he left having seen the full email exchange where I had said that I wanted to leave the label. I was desperate for that to be reversed in the hope that it might stop the other negativity. I even told him something insignificant but important to me. Verity had called me in tears after Simon had lampooned the last series of the show. He singled Verity out as being 'terrible'. She was devastated, as he had been so supportive through the series. A 51-year-old woman who taught children to sing branded 'terrible' by the man who a year earlier was using her to sell his show. It disgusted me.

James handed me the letter: "The *News of the World* agree to make a donation of £5000 to the NSPCC on publication of an article on your time on the *X Factor* and subsequent events since winning last year. We will pay £5000 to the charity if no other article appears elsewhere."

I had told James other publications had been after the story, which was true, so the last part he had to add by hand! I knew my story had a monetary value but that was not a motivation. I just wanted someone to listen. It was time to go on the record. I wasn't about to give it away, though, but equally I knew that if I took the money personally, I would cheapen it. I purposely chose the NSPCC as a clue to what was to come.

Within days, it was clear. The word was out. You can bury Steve Brookstein.

Phil Tufnell had called me asking if I would sing at his engagement party. We had met on *The Match*, but I hardly knew him at all.

I didn't subscribe anymore to the celebrity mentality that if you did something for one, it might help you meet another or get further work, so I told him it would be five grand and I would put on a show. If he had used my agent it would have been three times that amount!

I knew, too, the danger now that it wouldn't be long before 'Steve Plays Parties For Free' could become the next headline.

Phil wasn't very happy about it at all.

Sure enough on 2 December, I received an email from a fan called Pam bemoaning that 'if the newspapers have nothing good to say about Steve I'd wish they'd say nothing at all unless you go by the idea that all publicity is good publicity'.

It was Richard Kay's column in the *Mail*.

"Cricketer Phil Tufnell got a nasty shock when he asked his mate Steve Brookstein, last year's *X Factor* winner, to do a turn at a party to celebrate his forthcoming marriage to third wife Dawn. Steve told Phil he'd be delighted to sing as long as he was paid £5,000 for his trouble, I'm told. Phil refused to pay and told him to come to the party as one of his guests. He has now booked another singer instead. Brookstein, 36, who was recently dumped by manager Simon Cowell, really needn't have been so grand. He was quite happy to sing last week at a pub in South London."

I was naturally disgusted by this. Firstly, it was a gossip column – the sort of journalism where somebody tells you something juicy over the phone and you write it down. There would be no need to check with Steve. It was also part of a business negotiation. It had no right to be in the paper.

Secondly, I hadn't been dumped by Simon, and thirdly, the 'happy to sing at a pub' narrative just proved that not only did you not have to be there, but you could then take as fact someone else's shoddy work and repeat it, creating a new narrative. It was now official – Steve was now the pub singer the TV show had always told him he was.

I needed that piece with James Desborough to run more than ever.

Friday 9 December 2005

'They've decided not to run the story. Sorry, Steve.' James seemed genuinely gutted for me, but also for himself. He had wasted two hours having lunch discussing a story then writing it up only to be told that the powers that be are going with a 'pro-Simon piece'.

He didn't tell me that the piece would include a couple of digs at me. I had had enough bad news for one day.

James gave me some advice. The same advice Max had given me. The story won't be coming out so it was better to stop fighting and just leave it. He told me that Max was way too powerful to take on and if I wanted any chance in the business I should apologise and thank Simon for the opportunity.

I don't know who the powers that be were but, strangely, Andy Coulson was the editor at the time.

When I tried to tell the story of my non-story on my website, Max Clifford took to the *Independent* to say that there was no story and that nobody was interested. It hadn't run because I wasn't saying anything new:

"If Steve had been saying something about Simon's love life then I might have got involved but that would have been worth £500,000 not £5000!"

That I had a letter from James and he had seen in black and white the electronic trail places that as a categorical lie.

There was nothing I could do. At that stage of the game, Max was King.

To add insult to injury, when I did watch the 2005 final, I shook my head in disbelief when I saw a choir and the winner's song.

Journey South were doing a gospel version of "Let It Be" and Sir Trevor McDonald was swaying in the audience. It had come full circle.

'Simon, the standard is *so* much better than last year,' Louis emphasised, and had no longer seen the choir as cheating.

From quitting the show, he was back on message.

"That's My Goal" was the original song that Simon had talked to me about. Straight off his conveyor belt of bubble gum pop and into the mouth of a younger version of me, the process of erasing me continued.

Shayne went on to reportedly shift over 300,000 copies in two days. It became the fastest-selling single of the year and awarded Simon that Christmas number one slot without the moral distraction of a charity song. Originally positioned as the UK's Justin Timberlake, poor Shayne was stuck in a black suit and white shirt, singing a song that was offered to a 35-year-old 'pub singer'.

Furthermore, runner-up Andy Abraham was also signed. His 2006 album was going to be called…"The Impossible Dream". You couldn't make it up.

2006

At the turn of the year my focus was simple. I had to move on. I had a marriage planned and I wanted a family. I would have to park my desire to set the record straight. The message was clear. I was a nobody.

I hadn't really got very far working on Eileen's album but had a number of people advising me to get my music out. Time was ticking by and, as the negative press continued, things would become increasingly difficult for me. I felt uneasy, as I saw it as a way for them to keep attacking me, but I agreed and I teamed up with a small company called Create. They were an agency and one of the partners had owned a bar I used to go to many years ago.

I have had bad experiences with three managers who had all been well connected so this time I was trying something different.

Deep down, I think I was looking for an administrator and a yes-man. They were a small company who liked to think big.

There had been other meetings and lots of talk of books, deals and marketing but much of it was hot air. Almost without exception I was suspicious of any new piece of work that came in. I was supposed to be on the bill at an event with the Sugababes, but was later told that they had a potential veto on the other acts. Was it really true they said no to me?

At a premiere – one of the few I was still invited to – the *News of the World* sent a homeless man to stand next to me to have his photo taken. The implication was that only a down and out would tolerate me. It was classic gutter journalism because you couldn't actually put words to it. It was a photo, not a story, and it was a stitch-up. The papers were all quick to report that I had won Music Choice "Worst Album" Award, even though it was a Simon Cowell product. I did insist on actually receiving it and for years it became a doorstop!

On another occasion I heard Vanessa Feltz reviewing that day's newspaper stories on the radio.

'Steve Brookstein is in the papers again. Why can't he just go away?'

That hurt because I wasn't the one putting those stories out there and was unable to stop them. The media were making me out to be a joke and it was spreading to the music industry and the public.

Then *The Sun* ran a "Where's Our Steve?" campaign to find out what had happened to me. I was keeping my head down, though someone did spot me out in Crawley. I became very self-conscious. They were getting into my mind.

To the outside world, who had only read this negativity about me whilst seeing a new champion crowned, it might seem I had been away for longer than I was, but the reality was that it was only in my own mind that I had gone so far as to Hell and back. Other people saw I had further albums in me.

Once I got reeled in and started thinking about what it could be, it was very hard to withdraw. I was far from ready but when new people take an interest in your work while it seems the world is against you, then that is a massive personal investment in you. Given that my voice had been virtually stripped from my soul through the inability to reply to the rubbish in the press, I took it as a huge vote of confidence.

I wasn't about to make an album cover with a big, smiley-faced me on it. The damage from the Fred West comment still meant that I found it difficult to smile again in any photo shoot or filming capacity. I wanted all that stripped down.

In terms of the material I am sure that my mood reflected the song choice – my melancholy leaning me in a very specific direction. The switch from Eileen's album back to mine came when I wasn't ready, though: a long way from being in the right frame of mind to write songs for myself. Instead, we ended up using songs that I had already written for other artists.

I chose tracks that I hoped reflected the journey of life within in a relationship, but an album that doesn't tell you where that ends. I think.

My first very simple problem with the album was the title. I had tried to put it out there that it was going to be called "I Am Steve Brookstein". Clearly this was me defining myself in a way which my previous album hadn't.

Again, I was ridiculed for it so I backed away from it, afraid it would be seen as cocky and arrogant when in fact I wanted to use it to help regain my confidence. I went with "40,000 Things". It was just a line from "Then There Were None", a track I had written with Livingstone and Katie Jackson when we were in Los Angeles signed to Columbia way before *X Factor*. My scrambled brain was constantly thinking about the ramifications of my actions even down to the title of my album.

The album itself was mostly original songs with three covers: I was convinced "Every Kind of People", which I recorded with Maxi Priest and Sonna Rele, was a summer hit. "Won't Last A Day Without You" remains one of my favourite recordings. The lyrics seemed to sum up my situation. I also included "Smile" despite the overtones of the show. I had 'made it my own'! The version I did on the show felt happy. This time it felt incredibly sad.

The last track on the CD was called "Can't Get Any Worse Than This".

I had written it just after I had lost my deals in America and was breaking up with Katie. Our house was sold and my life was in boxes in the hall. A totally depressing song. However, as someone who suffered depression, it was a reminder. Things will get better.

Back then, after signing to Columbia they decided our band "Maker" wasn't what they wanted. They wanted Katie Jackson.

They didn't understand the concept of a studio band. At one meeting with the renowned producer/songwriter Patrick Leonard at his home in LA, he listened to one of our songs.

'Let me get this straight, she's the singer, I write songs, why do I need you two guys?' He made a good point.

He had worked with Madonna, Bryan Ferry, Pink Floyd, Bon Jovi, Fleetwood Mac and Elton John, to name a few, but should never have been in meetings with songwriters. We had the songs.

Pressure grew on a volatile relationship, and Katie and I broke up before the album was finished. I was back in Blighty while she performed showcases in the US. Things got worse when Joanna Ifrah was headhunted by Warner Brothers. The President Donnie Ienner was reportedly so incensed he dumped all her acts except Katie. However, now without an A&R manager, Katie's album sat on the shelf for over six months before she was eventually dropped. All I could think about was that Sylvia Rhone phone call. With the loss of the Columbia deal, I lost my publishing contract. My further advance of $70,000 was dependent on the release of the album. One minute we had the world at our feet, the next it had fallen apart.

So now I had my album of original songs, but, of course, the major difference between being with Simon and making this album was resources. You have to take ownership of everything – which is a different mentality to trying to control it all.

It was a difficult time. I disagreed with Create on many of the issues, and the compromises we made meant that neither side was entirely happy. I had gone down the road of a small company because I wanted yes-men, but I just found myself having different battles. Considering the budget, the album had turned out well. The artwork didn't. I just hated my image and didn't want to be on the cover. It was becoming even clearer that I wasn't in the right mindset to make or promote an album.

By the time the new series of *The X Factor* began I had learned a life lesson in avoiding getting sucked in. I had booked a stag week in Portugal.

I was well aware that Simon was tinkering with the show and knew exactly where he wanted to take it.

I had seen him on *This Morning* announce that 'the next international boy band or girl band is what I want to see in this year's show'. By that point, the previous winner Shayne Ward had released a single which got to number two and his album came out in the April with reasonable success. It looked like Simon didn't want a single male vocalist to triumph for a third year running.

There was talk of a fourth judge, too, but it only materialised in the shape of guest appearances from *American Idol* judge, Paula Abdul. With a new colour scheme and website it looked like reinvention was on the way. They were moving on, and so was I.

On 26 August, Eileen and I were married.

"This is the end of a beautiful friendship and just the beginning of love." Stanley Styne

Though my professional life was a mess, my private life couldn't be better. I had never met anyone like her. As I had got to know Eileen, the more I fell in love with her. We took it slowly, but when *X Factor* came along in 2004 it became a real test of where we were heading. The time on the TV show clouded things.

Life was going to change dramatically and we both questioned whether we could survive it. We were close, very close, but marriage felt miles away, even though we both wanted to grow into something more. I only realised how irritable I had become, how my attitude stank of 'If you don't like it, go', where the old me would have apologised. My temper was short and not being in control of the negativity coming into my life. I took it out on the ones who loved me the most. My parents and Eileen got the brunt of it. Sometimes you feel that it is worse than it is because if everything else is going wrong in the outside world, and there is a slight pause or hesitation when you are seeking reassurance in your own, any lack of confidence radiated your way from your partner counts double. I know that's how I took things when everything else was going wrong. The truth is she felt my pain, too. She remained unflappable – calm and beautiful and helping in my media when she had a career of her own and hated the circus of it all. People told me then I was lucky, and they still do. I am.

The tabloid media constantly wanted to take my joy and I was afraid that marrying Eileen was seen as a vacuous gesture on the back of losing so much from *The X Factor*. I had a new album coming out and we were going on tour together. I guess if it was a stunt, eight years together quashed that.

In the days before the wedding, we had begun to laugh about the mocked-up engagement they had wanted us to take part in. It really was so far from reality, it was ridiculous. Yet, we've seen so many couples since pull off similar, sometimes more than once. I'm not sure a marriage can last that starts in such a way – though the money would be tempting. I can't lie, there was only a little media interest in us getting married which, considering all the front-page headlines about whether or not I would propose and all the articles in *OK! magazine*, just demonstrated how quickly I had fallen. Eileen would never have allowed me to sell pictures of the day, but for me it was more about coming to terms with my situation. The big wedding that week was Chantelle Houghton marrying Samuel Preston from The Ordinary Boys. A marriage that managed to last fourteen months. This was the world we had momentarily lived in.

At the ceremony at Aberdeen University, members of the public were snapping away anyway. The *Daily Mail* did make a small contribution, but it was more really to ensure that they actually took a decent picture of us, rather than having them sneaking around and getting something compromised. They didn't linger and we didn't want all that fuss.

Most importantly, I felt really free as I took my ball and chain. We were now man and wife.

After our Rome honeymoon, it was back to reality and a bit of a shambles.

The dates came before the album – the single "Fighting Butterflies" was released on 18 September but only registered on the C category of a few radio playlists. I was realistic about what we could achieve but I wasn't aware just how quickly shops give up on a product. Things started to implode and there was nothing I could do.

Create ploughed £30,000 into TV advertising which seems a lot, but in the great scheme of things we were small-time. Much of it was not on the main channels but ITV2, meaning what little exposure it got wasn't my market. I needed to reach the ITV1 viewers who voted for me week in, week out. I was desperate to get *GMTV* and *This Morning*. Everything relied on me promoting the tour and the album on these shows.

After the initial meeting with the marketing team I felt sure we would get *some* good exposure. After all, my first album had been a hit and I was the first *X Factor* winner. It was a body blow that by the second meeting, it was clear there was very little media interest in me. This came as a shock to both Create and myself.

We needed this. I felt abandoned by *GMTV* and *This*

Morning. I had done so much on those two shows and now I was no longer an *X Factor* product and not welcome. I was fortunate that I had met Jane McDonald at a gig and she loved my version of "Won't Last A Day Without You". I had one bit of ITV exposure on *Loose Women* two weeks before the release of the album. Bad timing, but better than nothing.

I was told by our TV plugger that ITV were cutting back on promoting *X Factor* artists which I accepted until I saw Chico promoting his single, "Curvy Cola Bottle Body" on *This Morning.* It was a massive kick in the teeth. If it wasn't so business-critical I would have laughed.

Eventually, we moved around 7,000 copies of the album in the first few months. They were my core fans who were still with me and remained uninfluenced by mistruths about what had gone on. In my new world this was pretty decent, though unacceptable as an *X Factor* winner, of course. In isolation it was a great album, but I knew it wouldn't have mass appeal. It was also falling between two stools. It wasn't a covers album, so wouldn't really appeal to *X Factor* viewers, and it wasn't an out and out soul album. Mentally and musically I was losing my way.

Some of the venues were adding to my headaches, too.

A few were perfect like The Stables in Milton Keynes, but I remember getting to Worthing thinking what the hell am I doing here?! It was awful and with the lack of promotion it hadn't sold well at all. Luckily the *Daily Mail* was aware of this disaster and were keen to share my continued fall from grace with the world! I had yet another page in the national press and another embarrassment. The injustice was making me see red. They hadn't attended the popular shows or even commented on my tour before it had begun. It felt like the press were not ignoring me, but instead quietly waiting in the bushes for me to trip up so they could jump out and laugh.

Despite being a commercial failure I believed that creatively it was a decent success. I just wish more people had seen the shows. We had a fantastic band and great songs and in isolation it was empowering. Sadly, we had failed to promote it properly, choose the right venues, or anticipate the level of negativity still out there to keep me buried. In total we worked hard getting out to around fifteen venues from Salisbury to Aberdeen, but it had been another mistake.

As the tour ended, my relationship with Create was now breaking, too – for totally different reasons to what had gone on with Simon. They were really good guys and I still keep in touch, but we had both been burned by the tour and album release at the same time.

We had done some stuff well, and I was grateful that they had come to me with no preconception other than that we might succeed together. The negativity that surrounded everything we tried to do made for too hard a mountain to climb.

I was left with these conclusions:

Somebody would always write a negative review from now on, given that there were blocks in place against me in the mainstream media. Radio play was small, and ITV was almost out of the question.

At times, I thought I should have perhaps embraced that album of covers and established myself, but I had mistakenly thought that *The X Factor* had put me on the map. It only served to underline that there was the TV show, and then there came the possibility of a career and that other factors would have a say in that.

Any chance of getting the truth about my treatment out to the public was now in tatters along with my career. It would have been more accurate to say that my 'difficult second album' was in fact the impossible dream.

Some of those fans who had been loyal up to now were moving on and, by Christmas, I put on a brave face but inside I was calling it a day. People were still making jokes about me in the media and it was incredibly hard to take.

I had just one other business to put to bed. I had received a weird email in late-November asking me to meet up at the Mandarin Oriental Hotel in Knightsbridge. Then another one followed. It was truly bizarre and was playing with my mind that was already slipping from my grasp. I was well and truly buried and could not see why Simon or Max would want to contact me unless they wanted to see the state I was in.

I had no interest in pursuing it at this point, but I thought I should meet all the same.

"Appear weak when you are strong,
and strong when you are weak." Sun Tzu

As I made my way to the hotel I still couldn't believe I was meeting Simon Cowell's brother, Tony. Two years after winning *The X Factor*, what would his brother want with someone he must have known Max Clifford had buried? Why dig me up? I had Googled him, obviously. His most significant book seemed to be to co-write Simon's autobiography "I Don't Mean To Be Rude But..."

Simon Cowell's brother now wanted to write my book. I was unable to deal with the absurdity of this situation. I refuse to believe Simon was unaware of this meeting. This was about letting me know who was in charge.

As if I would let someone called Cowell write my book. Are you mad?

I smiled, I joked and I told him things. I said just enough to make him believe I was stupid. We shook hands and I left the meeting with a new lease of life.

After the meeting I received the following email:

'Steve, still awaiting your thoughts on the book synopsis. Please let's have a chat before Christmas.

I am going away on 17th Dec with the family till 3rd Jan. Would like to take that opportunity to talk to Simon re your song.

Would also like to talk to you about PR before I go – and see if we can work anything out for the new year. Perhaps adjust my fees to help you out to start off.'

I didn't reply.

On 16 December I sat and watched Leona Lewis beat Ray Quinn in a one-sided *X Factor* final. Gary Barlow told Simon that he had finally found a star, and warned him not to mess up her career. I poured myself a drink.

2007

The contrast couldn't have been starker, and the pointers were all there. Leona had raced to a Christmas Eve number one and was well away to becoming the show's real success story. She had released a cover of Kelly Clarkson's "A Moment Like This".

Clarkson was the first winner of *American Idol,* where Simon spent much of the year. She was now a true star in her own right. 2007 was also the year Max had indicated Simon had wanted to launch *X Factor USA*, but there seemed no sign of it coming. It was obvious, though, that he was looking at the model and seeing what the best bits were, and now he had a female vocalist on his hands and his hunt for One Direction would have to wait, but it seemed to be a sensible place to begin for Leona. Kelly Clarkson was huge.

I began the year tying up the loose ends with Create. There is nothing more deflating than returned stock sitting there gathering dust. We couldn't guarantee a further single, so back it had come and quickly. It was almost immediate. The business was in changing times, too – the record store Our Price had closed down in 2004, and there was almost nowhere left in the High Street to buy music. iTunes was already six years old but had not yet reached the moment when it would change the entire complexion for anyone like me. At the crossover point just when downloads were expanding, it was still felt that you needed a physical release for media and reviewers to hold in their hands. The truth is it was rapidly becoming a waste of money and a burden on time.

It was like when I became an estate agent in the crash of 1988. I joined the business just as the bubble popped. We would value a house only to see it lose thousands before we had printed up the details. Everything was on sale, every buyer was a waster, and every vendor was desperate.

The music industry didn't have a clue where it was going. As Simon had told me, the future was albums and singles were dead. CDs were on their way out and the industry was in turmoil. Nobody knew what the future was going to be.

I decided to do something completely different. It was a wild card. I went to Midem in the South of France. It was a music conference where labels big and small gathered from around the world. I was slagged off for going but I knew it was a place to meet people and build relationships, and right now, I needed to see who was out there. In London I had just met a manager who had a relationship with a label in Estonia that had money and loved Eileen.

I ran into a live music agent called Tony Denton who invited me out for dinner. He wanted a chat about a possible show he had in mind. It wasn't ideal but I had nothing else to get excited about. Showbiz agent Jonathan Shalit, possibly most famous for propelling Charlotte Church to fame, walked in and gave me some advice. We had met before, backstage at *The X Factor* final, though hadn't spoken much, but I didn't warm to him greatly. I took to him even less when he suggested I should be looking at a *Celebrity Big Brother*-type show or *I'm A Celebrity.*

That told me clearly he knew how to work fame but he didn't get me. He said that was the best way to get my career back on track but that wasn't my career. I didn't value fame and didn't want to discuss it. I was at a music conference. Without being pretentious, I didn't want to be a commodity, I wanted to have lasting worth. Then I could become a product! It didn't work the other way round. I could have explored it further but it wasn't for me.

Tony Denton's offer of an *X Factor*-type tour with stars of Series One, Two and Three was at least music-related. I had hoped to get away from the tag of the show, but that was never going to happen. They had no title for the tour at this point – presumably for legal reasons – but someone had seen a chance to make a buck and I just honestly thought 'Why not?' It was almost £40,000 and just 25 shows. Most people would think that was a good year's work and, after putting so much into the previous autumn whilst banging my head against a brick wall, it seemed a no-brainer to let someone else do the work and sign up for what I knew, comfortable that it was the best part of a year away. It went against the grain musically but I would use the money to fund what I really wanted to do in the future. Food, accommodation, transport, musicians, engineers and lights were all included. I literally had to turn up, be professional and deliver the goods. Despite everything, I would probably still be the biggest name on the bill.

The tour never happened. As I waited to sign contracts, Tony finally admitted that, as he couldn't get clearance to use "*X Factor*" in the title, it was too big a risk to take on. It sounded bigger than that to me. You wouldn't get that far as to send out contracts only to fall foul on the logo, would you? To me this was about relationships. Tony was well connected and so was Simon. It wasn't in his interest to piss off Mr Big.

All in all, it was hot air season. New Year was a traditionally quite time for the biz because it had been all about the Christmas market and, with *X Factor* on, the whole industry could piggyback on the back of a music-buying culture. That meant, come January, there were a lot of meetings, a lot of plans, and a lot of things that never got off the ground.

I couldn't go forward with Create. I wanted to push Eileen, and that gave me security to hide behind whilst at the same time nervously still putting out feelers.

In my head I knew it was small, intimate venues from now on. No financial or PR risk and maximum appreciation.

By March, things were put into context. My mum had breast cancer and Eileen was concerned with her dad's health.

I was fighting demons, and when loved ones were taking on bigger challenges I felt selfish. I was angry that my mum had seen me reach so high and come crushing down and I now blamed myself. I was married but I had no children and this was something else that hurt. Would my mum get to see my children? Why didn't I just play the game? I often talk about Simon's, but how big was my own ego?

Back in 2002 after things went wrong with Columbia Records, I read a book called "Who Moved My Cheese?" by Doctor Spencer Johnson. Cheese was a metaphor for the things we want in life. It was suggesting we should simplify our thoughts and act more like mice. It wasn't long but the 96 pages were deep. I stepped away from it learning that when things go wrong you must keep going forward. I had forgotten that, with change, you must adapt. *The X Factor* had opened doors that I never took advantage of. I started to doubt my decisions more than ever.

I did a few gigs here and there but they were mostly for charity events and private parties. I was more susceptible to doing charities and I knew if I 'gave something back' it was very hard to be criticised for it. I was keeping my head down.

Yet, I was still being slated and those dishing it out – just like Max in *The Independent* – continued to deny any wrongdoing.

On 26 March, amidst all that was going on, I received more bullshit.

Dear Sir

I refer to your complaint in respect of the article entitled "*They Don't Know Who You Are Steve*".

I have now had the opportunity to conduct an investigation into this matter. I have been given first-hand information that the article complained of events exactly as they occurred. As such we cannot agree to an apology.

Whilst we do not, therefore, accept the assertions contained in your email dated 21 March 2007, in the spirit of being helpful we have marked our archive cuttings database appropriately and have removed the article from www.thisislondon.co.uk.

We have done this without any admission as to liability and in order to adopt a reasonable approach to this matter.

I trust this brings an end to the matter.

Yours faithfully

Spencer Davis
Group Legal Adviser
Associated Newspapers Ltd

It was a sham.

I had arrived early in my local to watch the match for an afternoon of drinks in Southfields with my mates. It's what normal blokes did. We had got there well before kick-off to get the best seats, and ordered Sunday lunch. We were in for the long haul. The pub eventually packed out for a Spurs game, but it didn't matter as we were in a prime position.

Then, with the venue showing two games, all the Chelsea fans turned up and they switched the matches being shown in the two rooms. Obviously I was unhappy about this and made my point to the landlord that we had been in situ for some time, had ordered food, and had even made a point of checking which room was showing which match. He apologised for switching channels. I was irritated, but there was nothing I could do.

I was staggered when I began to read in *London Lite* that I had kicked off and given them the 'Don't You Know Who I Am?' spiel.

I have never played that card. There *were* two journalists in the pub but they totally made the article up.

Once again I get the legal letter and a supposed investigation and then a cover-up. What happened next is brilliant.

The landlord of the pub wrote to the Press Complaints Commission who had been toothless in their verdict because it was a two-against-one scenario.

London Lite had to apologise, and they did so in typical British press style. I got a couple of lines tucked away in the middle. As ever, there was no real context to the apology, and its size and placement bore no resemblance to the original.

'Sorry, Steve, misunderstanding all the best, mate,' it read insincerely.

And it didn't stop there.

By June, my agent had offered me a 'mini-cruise'. Having never sung on a ship before I had no idea what I was letting myself in for. I was oblivious to the implications of singing on a ferry. A good gig but I paid the price.

I flew to Spain, boarded the boat, got seasick, performed the following night and got off at Portsmouth. It was easy money that sorted the bills for a few months and I was unaware of the other acts even being on the boat.

I couldn't see why this was tabloid news.

I was branded 'failed' and a 'flop'. One paper even referred to 'poor Chico' for having to perform with me.

Another billed it as 'Chico joins *X Factor* Flops Ferry Tour'.

It wasn't a tour, I had won the show, whereas he came fifth and he was issuing quotes, as was a source. It didn't take a degree to work out where those were coming from.

It wasn't just about making me look bad, it was about warning people what bad press working on a show with Steve Brookstein would bring.

I was rightly becoming paranoid. Anything I did was either mocked or ignored. So I did the bare minimum. I had done a few favours for Ian Levine over the years and did a gig under the name The Four Vandals. It was a Northern Soul gig with a live band and a packed house, so wasn't of any interest to the media. It also was an example of how I lost my drive. Here was a situation to get involved with a Northern Soul band under a new name and I just wasn't interested. I had to force myself to do anything.

Before *X Factor* had even started, we had recorded a track called "Wrong Side Of Town" together. Ian had messed around with it, sent it to the States and got it all scratched up to make it sound like rare 70s groove, only to then import it back into the UK spinning the yarn to the Northern Soul DJs who were always looking for the hottest rarest import at the time. I felt bad when the guy who paid £300 for the track asked me to sign it at the gig. I joked that it was probably worth less now.

At the time of *The X Factor* live shows, I knew some people in the know had put two and two together and worked out it was me, but I kept relatively quiet about it. Yet, at the same time, Sharon was going through all that 'why do you sing like a black man?' nonsense as if it were something I was affecting for the programme. It wasn't. It was how I had always sounded and always would, and here was the proof.

I was actually booked in for the Northern Soul In Crowd Weekender itself in late-May – this was my kind of audience. But as I took to the stage, I was also clearly aware that Simon's empire was expanding further. The first series of *Britain's Got Talent* was heading towards its conclusion, and Paul Potts, a manager at the Carphone Warehouse, was on his way to victory in his new search for a star. It was meant to be a competition for jugglers, dancers, impressionists, illusionists, anything which stood out that couldn't get a platform on British TV, as variety had been perceived as dead. These shows had been on before but not for some time, and now they were back and Simon had found… a singer! The TV market was now totally dominated by Simon's shows. I was unable to escape this world and it was getting bigger.

I really didn't want to go out and had become very cagey about accepting any invitation. These were very dark days.

Carol Meehan at Star Management Ltd emailed:

I haven't heard back from you regarding the Breast Cancer Care gig in September, can you let me know if you don't want to do it as they've asked me to approach Andy Abraham as their second option.

Cheers, xx
Carol

The interesting aspect of this request was not that I was still valued, but that I had to be chased up to actually do anything. I don't know how many gigs I've missed out on but I found myself regularly letting emails go. If people didn't force me, things would simply slip by.

Though I had never opened up about my own experience since talking with Tim, I found it easier to drag myself out for such causes. It was always an honour to be asked. I managed to sign up for the NSPCC Cinderella Ball later in the year.

One email that did catch my eye on 28 August made me roar with laughter:

From: Jonathan Lipman
To: Steve Brookstein

Hi Steve, hope all is well,

Sharon Osbourne's manager in the States has called me to ask if you would do a quote about Sharon for her new autobiography, if you want to do it just email it to me and I will email it over.

They just want you to write what ever you want about her, your thoughts about her whilst in the *X Factor*, your thoughts now etc etc…

Let me know,

Thanks

Jonathan

I called out to Eileen immediately to come and see. Sharon was either extremely arrogant and didn't see she had done anything wrong; or thought that sufficient time had passed for it to be water under the bridge; or believed I was desperate *or* possibly was giving a very honest and transparent account of what went on and that included the good, the bad and the ugly.

The only problem with all of that was that I was still living with much of her narrative. The request amused me, so I replied:

Hi Jonathan

Sure not a problem:

'Sharon Osbourne is complex character who has experienced many of life's difficulties. Although I found her treatment towards me on *The X Factor* unfair, untrue and most of all deeply upsetting to me and my loved ones, I still like to believe that Sharon is fundamentally a good person. She's just a product of her circumstances.

It has taken me a while to come to terms with all the negativity that I've been subjected to over the last few years but I have a close family that have been a tower of strength. Winning *The X Factor* was meant to be a good memory not only for me, but also for my parents. It still upsets me that they don't want to watch the video of that night because of what Sharon did. I don't think she'll ever realise how much hurt she brought to them.

I have now married 'the reliable Volvo' who Sharon mentioned in the final and we are planning a family. I guess I'm finally moving on from *The X Factor*, Sharon, Simon and Louis.

I never thought I could say it, but I wish her sincere best wishes for the future.'

I hope the above will do.

Take care
Steve

I hadn't actually seen her since the Brits in 2005 when I asked her why she was so cruel towards me – she replied that she didn't think I liked *her*!

What I didn't know until much later was that the story that I had hit her assistant had made the press just after the final in 2004. Somehow I hadn't seen it. I was buried in media at that point. If I had, I would have actioned it because it was a total fabrication.

To this day, I have no idea what Sharon made of my book quotes but I meant every word. Though I occasionally still get angry about what she did, I know she did what she did because she is troubled.

My sister, who is very religious, always tells me two things:

'Stephen, hurt people hurt people' and 'The truth is the truth'.

I knew Sharon was erasing the past, too, but I remembered clearly how she had said 'I hope you fail' and she got her wish. In publishing her memoirs, there was also an element of saying she was riding high – take a look at you now, Steve.

On 22 October, I sent this out to my email fan base:

Hi Members

Today the *Daily Mirror* have spent the day at The Lodge Tavern trying to get an interview with the manager. They had received photos from someone. I spoke with the reporter on the phone and expressed my disappointment.

I play the 606 Club and duet with Ian Shaw, they don't mention it.

I get a good review for Pizza Express Dean Street gig, they don't mention it.

Album released in 2006, 40,000 Things, they don't mention it.

However, Steve Brookstein at The Lodge Tavern is in the public interest.

X Factor, Cowell propaganda machine rolls on.

Best wishes
Steve

It must have been a quiet news day or someone had an agenda. I doubt Simon knew anything and I don't believe Max's hands were all over it, but I am sure that, by this stage, some three years on, the narrative that those two began was now the accepted tone towards me. Max wasn't burying me here. All written media were so versed now in digging my grave that they could do it themselves. Clearly, too, the only place left to set the record straight was in my *own* media.

And it's lines like this in my own book that will be taken out of context and reprinted again to show that I am still bitter, whereas the truth is that I am simply outlining the volume of acidic copy on me one by one so that decent, fair-minded people can see for themselves the accumulative effect.

The Breast Cancer Care gig in Scotland just further underlined what nonsense all this was. It was a great success for the charity and I had received a lovely email saying how much everyone enjoyed my performance, and with my mum on the mend it was one of the highlights of the year. The icing on the cake was that Eileen had been pregnant for twelve weeks and we could finally share our wonderful news.

By the time Leon Jackson won the show a journalist called Matt Roper wrote this about me:

"It's funny to see the same tired lines being wheeled out about Steve Brookstein yet again, though, if you're Steve, probably they're wearing a little thin now."

"As Leon landed the £1 million recording contract, a former winner was singing to 50 diners in a pizza restaurant."

My friend and bass player Jonty Fisher could see that I couldn't get anywhere taking this up, so he wrote to the *Mirror* himself:

"Just to be clear, was the 'pizza restaurant' in question The Music Room, which between it and its sister 'pizza restaurant' in Soho has hosted such names as: Norah Jones, Stacey Kent, Jamie Cullum, Humphrey Lyttelton, Diana Krall, George Melly, Brad Mehldau, Clare Teal, Amy Winehouse… (I could go on but my point is it's boring to go on)?

50 diners? 'Full house' or 'Sold out' are maybe a little less misleading.

I was playing bass on the gig in question and have played at the 'pizza restaurant' before… also the Royal Albert Hall, Queen Elizabeth Hall, Ronnie Scott's, the 606 Club (…another opportunity to go on). I hope to play at the 'pizza restaurant' again, too, fantastic venue.

Hope Matt enjoyed his Salsiccia al forno, did he hear any of the music? Hmm, I guess that music wasn't in the brief."

I *had* announced that Leon was crud in between songs, but what I meant was that it was crud he won. I corrected myself on the night. He wasn't ready. His performances just said timid, and he needed much more stage experience. His voice had huge potential and he looked like a star, but he was just way too nervous. Simon still didn't have his boy or girl band but he did have an international sensation in both Paul Potts and Leona. To a degree, the pressure had been off. That probably had made it the right time to reinvent the show.

Leon went on to release three singles and an album. I don't recall the title of any of them. Bizarrely, he hosted his own online TV show called *Leon's Life*. So soon after winning, it shouldn't be that a career in the making lives on the net within *his* own medium. That wasn't what the show was about. Leon should've been gigging and learning to work an audience. He came back the following year like every other reigning champ since me, and looked even more nervous than when he had won the thing. I didn't feel they looked after him.

Many musicians contacted me, too, to say that the paper were rubbishing Pizza Express, too, and that was bad for all of us. Those people in my audience obviously didn't care enough to stay in to watch this year's final.

This was the year where there had indeed been four judges, with Dannii Minogue joining the panel, and it was Dermot O'Leary's first series as host. Back in March, there had been a ridiculous stunt again when Louis had reportedly been sacked, replaced by the Creative Director Brian Friedman, but it was laughable and few people bought it, just as it had been him quitting a previous year.

At the autumn launch, Simon had played down the role of the judges, saying: 'There's still competition within the judges but our job is essentially to find a star'. He seemed to have finally cottoned onto the distraction that brought and the destructive narrative it created.

I had actually always felt Kate had done a good job and captured the spirit of what was a new show in 2004. I could see the American influence kicking again on the few nights I had watched. I think getting rid of Kate Thornton, Ben Shephard, the red X and adding a fourth judge was all part of making Series One look a distant memory. But I also suspect that this perception is part of my increasing paranoia.

In the States, the results for *Idol* were not delivered on the same night for the show. That was now happening here. I used to boast in previous years that I had always had the most votes out of all the winners. That was now unlikely going forward with the Saturday and Sunday show. In other words, good commercial sense from ITV and Simon, and a little bit more of me erased from the show's history.

2008

This was a massive year for us as a family. My mum was on the mend, but the personal highs and lows continued:

COMPLAINT:

Steve Brookstein, the musician, complained that an article had inaccurately portrayed a performance he had given at a jazz club. He raised the following specific issues: that the venue was described as a pizza parlour when it was the Pizza Express Jazz Club; that he was described as "slamming" Leon Jackson – the latest *X Factor* winner – as "crud" when he had been obviously joking and had also complimented Leon on his voice; and that the article had given the inaccurate impression that he had given an interview to the magazine.

RESOLUTION:

"The magazine sought to explain that the information for the article was obtained from a report in another publication. It made clear that the day after it was published, complaints were received from fans about the manner in which the complainant's gig had been portrayed. The magazine immediately amended the online copy to take account of the three points of complaint. The complainant indicated that he was happy to resolve his complaint on this basis."

This was *Now* magazine. I am sure you can read between

the lines yourself to understand that 'the article was obtained' tells you this was shoddy, cut-and-paste journalism.

And yet, the recompense for this is minimal. I am not talking money but integrity. Most of these publications trot it out, respond with a meek innocence distancing themselves from the blame trail and then go and do it all again. Is the best they can really do to say they stole it from another publication? Seriously, they stole it and that is their defence!

I took it on because enough was enough. My first attempt at a fightback served little except warning to the publication in question that I was reversing that Max Clifford phone call of August 2005. If I didn't show some metal, they would continue to bury me.

At the tail-end of last year, I had got lucky. I had no idea where my life was going, but out of the blue two things came along that would change my life. I had been requested to audition for *Our House*. Written by Tim Firth, directed by Matthew Warchus and produced by Andrew Welch, Christopher Malcolm and Brian Eastman, it would turn out to be the most exciting project I have done to date.

The second moment will stay with me forever as I awoke one autumn morning to Eileen holding an envelope and a package.

'This has come for you,' she said straight-faced.

It was a card 'to Daddy' and the package was a Babygro.

'Who is this from?' I was disbelieving.

Was this some kind of sick joke? For a moment I thought I was being stitched up. That's how paranoid I had become. I was barely awake and slow to cotton on. Then she smiled.

We hugged and for the first time in a while I had tears of joy. These two events sat side by side for much of this year.

I had met the director and was nervous as hell but didn't want to let on how much I wanted the part. I needed to work, but also I needed it for my sanity. Somehow I impressed in my audition and after getting together with the producers I was offered a contract.

Rehearsals for *Our House* began at the end of April and Eileen was due late March. I was now given a purpose and was forced to dig deep. I didn't want to get too excited but I was being given a chance. I didn't care that I was potentially out of my depth doing musical theatre in a genre I didn't understand. I am talented, I told myself. I can do this.

We made our way up to Aberdeen two weeks before our son was due, just to make sure. We had decided that, because my family was a mixed lot from all over the place, it would mean more that he was born in Scotland. It would also be a great excuse if he turned out to not be very good at kicking a ball. I had always wanted to be in a pub smoking a cigar waiting for the call, but things had changed a lot in the last few years and I was expected to be there having my fingers broken as she clutched my hand shouting obscenities at me.

I had even been dragged kicking and screaming to St George's Hospital in Tooting to antenatal classes. I hate to admit it, but it was worth it. We were confident we were ready.

But the due date came and went. Now it was getting exciting. We started going for walks and having curry, but days went by and nothing. Crucially, Eileen's dad Alastair was feeling unwell and went into hospital for tests. More days passed and still nothing, then the tests came back and Alastair returned to the Aberdeen Royal Infirmary.

Eileen's brother Russell came up from Edinburgh to see us and was hoping our son would arrive on his birthday, 5 April. This was starting to look possible but more days passed and the news was devastating. Alastair had cancer.

All the excitement suddenly turned to concern, but that night as we sat by the fire Eileen's contractions began. Nervously we laughed and carried on talking. We started to note the intervals. It was like our son was coming to cheer us up. Every twenty minutes they came, but he wasn't close. We were told that we had to wait until they were down to about three to four minutes before even thinking about going into the hospital. That Friday night was long.

I spent it rubbing Eileen's back. Saturday was more of the same. It was ridiculous. Eileen had done months of hypnosis and was calmly breathing through each contraction like it was a minor inconvenience, but the tiredness was destroying her. I was exhausted, too, but I really couldn't complain.

By Sunday it was time to go in. The contractions were every four or so minutes. Calmly we sat down with the midwife. We were delirious, starting to find everything funny in our sleep-deprived, nervous energy. We had been up since Friday and now it was Sunday lunchtime. I can recall so much of what happened in those hours like any father, from the tremendous fear of the low heart rate to the immeasurable joy hearing his first cry.

At 04.38 on Monday 7 April and weighing in at 6lb 4oz, our little boy was born.

It was like nothing I'd ever known.

Eileen had been awake for almost 70 hours and was past exhausted, and, as our son was slightly jaundiced, she was staying in for a few more days. Eileen's mum and brothers came to visit but, even though Alastair was in the same hospital, he was too poorly to come to the maternity ward. Alternatively, we couldn't take our newborn to a ward where radiation treatment was underway. Luckily I had brought my laptop up to Aberdeen, so I made a great little video of Eileen with our baby so that Alastair could share in the moment. It was lovely.

The night before Eileen was due home I promised to bring in some food. The ward was still and peaceful. A warm, dim lamp lit the corner of her room and we sat on the bed eating some Chinese and deciding on a name. He was tiny, weak and softly stirring, but our wee man was to have a strong Scottish name – Hamish. By midnight I found myself drifting off with Eileen in my arms. It was the most content I had ever been. I kissed them both goodnight and left.

Alastair died that evening.

The following day as I prepared to pick up Eileen I could only think that she had not had the chance to say goodbye and that Hamish had not said hello.

Eileen's other brother Graham had arrived at the house and we agreed that if she asked how Alastair was doing then I would break the news. I prayed she wouldn't. Seeing her packing her clothes and smiling at Hamish knowing what I did weighed heavily on my heart. Eileen looked radiant as we left but I looked at her differently. She was not only my wife but now the mother of my child. I couldn't bear to hurt her.

The house was just a stone's throw away and I was making sure I kept up the conversations about Hamish, the speed I was driving, the baby seat, and even how great it was that the hospital had given us so many nappies. We pulled up at the house and I immediately jumped out of the car to collect Hamish from the back. Graham looked at me from the door and I shook my head.

By the time Eileen entered the house her mum and two brothers were in the lounge. I think she knew as she walked in that this was their moment. I stood in the hall and closed the door.

19 April. I had to make my way down to start rehearsals on *Our House*. I had a lot of time to reflect on the long drive back from Aberdeen.

I hated leaving my new little family and I worried for Eileen. I filled the long hours on the road listening to the Stephen Sondheim musical 'Into The Woods'.

I wasn't the man I had hoped I would be and, even though I had let go of a deep childhood shame, it had been handed back to me. It took a long time to say 'it wasn't my fault' so I wasn't prepared to accept this new guilt. The interview with

Closer was never far from my mind and neither was my argument with Tim. If they had asked the question, then how could a truthful answer be wrong? I was touching on something that was uncomfortable for people and caused embarrassment. Why else would two articles be stopped?

I did not want my son to ever experience what happened to me, but equally I did not want to pass my anger and resentment onto him. I was determined to make his childhood a happy one. Children *do* listen and dreams can come true. I was in a far bigger battle with myself than the one perceived by the public.

At the same time, I had to learn lines and quickly acquire new disciplines. I was working with young professionals and I had to be at the top of my game just to keep up. They were hugely supportive, but nobody was going to carry anybody and I was desperate to be credible.

I was also daunted from the first read-through. I was given an older version of the script and didn't follow. I felt I looked an idiot. I could imagine a few thinking it was a joke having some bloke from *X Factor* doing musical theatre, but I couldn't listen to those voices in my head.

I have no idea what the musical director Phil Bateman must have made of me. It was just a whole new genre for me. I loved Madness but to sing their stuff was an entirely different thing. I tried to be fun and socialise with the cast as much as possible but I often wasn't in the mood.

When it came to the publicity for the show, I was obviously somebody whom they could use for media, and still, despite this sideways career change, when I did *BBC Breakfast* all the usual rules applied.

'He's got the look…he's a charmer already…' Sian Williams and Bill Turnbull began. It was nervous awkward banter, and as usual much that followed harked back to *The X Factor*. I just had to accept it.

Sometimes over the years I would use it to my advantage. On others I didn't fight it when they used words like 'dropped', even though this wasn't the truth. In the context of an interview plugging something new, it didn't serve to get into an argument about it if I was promoting *Our House*.

The show itself was a fantastic romantic production that should have stayed in the West End longer, and I felt "It Must Be Love" would have served it better as a title. I was to play Joe's dead dad – the ghost. At a time when I had become a dad and Eileen had lost hers, I felt that this show was sent to help us through this emotional time. It was such a blessing.

It was also scary, at times embarrassing and often hilarious, but I remained in awe, fascinated at how it all worked, and I was acting opposite Cassandra from *Only Fools and Horses*! Gwyneth Strong played my wife, and if I was rubbish she never made me feel like it. She was an absolute treasure and made me feel so comfortable.

I was doing such a good job they gave me more lines. Big mistake: I forgot them!

I remembered just half of one sentence and so blurted out a pathetic 'Oh Joe'.

I could see Joe trying to keep a straight face. Hey, I was a ghost. He wasn't meant to be able to hear me anyway!

On another night, a replacement musical director forgot to give me my normal two beats intro, so I was all over the place with a song, mumbling all sorts of nonsense. I felt humiliated. I didn't know the culture. Half the cast backstage were pissing themselves laughing. One guy, Will, laughed so much I threatened to knock his 'fucking lights out'. I felt so bad. It was the way the cast were with everything. It wasn't personal.

By the time we got to Glasgow, I felt I was doing well and really enjoying it.

I was ahead of myself. Up to now, I would wait in the wings well in advance of my cue, but now I was leaving my dressing room with 60 seconds or less to get there. Backstage was like a rabbit warren and I took the wrong stairs ending up at the stage door. I couldn't find my way back to the set.

As I heard one song ending, I knew I was due back on in 30 seconds but was nowhere near where I needed to be. My song was going to start without me. This wasn't a gig. I couldn't just stroll onstage as the band went around the first eight bars, I had to be there. I have never panicked so much. Breathless, I arrived just in time.

But these were isolated instances and most things went smoothly. Oh, then there was one scene where a motorised boat went across the stage and they wanted to try me out singing "Night Boat To Cairo" wearing a fez. I was a fez-wearing ghost. I wasn't happy about it, but I can see the humour. Then halfway across the stage the boat broke down and I had to get out and push it. It got a laugh and it was just one of those things. This time I wasn't angry, I joined in with the laughter! Good times.

Looking back, it showed just how much I had changed. It was nothing like the ribbon falling from the stage on *The X Factor* tour. This wasn't a competition. We were a team, all in it together. Every night we ended on an amazing high and a standing ovation. Each time I was growing stronger. Eileen needed to get out of the apartment at home so had come and spent time coming to many of the cities with Hamish. The cast got to know them and we were finally as one.

By the end, I really wasn't sure if they respected me or not, but I felt the love. We had an Our House award ceremony and I was the proud owner of "The Best Cock-Up Award" for my 'Oh Joe!' comment but the public did send dozens of lovely letters and I have kept in touch with some of the cast. They never knew just how much they saved me in 2008. The entire *Our House* team had built me back up and I am forever grateful.

As a result, I had met a couple of agents with a view to

doing more shows, but it just underlined that I had unfinished business as a singer-songwriter and however much I was mocked, you couldn't take that away from me. I was told I would have made a great Billy Flynn in *Chicago,* but I wasn't offered any West End parts and I wasn't ready to tour again. I wanted to be home with my young family.

In October, Carol Meehan at Star Management forwarded me this email marked 'urgent':

Dear Carol,

From the comedy entertainment team that brings you *Q.I.* and *Never Mind The Buzzcocks* comes a brand new comedy panel show *Celebrity Juice. Celebrity Juice* is an irreverent, topical, tabloid-based panel show where *Heat* magazine meets *Shooting Stars.* The show is hosted by **Leigh Francis** in character as businessman-turned-celebrity **Keith Lemon**, with **Holly Willoughby** and **Fearne Cotton** as team captains. Each team will be completed by a combination of comedians, celebrities and celeb journalists. Inspired by the world of *Closer, The Sun,* and 'PerezHilton.com', the show breaks, and makes, the showbiz stories that fill our national tabloid press. Recorded the night before transmission the show will probe the spicy, ridiculous, and funny gossip that the nation is talking about, through a series of traditional and not-so-traditional panel show rounds.

We are shooting a light-hearted sketch for the show on Monday that we would like Steve to take part in. The basic premise for the sketch is that Simon Cowell has been kidnapped. At the end of the sketch it will be revealed that Steve is the kidnapper. It will be no longer than a couple minutes long and is a bit of fun in the vein of *TV Burp.* It will take no more than half an hour to record and we are looking to record it before 2 pm

231

on Monday. We can pay a fee of £1000 for Steve's time on a full media buyout. For more information please don't hesitate to get in touch.

Many thanks,

Evan Ray, Talent Director.

I turned it down. It wasn't the first time I was getting offered money that could make me look stupid.

Firstly, *Buzzcocks* had always been trying to get me on in one of those skits where they ask the panel to identify people who were once famous; secondly, he couldn't have known how stupid it was to try and sell it to me on the back of the two publications he mentioned, and finally, he, too, clearly thought I was fair game – that a grand would happily see me kidnap Simon, therefore underlying the narrative that I was somehow bitter and wanted revenge. I knew I was only there to be ridiculed. It was better not to be on TV if this was the TV on offer. I tried to cling to the positive energy I got from *Our House*.

My mind was now back to discovering talent and making music. Through YouTube I found a great singer called Laura White and got in touch and agreed to meet up. I had invited her to come and meet me with her parents when *Our House* came to The Lowry in Manchester in May.

Laura was lovely and had a terrific voice. She had great potential and I wanted to work with her. She confided in me that she had entered for this year's *X Factor*. I wasn't pleased with her decision to go on the show but couldn't advise her against it. I told her to use it and to get out of it as much as she could. *X Factor* takes any credibility that you think you have, so it was important to get as much coverage as possible.

The show opened to its highest first-week figures at the time – 12 million viewers. However, this was the year that *Strictly Come Dancing* had its first Saturday night victory against the boot camp shows.

Ultimately Laura was eliminated in week five on the night Diana Vickers had a bye and Laura got more votes than Ruth Lorenzo. (In the first week, she had got 16% of the week – Alexandra Burke managed 7%, and JLS a mere 5%.)

How could she lose support so quickly? For me, it was another example of mismanagement. It was an injustice in a poor year that she didn't get to the final.

Instead it was Alexandra Burke who went on to win and with runners-up JLS, Simon almost had his boy band.

2009

I was *still* working on Eileen's album so had approached Caffè Nero. It was a classic synergy as we looked at promoting the album for September. It was also a gentle way in of getting her out there. They did live music for independent artists, and Eileen had recorded a wonderful version of Sonny Burke and Paul Webster's "Black Coffee". Angus Moncrieff had done a superb arrangement and Livingstone Brown's production was excellent. We were still some way away from completing the finished product, and Hamish was taking up a lot of her time, but we were moving in the right direction.

The delays meant that we were finally being allowed to record "I Miss The Sky" by Jesse Harris, which we had first discovered back in early 2004 when Eileen had a development deal with Jive Records before I was even on *The X Factor*. Jesse had written "Don't Know Why" for Norah Jones and we had been sent a number of his songs. I was keen to record with Eileen, but when she got the chance to duet with the BBC award-winning jazz vocalist Ian Shaw, we knew that was the sensible option. Together, they performed a beautiful rendition of the theme to Mahogany, "Do You Know Where You're Going To?"

Even though Eileen is a jazz singer, whenever she crossed over into soul to duet with me she had a stunning tone that echoed Motown legend, Diana Ross. This song suited her so much. I love what they did with it and was a little jealous of what Ian was doing to it.

I knew we were making a great album and one I should've finished in 2006 instead of being swayed into recording my ill-fated second album.

The one thing people couldn't ridicule was the quality of our work. It may not have been everyone's cup of tea but the standard of craftsmanship was undeniable. We brought in a great string arranger, Steve Hussey, and guitarists Nigel Price, Robin Trower and Tony Remy all played on the album. Drummer Jeremy Stacey was magnificent. I was immensely proud to be involved.

I had also been doing some writing and recording again with Ian Levine and Clive Scott. We were still all disappointed that my debut album "Heart and Soul" was just covers. I was slowly getting myself back in the studio.

Clive sent me a track that he had been working on that I fell in love with and we agreed to finish writing it. This was the direction I wanted to go in and I was finally ready to go again. As soon as he finished jury service we were going to be back recording again. This was it.

March was Comedy Store season. Every year for as long as I could remember we would celebrate my best mate's birthday by sitting in the front row of this famous London venue watching the best and worst of new comedy talent. I still dine out on being there watching an unknown Micky Flanagan doing his "Out out" routine and nearly falling off my chair with laughter. We would never heckle, but if the comedian tried it on we would just snigger and whisper. They know how to deal with drunken fools who shouted out nonsense, but we found them less comfortable with this form of response. You can't compete with a man onstage with a microphone.

That night Terry Alderton was hilarious. I had seen him a few times and if you knew his routine then you'd know sitting front row was scary as hell. On this occasion he knew who I was. He was subtle with his banter and I thought I had gotten away with it. Then at the end of his set he mimed to my version of "Against All Odds" and went crazy sticking the mic in his mouth. He pulled it out and started hitting himself on the head. I was finally learning to laugh at myself.

However, later that night an unknown comedian, who will remain nameless, just put me down. If it had been funny I would have embraced it, but it was just insults. He had taken his lead from Terry, but without the touch of class, saying I was shit and attention-seeking for sitting in the front row. It wasn't comedy, it was just abuse. People loved it and laughed at me. I haven't been back since.

I was starting to get annoyed again by the narrative that surrounded me since 2005. The put-downs were too numerous to mention, but it started with national press and had worked its way to mainstream comedians and broadcasters and now down to comedy clubs and independent bloggers.

I don't like to believe in evil forces but things seemed to be going against me. I tried to remain positive, thinking it would all be OK. I had long left the comfort of Jesus Christ and continued to question my faith.

Then my phone rang and it was Ian Levine.

'Steve, Clive is in hospital.' He was alarmed.

Ian was a big, gay guy and was very often a drama queen. It was serious but he was stable. This was going to put back recording which was just my luck.

I had arrived home with a Get Well Soon card for Clive with an old tortoise on the cover. It was mildly amusing and true to character.

But suddenly Clive was dead.

I stared at this card as Ian told me how Clive had finished early and had decided to fix his roof gutter. He had hit his head. That was his last goodbye.

Clive left his wife Ann and their son Sam. So often people say 'he was one of the nicest guys I've ever known' – but Clive really was. Five years on, I still miss him, the great times we had working together, and that song we never wrote. Life can be so unfair.

One of the good guys was gone and the path I wanted to walk was blocked. I was honoured to do him justice and sing at the funeral.

The Tony Cowell conversation had reared its ugly head again, too, but this time it was with a man named Richard Hillgrove who approached me saying he had represented Charles Saatchi and James Caan. He had some big ideas about me doing a book and wanted to get me to see an agent for the deal. I thought it was worth a conversation.

On 18 April, I read an appalling article in the press announcing my non-existent book. Despite initial chats, I wasn't in the right place then to tell everything and I certainly wasn't once I read the piece. I felt a pawn in somebody else's game. The feature said I would be talking to Leon and Michelle McManus in an 'explosive tell-all' book. I wasn't.

It said the book was being written 'at the moment' when no such thing was true. It also added the line: 'Are you excited to find out what Steve and Co have to say about what really goes on at *The X Factor,* or should he just let it go now?'

There was that narrative again – letting it go implied I couldn't let it rest when all I had done was leave the label after a vacuous relationship and suffer an intolerable amount of abuse at the hands of the press.

Worst of all, the title of the book was *X Factor Nightmares: The Manipulations. The Greed. The Deceptions.*

It was a shabby, negative title and not even catchy, focussing on the wrong themes. It didn't in any way suggest that it was my story, and it wasn't.

On 19 May, I killed the whole thing:

Dear Richard
    Further to our telephone conversation I would like to confirm that you are no longer involved in my PR or

237

management and you are not looking to receive any fee if I was to get a book deal. However, as a sign of goodwill if I was to do an autobiography within the next year using Robert Smith as literary agent I would like to offer you a 3% fee for the introduction.

I appreciate that it was well intentioned to get publicity for me but the negativity and problems I get as a result of fighting Simon Cowell don't seem worth it. I would rather take my chances on writing a book called 'Getting Over The X' which is a lighter, funnier look at the show and its part in my life.

I have also received a letter from Simon Cowell's lawyer threatening legal action regarding the book and press release

'X Factor Nightmares: The Manipulations. The Greed. The Deceptions.'

Please can you confirm that this press release went out without my prior knowledge or consent.

Thank you.

Steve

It said it all – from the negativity surrounding the article to the threat of legal action. Simon's people had wanted a first look at any early draft, of which there was not even a word written!

The arrogance was stunning. I left the label with a lot less money than I should have, and without much more than a beer mat of an exit agreement. The assumption, though, that my story was all about him in somebody legal's eyes just told me I was right all along about control.

This man, whom I never even knew, had shaken up the hornets' nest and the papers were after me again. I noted just how little these tabloids had said about my involvement in the award-winning *Our House* and suddenly I had become newsworthy. This was clearly bullying.

By 15 August, we were back in tabloid fantasyland at Pizza Express. Two reporters – yes, it took two to write the story – ran *"Steve Goes From Superstardom To Dough Ball"*.

The reporters were Dan Evans and Simon Ward, and the paper was the *News of the World*. I had made a full page once again.

Though Andy Coulson had resigned from the paper in 2007, he had been singled out by an employment tribunal in 2008 for making bullying remarks in an email. There was definitely a culture at the paper and they were forced to pay senior sports reporter Matt Driscoll £800,000 for unfair dismissal. He had set a tone with regard to me and it was still going strong.

I had struggled to get a band together as all my players were already booked out, but Ian Shaw said he would help me out. Unfortunately, Ian rang the week before to say he had been double-booked at Ronnie Scott's in London. That left me with a bit of a hole. On reflection, I should've cancelled but Ian recommended Anthony Strong, an up and coming jazz singer-pianist who could step in and do a job.

We could only find four hours that week where we could get together and rehearse. I was still confident that we could deliver a good show. Anthony was brilliant.

It was better to perform than cancel in almost all the cases, especially as the press would have had a field day.

I had worked with Ian before on a piano/vocal gig and it worked well, but this time with so little rehearsal it was a little disjointed, but we were carrying it off. The show was going fairly well until we performed "Smile", which I had performed on *The X Factor* and had recorded a new version on my new album. The latest version was a new arrangement with different chords.

And on the night, Anthony played the wrong chords and I couldn't get back into the song! It was carnage. So I stopped the track, made my excuses and moved to the next song. The next song was "Since I Lost My Baby" and I made sure it made up for the previous mess-up.

It was staggering that in 2009 they were still after me. It was as if by magic that I was being ridiculed as a new series of *X Factor* was beginning. They also referenced the P & O gig and the "tell-all book". I am sure, given that it had alerted Simon's lawyers, that there was a renewed interest in my burial.

I had joked at the do that "It's better to be shit than cancel". But in truth I knew that me being bad was still good. I wasn't brilliant that night but *some* of the show was outstanding. I was just overly apologetic as I was extremely disappointed that "Smile" was a disaster.

The problem with all this was when other people assumed the narrative as fact. In September, I was on Richard Bacon's show on 5 live. The BBC had been mostly decent to me. I was on with another of Andy Coulson's boys from *The News of the World.*

Earlier in the interview, Jules Stenson had mocked me, reminding everyone of the Pizza Express. 'The gig didn't go down too well, though, did it, Steve? You forgot your words,' he said.

I was not in the mood to accept this rubbish.

'Do you know what? You've got a guy from the *News of the World...* So when it comes to music I can't really get into a conversation about them not understanding what I do and about me getting a session player in to play piano, who doesn't know the chords. It's a waste of time entering into a conversation like that really.'

Stenson followed up by suggesting I was resentful, so I just cut in:

'Woah, woah, woah, wait there! Wait there! This is the spin and propaganda, tell the truth. I did an exclusive interview with you guys and I've still got the paper that I signed and it was a paid thing. But because of Max Clifford and because of Simon Cowell, you didn't go with my story and you ran with Simon Cowell's slagging me off. So don't even start on me. Don't start on me being dropped twelve weeks after having a number one record. Don't even go there. You don't know the facts, you don't know the truth and even if you did, you wouldn't print it. So don't even start!'

I had put it out there at last live on the BBC… but it still didn't cut through.

Irony of all ironies, I would meet the man behind this narrative one final time. On 28 September, Eileen and I found ourselves at the Rhys Daniels Trust Butterfly Ball at Lancaster House as guests of the actor Bill Murray and his wife, Elaine.

The broadcaster Chris Tarrant asked me if I was still whingeing. I am not sure if I had even met him before.

It was on the dance floor, though, that I found myself in a bittersweet moment. Billy Ocean was performing "Red Light Spells Danger" with his band, and Eileen and I were up and having a great time.

In the half-light, I suddenly felt the heel of my shoe tear into the shin of the dancer behind, only for cries of agony to follow.

'It would be lovely to see you at these charity balls in three years' time,' Max had said in August 2005.

He was right. It was lovely – he was just a year out.

I turned to watch him hobble away back to his table!

I did join him briefly for small talk, but you always knew the clock was ticking on the conversation.

He was aloof, as he often was, but filled the void with talk of Simon getting things going in America and how he had long since moved on from me.

The feeling wasn't mutual.

In October the website *Digital Spy*, which had previously banned me, approached me to 'give my side of the story' about

The X Factor. Alex Fletcher from the website wrote 'I can understand Steve's history with the show and tabloid press, so I can understand any reluctance. However, I like to consider us to be slightly different from the *News of the Worlds*. We are not looking for gossip, just some nostalgia!'

Alex may have been the loveliest person on the planet but I was no fool, and still today I am aware of the often acidic tone of that website. In the unpoliced world of the Internet, it actually placed them as more untrustworthy than the publication cited, through no fault of their own. You can see in my reply just what I thought.

Hi Alex,

It sounds good but I have been burnt too many times and get too much negativity from anything remotely tabloid. I appreciate the offer but I'm going to have to pass at the moment.

Kind Regards
Steve.

Instead I went to Paul Morley at *The Guardian*.

To date, this remains the fairest and most balanced article I have done. Paul was a good old-fashioned northern music journo. I don't think he had much appreciation for Simon's musical pedigree (or mine) but he could see the process as clear as day straight through the needle of an eye. He totally got the whole 'inventing an Over 25 category' only to then criticise people for being too old. He was the first journalist to articulate intelligently this level of manipulation that had so upset Verity and positioned others as 'desperate' because it handed them the 'last shot at the big time'.

I am grateful, too – he was also the first to say I came across as a musician, which was an acknowledgement that I wasn't desperate and that I had cut those deals in the States prior to the show and had been about to support Lionel Richie.

'They're very good at putting their arms around you,' he noted, referring to what you saw on-screen.

I told him that they refer to you in the press by your surname so they can put distance between you and the show when it all goes wrong.

I liked the piece a lot, partly because Paul was respected without being mainstream. He had no agenda. It was more like being a Media Studies guest speaker. But at least a balanced truth was out, if not the whole story.

2009 was, however, the year Simon Cowell turned 50 and Max Clifford made sure this was big news. It made all the papers and the story ran for months leading up to the big event. I was surprised there wasn't a national holiday.

'All his recording artists – bar Steve Brookstein – have been invited. And all the judges on his shows from both sides of the Atlantic,' said a source.

The *Mirror* on 8 September 2009 made the point:

"But singer Steve Brookstein doesn't need to keep the date free. He's not invited.

Although 40-year-old Steve was the first-ever *X Factor* winner when the talent show phenomenon began back in 2004, he fell out with Simon.

Then he was dropped by his record label after just a year. Steve now has the fresh embarrassment of losing out on a party place to zany Big Breakfast puppets Zig and Zag. Oh the shame!"

The *Daily Star* kept it going on 3 October 2009.

"Singer Steve Brookstein, who won the first series of *X Factor*, is not on the guest list.

He fell out with Simon some time ago. The 40-year-old was recently spotted singing at his local Pizza Express in Maidstone, Kent."

It was constant and it was tabloid media bullying me. As if I even wanted to go to Simon Cowell's birthday party! Obviously when my birthday came around in November, I told the press that Simon could come but he wouldn't be allowed any jelly. That'll teach him. It was ridiculous. Of course, he was way past me. He had a new series to promote.

On *X Factor* the judges' houses now began to eek opulence – Cheryl Cole was in Marrakech, where I don't really think she lives. Dannii Minogue was in Dubai and Louis wasn't taking boy bands back to his flat in Dublin anymore, instead pallying up with assistant Ronan Keating in Lake Como. Ronan later went on to judge *X Factor Australia* – further evidence of the show's incest – while Simon was in LA where he *did* have a home and was assisted by Sinitta wearing a few leaves to cover her private parts. It was all good, clean family fun.

2010

"Every year it get's harder and harder for any person of principle to be in tabloid newspapers, because if you don't do it you're sacked and they'll get someone else in." Max Clifford

I was looking for new management but at the same time my heart wasn't in it. I couldn't get my head around writing after Clive died. I really had so wanted to work with him further for his skill and experience but also because he was a lovely man – the antithesis of so much I had seen since 2004.

The year got off to a good start with some fantastic work booked in for later in the year. My agent had set up a mini-tour with 80s soul legends Shalamar ("Night To Remember", "There It Is", "Take It To The Bank", "Friends") and Kenny Thomas, who was best known for hits "Thinking About Your Love" and "Outstanding".

I was also booked in to do a performance at the Monaco Grand Prix on Kimi Räikkönen's yacht. It was a brilliant opportunity that I was so looking forward to. As a favour, my agent also asked me if I would help a friend of his who was trying to promote his pub in Cornwall. It was in the middle of nowhere and, as Alexander O'Neal and Junior Giscombe had been down there, I thought nothing of it.

X TRACTOR became the headline in *The Sun*.

"*X Factor* winner Steve Brookstein has gone from singing to millions of TV viewers to playing a £2.50-a-ticket gig in a Cornish village pub."

It made all, and I mean all, the tabloids. I couldn't believe it. I felt sick that it was such a huge story. 2010, and I was back in the press getting ridiculed. It definitely had an impact on my work. Suddenly people were offering me gigs for less money than before I had won *X Factor*.

'Don't worry, Steve, I'll look after you.' Simon had been a man of his word!

I was unaware the pub owner was going to charge such a stupid figure of £2.50. Someone even joked that the door charge was waived if you bought a pie and a pint. This lie became the truth and was also reported. It was just terrible. To make it worse *The Sun* had cut and pasted my head on the body of a farmer next to a sheepdog. It was my Graham Taylor turnip moment. The phone didn't stop ringing with people chuckling, asking if I had seen it. I laughed it off but inside I was humiliated once again. I sunk to a new low. Into a new and black depression.

I took the image from *The Sun* and posted it on Facebook. Underneath I wrote: "This is what happens when you fall out with Simon Cowell", just to show people how powerful these people were. Before *X Factor* that paper couldn't get enough of me, and now five years on, they ran a full page destroying me. *The Sun* was responsible for not running a story that was embarrassing in the past, but now it would be seen in a different light. I had to stay buried.

After the gig it got worse. All the papers ran full pages again mocking my performance, the venue and the audience. They even turned round the comment I had used on Facebook as though I had said it at the gig. The truth was well and truly buried. For the avoidance of doubt, "This is what happens..." was now referring to my fall from grace, not their propaganda. I was livid. The sensible person would know when he was beaten and stay down.

In May, I flew out to Monaco and then got a helicopter

down to the racetrack. This beautiful location didn't wipe away the bad memories as I ran into a host of stars including Eddie Jordan and Nigel Mansell, but the gloss had been taken off one of the showpiece events in the sporting calendar. It didn't matter what I did. I was feeling broken. Every time I got up, I got knocked straight back down. I could no longer see the point. I knew nobody would report on this gig as it didn't fit the narrative.

Understandably, despite the black dog hanging over me, as gigs went, it was a dream come true and significant, too, because a friend of mine was on the next yacht and overheard me singing. He loved what he heard and promised to introduce me to someone very well connected when we got back to London. That, at least, was a boost. But, despite spending two nights on the yacht and being asked to stay on for the Grand Prix, I just wanted to get home.

2010 hurt more than any other year because this negativity was relentless and so vicious. It was also five years after I had fallen out with Simon and I wondered how deep they wanted to bury me. I took heart from my friends' kind words but it always felt one step forward, two steps back.

At home, Eileen had done a gig with Courtney Pine and together we planned to record Peter Gabriel and Kate Bush's hit, "Don't Give Up". That would be the icing on the cake.

Her album title was changed from "I Miss The Sky" to just "Eileen Hunter", and finally came out in June on Jazz FM's new artist label ironically named "Clifford Street".

Even through coincidence I couldn't escape that man. I had originally sent it to Mike Vitti at Jazz FM in London in the hope it would be playlisted, only to be offered a record deal. It was a rare, unexpected moment of pride. Once again, Eileen's work gave me a focus and a mask my own couldn't find.

She went on to play Ronnie Scott's, Hideaway, the 606, the Elgar Room at the Royal Albert Hall, and as part of the Jazz

FM stable she was also Artist of the Week on the station. I had co-written the original songs on the album and was executive producer. This was hugely credible – so there was no danger of anyone writing anything about it! – and, most importantly, it was another new start.

Other good things were happening, too. The relationship I had been building with the coffee chain Caffè Nero went all the way to the top of the company and they agreed to playlist Eileen's album in the coffee shops. That was a huge endorsement.

It *was* easy to get behind Eileen but I really feared every gig I did from then on. I didn't trust anyone who took photos, I was nervous of people who wanted to chat. I stuck to company I knew and the venues I was familiar with.

What I didn't expect to happen was to be taken in by a crackpot. A 23-year-old man called Christopher Matt was putting it about that he was a hotshot songwriter and was making a charity single with Sting for Help for Heroes. He had bragged he had written a song for Cheryl Cole and had approached several other former contestants from *X Factor* about being on a charity record. He had even offered Bad Lashes (who had been eliminated in the first round of 2008 with 1% of the vote) a two-year deal. He had somehow managed to fool the local press who ran a piece on him, and that in turn helped him con people in the industry. He was passing off other people's demos as his own and that's how I got suckered. That I was at all probably indicates my state of mind.

I met up with him for a writing session which turned out to be weird, to say the least. His house was modest but that wasn't unusual. Publishing can take time to come through. I was renting a little flat when I had signed a massive publishing deal so that didn't start any alarm bells. What raised my concern was that he was total and utter rubbish! He then made the excuse that he wrote better on his own under his bedcovers with a torch strapped to his head. Of course you did, Chris! I couldn't believe I had driven a 220-mile return trip to work with Walter Mitty.

All the time, Christopher Matt's modest house was actually just his mum's in Nuneaton. Embarrassed, but aware of the potential dangers that he possessed, I told Susan Hill at the *Daily Star* and, of course, the police. The last I heard he was on the run. I can laugh now, but even a crackpot thought I was there for the taking!

The tour with Shalamar and Kenny Thomas went well. There were no slip-ups or empty venues. That meant there was no press. I knew the score and had to change my approach. Twitter was now the platform for the intelligent man in the street. You at least had a voice there.

If I became aware of anyone in the press starting negative propaganda against me I would confront them. Enough was enough. It was time to provoke transparency. I had to avoid the bullies in the playground by staying in the library.

"If your enemy is superior in strength, evade him." Sun Tzu.

I began showing an interest in alternative media from Alex Jones, Ron Paul and David Icke to Noam Chomsky, Ralph Nader, John Pilger and Gore Vidal. I was still struggling with my demons so I wanted to discover more ways of thinking and exercising my mind. Many of my battles were in my head which led to sleepless nights overthinking my problems. I was convinced that understanding propaganda was key to overcoming my obstacles. After all, it was this that got me in the dire situation in which I found myself.

I was aware of my enemy but more importantly I knew myself. I was still struggling with my demons but my personal life was good. I had some foundation on which to build. Eileen and I were very close, Hamish made us happy every day and from nowhere came the perfect tonic. We were expecting again.

We had struck a deal for later in the year to do a 'tour'

around Caffè Nero coffee shops to promote Eileen's new album. Eileen would play her new album and I would join her for a few songs. It wasn't promoted in-store, more a case of turning up and playing – very relaxed and casual as suited her music and their brand. It wasn't about playing to 30 people in the coffee shop, it was about the subsequent BBC radio interviews and interviews with local newspapers that being there induced. We were working the album.

We decided any profits from "Don't Give Up" were for the StreetSmart homeless charity, and had also agreed to go to Mustard Tree homeless charity in Manchester. November was looking busy. I was fully aware we might get some bad press but this wasn't about *me*, now it was about Eileen and they've already played the "Dough ball" and "X Tractor" gags earlier this year. How much more could they do? I took a punt that we were safe.

For myself, I had been booked to do a concert with Jaki Graham, Kenny Thomas and Gwen Dickey from Rose Royce in Northern Cyprus. A long weekend away but I was hoping to get back in time for another of Eileen's gigs at Woolston Manor Golf Club in Essex.

I didn't think Cyprus was my next career move and I was keen to get home. It was just work in the end. The problems began when our plane was delayed so I wasn't going to make the gig.

But at Woolston Manor, unbeknown to me, tragedy struck. As Eileen was setting up with the band, the fears that she had since the morning had come true. She excused herself and went to the bathroom. She phoned NHS Direct and explained what had happened. She was told to go and rest.

Eileen replied, 'I can't, I have a gig.'

She wiped her eyes, reapplied her make-up and went back out to put on a show, all the while knowing she had lost her baby.

I have since asked her how she got through the gig.

She simply said, 'It wasn't a good day.'

In contrast, *The X Factor* was having the best year ever. It had reached its peak as I was about to hit an all-time low. Matt Cardle had won every week by a distance since the second live show, and was clearly on his way to the top spot with his cover of "When We Collide".

This year, other changes included a wild card element; at the start of each results show all the remaining finalists would perform as a group; Dannii Minogue was heavily pregnant during the auditions and replaced by a variety of guest judges from Katy Perry to Nicole Scherzinger; and the contestants' tracks were available as downloads almost immediately for the first time.

That potentially was a major game-changer. It also, of course, further undermined the notion that the prize was a record deal only achievable by the winner. In reality, you were facing a scenario where anybody in the show could have a song out before the winner's physical release, albeit without the might and support of a label behind it.

The 2010 series was also once again fraught with new and different controversies. The show had found its next Chico in the appalling Wagner – a Brazilian-born, retired PE teacher from Dudley who came onto the radar of the Department of Work and Pensions Secretary, Iain Duncan Smith, for claiming incapacity benefit whilst leaping around the stage on a Saturday night on live TV.

Contestant Shirlena Johnson was axed over concerns for her mental health; Gamu Nhengu was kicked out at judges' houses and was later revealed to be fighting a deportation order back to Zimbabwe, and crucially in the biggest cross against the show, the public were complaining en masse about the use of pitch correction software. Astonishingly, I had to complain to the Press Complaints Commission again when the *Mirror* implied I had used it at my gigs. Not once, not ever, but I was tarred by association!

What this meant for the show itself was that the process of manufacturing a star began much earlier. The manipulation of the act and the public began at the vocal stage and not just in the VT narrative or judges' comments in the studio. It was fake come full circle.

By the time Matt won, the now traditional attempt to slaughter me on the night was well underway. All the usual applied.

Only now with hindsight do I accept it was a mistake to sing at Eileen's Caffè Nero gigs. It gave the tabloids the excuse they needed to push me down again.

The *Birmingham Mail* (part of Trinity Mirror) reported that there were "certainly no more than 20 people" there and that "some of them got up to leave as he started singing…three tables emptied within minutes, although curious punters took their places after the volume was turned down".

The Sun was even worse at the Ipswich venue, saying not even "one man and his dog" turned up at "Caffè Zero". I noted the "one man and his dog" line was a continuation of the Cornish theme.

I could make my excuse as to what went wrong at the Ipswich branch, but the point is that a one-hit wonder from 2005 is never full-page headline news in 2010 unless there is an agenda to keep him down. *The Sun* had a reason to keep me down and so did Max Clifford. So they kept up their character assassination. This was Eileen's album promotion. We managed to get on many regional radio stations, including BBC WM and Manchester, and reached over 500,000 people by doing those coffee shops but that counted for nothing. And they couldn't know the effect.

I received an irate phone call from Paul Ettinger, the co-founder of Caffè Nero. They were outraged by the headlines.

Branding the chain 'Caffè Zero' was the last straw and they didn't need or deserve that association. The relationship I had nurtured for over a year was ruined.

It didn't end there. *The Sun* continued their attack by claiming that I was trying to beat Simon Cowell to Christmas number one. It was purely propaganda to make me appear arrogant or idiotic for even believing I had a chance of beating him. This, you recall, was the Kate Bush and Peter Gabriel song that we had recorded for no other reason than charity – a huge irony given my Tsunami number one.

2011

2010 had ended with a favourable piece in the *Daily Mail* with the journalist Kathryn Knight. It stands almost alone in my written press archive for its balance. That is not to say it is exclusively pro-me, because that would be dishonest, but it told my story from start to finish, reminding people that I had sacrificed Lionel Richie and alluding to the dressing room incident. I had also sent out a warning to Matt Cardle in the nicest possible way.

'Simon's has such an enormous ego, he believes that if he can't make you a star, then no one will. I should probably have never entered – but Matt's got a great voice and seems like his own man so I hope he bucks the trend. I wish him luck because if Simon's not 100% behind him, he's going to need it.'

I didn't know Matt at all but I was aware of one thing. 2011 was the year that Simon would finally launch *X Factor USA*. I am sure his priorities weren't Matt Cardle.

In fact, as it turned out, his priority from the show was actually the manufactured group who had been assembled after individual failure at audition stage but had gone on to finish third. Their auditions had been awful but they had soon progressed into what, in effect, became a four-month marketing campaign for them.

They hadn't won but Simon had finally made his boy band. One Direction was born.

On 18 March, I spotted that the We Will Rock You tour was beginning in Cardiff. The Ben Elton and Queen musical was set to tour for much of the rest of the year.

I felt slightly irritated by this. After *Our House,* I had received a call from the producers of this show. As a business decision, it always made sense. You were paid upfront for gigs, and at a time when other parts of my game were prone to ridicule, it would be hard for anyone to slaughter a show like this in its entirety just because I was in it. It was a chance to get away and do something different with no grief whilst banking the money so I could ultimately buy the time to do what I really wanted to do.

I was with my agent at the time when he took the call the previous year but he blew it for me, playing the big, pushy hotshot dealer straightaway, talking money rather than finding out what the part was. They never rang back.

To this day, they probably are put off me for life thinking I was that big cheese controlling the deal through a tough-talking middleman. I wasn't. I had been genuinely interested. When you see half-conversations come to fruition months further down the line, it's another kick in the teeth.

On 19 April, I received an email from Elisabeth Scott at Channel 5. Shayne Ward had been dropped by Simon. Would I like to do a piece for the 5 o'clock news?

I declined.

On the same day, Susan Hill at the *Daily Star Sunday* emailed:

To: Steve Brookstein
From: Susan Hill

Can I just say having seen Joe McElderry and now Shayne Ward dumped… YOU WERE so right. So Olly Murs won the battle of the boys then??!!

Hope you're well? Mystic Steve. Should've put a bloody bet on… xx

The next day, Nicole Lampert at the *Daily Mail* was in touch, writing a piece about whether "Simon Cowell can actually manage the talent he gets on reality shows following the sacking of Joe McElderry and Shayne Ward this week".

She continued: "obviously as the first winner who was quickly let go, I would love to hear your view on the matter".

It was ridiculous that I was only courted by the press favourably when it was to pour scorn on another contestant's demise. I did not want to be perceived as the original failure commenting on current failure. The only consolation I took was that people were starting to ask questions now that the number of winners who had been binned was totting up.

On 12 August, it was Eileen's birthday. I was gigging at the Savoy in London. To my astonishment, towards the end, Sir Tom Jones walked in. He had been playing in Newmarket and caught the last couple of songs. When I finished he just shouted 'More, more'.

I approached him after and told him I was a massive fan and that I had worked with Jeremy Stacey on and off since 2001. Jeremy was Tom's drummer.

When I told him I had done *The X Factor* and fallen out with Simon, he brushed it off, telling me I had a great voice before asking me to sing again.

I agreed but only in exchange for a quote for my website!

'Fucking brilliant,' he said in his most pronounced Welsh tones. 'Just say fucking brilliant.'

Amid reports I had retired, it was frankly the greatest endorsement I can remember since being asked to support Lionel Richie. It had been a long time coming and a brief interlude from the nonsense that followed me. Those six words counted for so much more than the thousands that had been written against me. He was a proven great and a timely reminder of something that had seemed to come full circle – all the negative narrative about me was never about ability. It was about character – just as though we were back in that first audition with Louis and Sharon. Musical ability was all that mattered to him.

The timing was extraordinary, too – was this the moment the written press were finally coming under the cosh?

Imagine my surprise on 18 August when I read that James Desborough – who had gone on to become the *News of the World's* Los Angeles-based US editor, had been arrested. Add to my amazement that it was being reported that *The Guardian* website had the story before James had even been asked to assist officers with their enquiries.

The *News of the World* itself had been dead some six weeks and now Operation Weeting was trying to round up the bad guys.

Obviously, I had seen James around on a few occasions. It was he who interviewed me after the *Closer* debacle. I had told him everything.

Even though the extent of alleged phone-hacking was not really known at this point, I began to wonder.

I sent this to Detective Constable Paul Adams at Operation Weeting:

Dear Mr Adams

We spoke about the phone-hacking at *The News of the World*.

I have known James Desborough for seven years straight after winning the first series of *The X Factor*. He interviewed me after I fell out with Simon Cowell in 2005 but he informed me that the story was stopped by senior staff at the paper. I have had negative stories printed about me ever since and I have won cases taken to the PCC against *The Sun* and NOTW.

James got in touch weeks prior to his arrest which I found bizarre. He had previously told me that he had left the *News of the World* when in fact I have learned he was promoted to the LA office. James has always seemed like a genuine person but now I am concerned by this latest turn of events. I have managed to find my old telephone number. My mobile telephone number back then was [xxxxx xxxxxx].

Please can you let me know if they had hacked my voicemail. I really like to think James didn't do it, but I really want to be sure.

Best wishes

Steve Brookstein

I sent that email at 10.50. By 15.23, the same day I had received a reply that their "enquiries into me are now complete". They couldn't find any evidence that I had been a victim of phone-hacking.

It was a remarkably quick turnaround at the Met, but I took it as the truth, as I had no other means to proceed. I've thought about it long and hard since. Let's put it politely, if I were a journo working for that publication, given they had written some of the things they had about me, I would have been near the top of my own list.

I was left wondering as the eight series began in earnest with a further reinvention. Simon was long gone to the States, where Cheryl Cole had been dumped as a judge within the first month. Gary Barlow, Tulisa Contostavlos, and Kelly Rowland were now on the panel at home. Dannii had left to be on *Australia's Got Talent.*

I laughed when I saw that Olly Murs was now presenting *The Xtra Factor* with Caroline Flack. It had been six long years since it had been suggested to me that this might be the route I would go down.

In some ways it had gone to a new level, though I felt the standard of talent was worse. In a new twist, the show had a fashion partner in Marks & Spencer, and all of the sixteen finalists were to appear in their 2011 Christmas ad with their version of "When You Wish Upon A Star".

Backstage, contestant Misha B was involved in a controversy during the live show when Tulisa accused her of making 'mean comments', and Louis piled in, too, naming her a 'bully'. Oh, the irony.

Frankie Cocozza was removed from the competition after *The Sun* claimed he had been overheard boasting about using cocaine. He had also sworn during a live show, prompting an Ofcom investigation.

As usual by late-October, the requests were coming in for me to talk about it all. Once again, it amazed me how journos approached me with such innocent wording in a bid to lure me into comment.

Lucy Vine emailed me, working on a piece for *Heat* magazine, wanting 'five minutes on the phone' to find out 'the truth behind talent shows'.

I simply replied: 'Sorry, Lucy, I don't do *Heat.*'

By the time Little Mix had won, the Leveson Inquiry was in full swing. Its job was twofold – to examine press ethics and the culture, including the relations between press and politicians and press and the police, *and* to examine unlawful or improper conduct at News International and other media outlets.

I felt optimistic that this was a landmark moment.

I knew deep down that inquiries made recommendations that often were hot air, but I was aware, too, that a lot of intelligent people with varied but shared experiences were going to testify. That meant J. K. Rowling and Gerry McCann. It brought Hugh Grant to the stand and Chris Jefferies, a Bristol landlord wrongly labelled as a murderer. Add to that the Murdochs themselves and, of course, the Dowler family whose voicemail messages were listened to by phone hackers after she had been abducted.

It is the bitterest irony that, amidst all this analysis into press ethics one detail from the inquiry emerged that resulted in an article by Julie Carpenter which only served to rubbish me again.

Charlotte Church had told a frankly terrifying story of how she had been offered £100,000 to sing "Pie Jesu" at Rupert Murdoch's wedding. Church told the inquiry that she had waived the fee in exchange for a promise of good press.

This was breathtaking.

However, Carpenter then ran a piece entitled "Stars Who Will Sing For Your Supper", notionally exploring that the fee for The Eagles might be £4 million, whereas you might get Leona for a million.

I don't need to tell you who was at the bottom of the list, do I?

Above me at a reported £10,000 was Howard Jones. Then I came in at £2.50. And it all started again – we were back to the narrative of the gig in the Cornwall pub and Caffè Nero.

At the height of the biggest investigation into the British press, which dragged in royals and the Prime Minister, yet another article was written by the British press ridiculing me. They either didn't see the irony or weren't taking any notice.

Then, on 19 December, *The Standard* in London announced Little Mix as the worst-selling *X Factor* winner since… obviously, me. I was the benchmark for failure.

2012

It looked like we had the worst possible start to the year. After becoming pregnant again, Eileen thought she had lost another baby. We had been so blasé when Hamish was born but, after losing our second, the third time was nine months of constant concern. It was only a routine check-up for a throat infection which confirmed we had been mistaken. Much to our joy, we were still expecting. I hoped it was a change of fortune.

And of course, the spring of every year always represented calmer waters after the frenzy up to Christmas.

On 5 January a journalist at the NME called Paul Moody had approached me about doing a book. His previous credits included a book called 'The Search For The Perfect Pub'.

He clearly had written for a decent publication in the NME that I also couldn't have imagined being pro-*X Factor*. It was always interesting to see what I got offered at the turn of the year.

People make big life and career plans over the Christmas period and put them into action when everyone is back to work. The book was to be called 'In Search Of The Lost Chord: How Pop Lost Its Soul', looking at how the music business had been taken over by corporate interests. It was to be a collection of interviews.

I declined, though it looked more credible than the usual approaches. That wasn't going to do me any favours about setting the record straight. My voice would get lost again.

By now, I was absolutely clear about the notion of a book,

though. I didn't want to be an example in someone else's study of the show, nor did I want to write a 'behind the scenes gossip' of it. The only way I could get a fair media was if I told it myself and explained the effect it had on my life – and with a second child on the way, that would put me back in doing so for at least another year but make it an absolute priority. I needed my children to read the truth in the future.

So, when I was approached to do *The Wright Stuff* on the anniversary of Andy Warhol's death – the man who said we would all have fifteen minutes of fame – I declined, as much as I liked Matthew Wright and he had always been supportive.

To: Jemima Headey
From: Steve Brookstein
    Thanks for thinking of me but I'm gonna pass to avoid going over my allocated 15 minutes.
    All the very best,
    Steve

Matthew read it out on the show! I was replaced by DJ Talent from *Britain's Got Talent* as if to demonstrate the point.

I did so, even though Simon had finally broken his silence. I must have niggled him.

The Sun reported that, at the fundraiser at London's Dorchester Hotel in February 2012, a girl asked him who was the worst person he'd ever dealt with. I couldn't believe that after all these years doing talent shows in the UK and USA I was once again number one!

"He was horrible, ungrateful and totally selfish. He just wouldn't listen."

At the end of the article the paper reminded the reader how great Simon was. Over £110,000 was raised for hospice Shooting Star Chase at the function, which was organised by… Cowell and PR guru Max Clifford.

By March, no further action was to be taken against the journalist James Desborough following his arrest, though realistically the News International saga was just brewing.

The BBC were launching their own equivalent singing competition called *The Voice*, in which judges would not see the vocal act until they had heard them, sitting facing the audience with their backs to the stage. It was a new twist on *The X Factor* and attempt to up the credibility, judging acts on purely their talent rather than anything else like image. What I liked about *The Voice* was that the contestants were not owned. They won a prize and went on their way. This would have been better for someone like me who just wanted a step up, not a full-on marriage to a control freak.

People will look at how few successes *The Voice* has had since, but equally you can look at how few failures, too. Everyone I know who had been on the show has gone on to improve their careers, maybe not to the extent of Leona Lewis, but still a step forward. *The X Factor,* by contrast, had some glorious winners, but it is littered with people left humiliated by the whole experience.

Then the most extraordinary booking of my life came in. Would I like to go out to Russia and play in a charity football match? It was for UK3Lions against a Russian team of ex-pros, musicians and politicians, including the Deputy Prime Minister, Arkady Dvorkovich. It was to be played at Luzhniki Stadium in Moscow where Chelsea played Manchester United in the 2008 Champions League Final. I still fancied myself as a footballer, so after the disappointment of *The Match* in 2005 this was a blessing.

It was madness but it was just what the doctor ordered. From the negativity of the UK press we were heading to a foreign land that seemed positive, despite everything I had heard, and, even though they had no idea who I was, loved the music. It made me realise that with 7 billion people on the planet I can take my career anywhere with or without the UK media.

I had been thinking that a third album was due. Because of the mistakes with the second one I was giving this one a lot more thought.

By April, Ian Levine and I were laying down some new tracks and I began to become increasingly interested in crowdfunding. It had a little bit of stigma within the industry. I suppose anything that cuts out the middleman and allows artists to engage directly with fans is frowned upon. I *was* a little reluctant and the thought that nobody would support a new album was horrific. The press would have a field day if I didn't raise the money.

Despite everything that they had read, though, the millions who voted couldn't have all disappeared. Many had made personal contact through my website; others were still seeking the whole truth as to what happened, and every time I played a gig I would get great feedback. My fan base was a reasonable size but was thinly spread around the UK, so reconnecting without mainstream press was going to be a long process.

By June, though, I was in Russia.

Despite the £30 price tag for three bottles of beer, Moscow was great – so good, in fact, that I went to Russia twice more. The hospitality was first class. It was an exciting time for the Russian people finding themselves again after years of Communism. Friendly but reserved is how I would describe them. It reminded me fondly of the best bits of my childhood.

My grandad August was a big Estonian carpenter. He had worked on ships during the war and ended up in London were my mum was born shortly after. His best friend was a Russian whom I knew as 'Uncle Nikki', though we weren't related. They would sit and talk in a foreign language whilst drinking vodka and eating jellied eels and sauerkraut. What a mix of culture. It's no surprise that I felt at home in the new Eastern Europe.

And here I was now, sitting on an old boat on the River Irtysh with twenty men drinking vodka and eating frozen fish and fish soup for breakfast! Then a group decided they wanted to go skinny-dipping. The boat stopped and for the next twenty minutes I watched aging Russian popstars splashing around in the water. When I stood on that stage having won *X Factor* I never imagined that my life would be going this way. But it was wonderful.

It may have been good fortune, it may have been God, but from the brink of despair came greater understanding of what life is about. It was little things like this over the years that have helped me through. I have very fond memories of my trips to Russia.

When I returned home, it was time to talk to Syco.

It was the first real dialogue in almost seven years.

It began when I started Googling. My album "Heart and Soul" had been taken off iTunes and Amazon back in 2005, but now they were taking down my video from YouTube. 200,000 views, and *Against All Odds* was gone from YouTube. My friends reinstated it, only for it to disappear again. This really was a literal erasing from the show's history. I didn't see what they were so embarrassed about, even though I do not think it was anybody's finest hour. You can't delete much from the history of pop – there are so many archives and the BBC is one of the biggest record libraries in the world, containing songs that never even made radio play, and here was a number one song and album wiped from history. In the modern era, Google made it hard to vanish, but so affected had I been by the imprint left in cyberspace of the written press that I would often search for myself. This was not vanity but self-protection as we moved from a culture where people would say 'today's news, tomorrow's chips' to an Internet where the chips were electronic and today's news was also tomorrow's news. Of course I would notice its deletion. This fight would continue forever while *X Factor* was a success.

I had already begun to weigh up the consequences of having had a public job, knowing that Hamish would one day Google me and that would cause him to question detail in our relationship. Could he really be sure of everything I said to him, if the words of a prophet were written on a Facebook wall?

All he would find would be this venom online. That would inevitably lead to him questioning the authenticity of what I had taught him in life. The book, therefore, was getting closer.

With that in mind, I wrote to Nigel Tait at Carter-Ruck solicitors:

Dear Mr Tait

I received a letter from someone at Carter-Ruck a while back requesting information on the content of a book I was considering writing. As I had not started it there was little point in replying. However, I have now decided to write my memoirs of my time on *X Factor* and thought I should let you know.

I know of no legal constraints upon me from doing so but wanted to inform the production team out of courtesy before I start. I have no intention of being controversial as my time on *X Factor* was on the whole very enjoyable.

If there are any reasons for Fremantle/Thames to object to this I would like to receive it within ten days. Otherwise, I will assume it's OK and I will go ahead.

If this is something you cannot help with, could you please pass this on to the right people.

Kind Regards
Steve Brookstein

I received no reply.

I'll overlook the fact that Simon's lawyers had requested a

look at a book which was essentially about me and not him, and which remained unwritten, and to which they had no legal say over.

The whole notion of putting it down on paper was becoming ever more real. Through the TV critic, Garry Bushell, I had begun a dialogue with a ghostwriter but none of it felt right. I had half-known Garry since the *Big Big Talent Show* in 1997 when he had played the nasty judge role but had said I was a star. On the other hand, he was an ex-*Sun* columnist.

Yet, even at an early stage, it felt wrong. Initially bogged down in legal questions as to whether I had a gagging order on me, I soon didn't like the tone. The proposal for the book was that it be called 'Take A Look At Me Now', and I hated that narrative because it was exactly the tone behind the choice of my winner's song, and that meant that a TV talent show could take you from pub singer to this regardless of your own ability. I also knew instinctively it was not for me when I was getting prompted with "I hope you've got lots of gossip on Louis Walsh".

That didn't sound like my book. It sounded like a kiss-and-tell, a tabloid sting, a trashy showbiz soundbite against which I had been fighting. It sounded like everything I had seen and hated at Leveson. Besides, I didn't have any gossip on him. I just had the facts on what went on and that was more telling than any hearsay.

Clearly it took me time to bring projects to fruition – from Eileen's album to the book, but I wanted things done properly and I was well aware of outside factors trying to muscle in with control.

It was always difficult sometimes to work out where that sincerity line was drawn. I knew the journos who had been decent to me, and I knew the TV companies who didn't just book me for an easy ridicule.

In a great irony, I received this exchange beginning in July:

Hi Steve,

I'm currently scouting talent for the 2nd series of the BBC talent show The Voice. I'd love you to apply for the show let me know if it's something you'd consider.

Thanks,

Jimmy Smith

From: Steve Brookstein
To: Jimmy Smith
Subject: Re: The Voice BBC TV – 2nd series

Hi Jimmy

Haha is this a wind up? Very funny! You got me.

Steve

No totally serious!

You in??

Jimmy

From: Steve Brookstein
To: Jimmy Smith
Subject: Re: The Voice BBC TV – 2nd series

Jimmy

Have you got any details? Just curious.

From: Jimmy Smith
To: Steve Brookstein

Steve

First auditions are Sept/Oct this year with a further 2 auditions in Dec and Feb 2013.

If you pass the 3rd round of auditions you'll be put forward for the blind auditions which will televised.

Think you would be great for the show let me know if you're keen to apply the producers would love to see you involved.

Thanks,

Jimmy

From: Steve Brookstein

To: Jimmy Smith

Subject: Re: The Voice BBC TV – 2nd series

Hi Jimmy

Sorry, I wouldn't be interested in doing auditions prior to the TV stages. If in the new year the producers feel my involvement would make good TV then I'm happy to have a conversation. I am acutely aware of the dangers of doing another talent show and the negativity it could bring me.

All the very best and thanks for getting in touch.

Steve

I saw no purpose in pursuing what would have been seen as my third attempt at 'making it'. Despite a second and a first place, I could only be perceived to fail and therefore desperate. The show must have known I couldn't win a second time, too, so that told me I was there to stir it up. For a brief moment, I was reeled in by the thought of working with Sir Tom, and regardless of what happened on the show, if that led to something after, then that had to be considered.

All in all, my business head overruled my dreamer's. The answer was emphatically no.

It was the wrong time to be starting new projects anyway. Our minds were focussed on a return to Aberdeen.

On 17 August, Esmé Malle Brookstein was born, completing our family.

Whilst it was obvious that Hamish would take Alistair as

his second name, Esmé had a free rein! Both Eileen and I have French blood so, even though we liked the name, the connection to our heritage added to the appeal. My mum's cancer had also returned and was under going chemotherapy, so "Malle" was an obvious choice.

Naturally, given the previous scares, we were both mightily relieved and ecstatically happy that it had been a smooth birth, still checking a thousand times everything was alright with our new arrival. Family had always been the most important thing to me and remained so. They were a great leveller in what you had and what you still had to do, and only they could put what lay ahead into some sort of context.

Just two weeks later, the trolls were back at me:

Message Could Steve perform for 15 minutes (all the hits please, no scrimping) week next Friday to a raucous crowd of drunk gay men. It would be such fun to see him croon his way out of every grope. Such fun. He might even fall asleep backstage and one of the lads could 'rouse' him. If you know what I mean. What larks! Do let me know. TTFN (I wonder if Steve gets the nuance of this...not the brightest lightbulb is he).

It speaks for itself. Seven years after winning *The X Factor* I was still reminded of the injustice.

In September, I received an email from Amanda Levett. She was asking my permission to make a visual and audio reference to me in exchange for £2,500 for the new Phones 4u commercial. The script read as follows (VO is the voice-over):

We open on a snow-covered shot of the UK seen from deep space.

VO: Ho, ho, ho, everybody! You can all get your Christmas gifts from Phones 4u!

We zoom into our island and see a woman up a ladder. She's nailing an illuminated Santa to the wall of her festive house.

Apparently I'm difficult to buy for...
VO: *Don't worry. We have Christmas gifts for everybody!*

We cut to a man in the middle of the lingerie section in a department store. He looks up and sheepishly asks:
Do you have something sexy for my wife?
VO: Err... we've got lots of sexy phones!

Then it came to my involvement.

We then cut to a young man wearing a Steve Brookstein T-shirt. He is working out in a gym in his garage. He asks:
I'm Steve Brookstein's biggest fan, do you have anything for me?
VO: Yes. Headphones.

The young man was to be a skinny nerd. It was an obvious pisstake. The narrative that had been set by Max Clifford no longer needed a push. It was still rolling along nicely. Though I had the support of credible people I was always encountering things that would knock me back. 'Get over it' was a common call from the tabloids, but it was starting to read as 'accept the abuse and go way'.

On *The X Factor* itself, Nicole Scherzinger replaced Kelly Rowland, whilst a whole load of guest judges from Leona herself to Mel B worked the audition stage.

A singer/songwriter Lucy Spraggan blew everyone away initially with her cheeky satirical songs only to then withdraw – you would sense – before she got sucked into the mainstream. I totally respected her decision. She had got what she needed out of the show – a great exposure and a bigger fan base. She was undoubtedly different. Beyond that it was one of the worst years ever with the novelty act – this year's Chico – Rylan Clark lasting longer in the competition than Ella Henderson who left the show in just week 7, a week after District 3 were eliminated.

I was watching District 3 closely. They were managed by Robert McIntosh whom I had been wanting to work with badly. He was from the influential McIntosh family and behind The Wanted who were dominating radio airplay. Indeed, before the shows aired, Robert had come to see me play at the 606 Club in London and told me to watch out for them.

Christopher Maloney won the first eight weeks of the show outright only to be routinely slaughtered by the press. James Arthur, who got few votes in the beginning, got better and better. He, too, was getting negativity – the tone was that he was too big for his boots.

And as for the judges, it didn't matter who sat in what chair. Gary Barlow had a go at Tulisa's breath; she in turn had used the word 'MILF'; and Nicole said "effing" live on the TV.

The show began on 18 August with trails featuring previous success stories. Shayne Ward was openly critical after being excluded. By the time it ended on 9 December, the final had its worst ratings since my year.

Better still was that the USA show was faring even worse and I had a blog with London24.com where I could have my own say unanswered:

"It's The Great Pumpkin Simon Cowell"

Simon Cowell can't be a happy captain. *The X Factor USA* is sinking. However, it still might be a while before it finally goes down.

There's plenty of car crash TV left in those old sea legs. (Maybe I should have said "shipwreck TV" as I'm going with a nautical-themed blog. Well, except for the title. "*X Factor* – All At Sea" was my first choice, but Great Pumpkin just made me laugh.)

Last year Simon said, "Anything less than 20 million viewers would be a disappointment". Yet the first series never went much above 12 million, and so far this year it is regularly slipping under 8 million viewers.

It is no longer competing with the other talent shows, *The Voice* or *Idol*, but instead it is losing out to reruns of "It's the Great Pumpkin, Charlie Brown" and "A Charlie Brown Thanksgiving".

You can understand his desire to sail back to Old Blighty where he is still loved.

Despite being the first to jump ship in 2010, charismatic Cowell is now returning to the UK to save ITV's Costa Concordia.

Captain Cowell will need to take drastic action if he is to salvage this stricken cruise ship, and in the panic a few judges will be lost.

Young Tulisa will be the first victim to be accidentally on purpose pushed overboard. Smoking, sex tapes and blaming the public for voting are unacceptable behaviour for any of Cowell's crew.

Nice Gary Barlow, who was responsible for bringing us Frankie Cocozza, will sneak into a lifeboat and will escape unscathed, just as long as he can resist the temptation of calling any of the women or children "fag breath".

Louis is going nowhere. He'll still be sitting on the deck listening to Jedward as the lights go out.

There will be an inquiry as to who is to blame for the show hitting the rocks and, luckily for Cowell, Christopher Maloney will be lost at sea and unable to testify.

Cowell will say sorry to the public for losing their trust (again) and he will pray that they believe him again. But one thing is for certain: this is one captain who won't go down with his ship.

"If your opponent is temperamental, seek to irritate him." Sun Tzu, The Art Of War

I had a blog and I had Twitter. Suddenly I could see a way forward.

The lower the ratings for *X Factor USA* went, the happier I got. It was the beginning of the end. I approached this Christmas in a happier state than ever. I was looking out for another result all together.

Max Clifford had been arrested.

2013

"None of this would have happened if it weren't
for Jimmy Savile." – Max Clifford

Historic abuse was now very much in the public consciousness. It had been in mine for over 30 years. For me, it was something you just put behind you. You survive the depression and eventually wake up not hurting and not feeling guilty. Until Savile, I had not even considered the thought of reporting my abuser.

The papers were consumed with tales of Savile, Stuart Hall and others. This wasn't good for me, and I would find myself overthinking the past once more:

It was a bright, sunny day. He closed the curtains and put the TV on. We had a 26" screen, but this one was twice the size. I was meant to be working at my Saturday job stacking shelves in a store room, even though I was too young to work in the shop.

'You'll like this,' he said, then left the room.

This was the first time I had ever seen hardcore porn. I was 14. I had only seen those underwear pages of the Freemans catalogue, and discarded soft porn magazines that my friends and I found in alleyways. I had never even kissed a girl. I was a typical shy young teenager. The screen was massive. Not only was this explicit sex, it was larger than life. My heart could have burst through my chest that day.

I got up and walked about. I had to think about anything else but what I was seeing. There was a large bowl of mixed sweets on the sideboard that included After Eights. They were special and in our house only came out at dinner parties or Christmas. I didn't think he would miss one, so I took one and ate it quickly then put the wrapper in my pocket. He returned five minutes later, turned off the TV, and just before leaving he handed me £20. This was twice my normal pay for the whole day.

'Don't tell your folks,' he warned. Not so much an order but a casual request like he really didn't care. He then offered me a chocolate from the bowl. I thought about what happened all week. Day and night.

The next time – nothing happened. We went to his house and I waited in the car. I got £10 for my trouble.

The following week I went in. The curtains were closed and he stayed and we watched. He sat by my side and asked me which bits I liked. I looked at the thin ray of light trying to break through the curtains and wanted so much to be outside. I looked back at the TV.

'The boobs,' I whispered. Everything else was totally alien to me. The light from the TV lit up his outstretched legs. Within twenty minutes the telly was off, the curtains were open and I had another £20.

Within a month he was rubbing the outside of his trousers. After two months he was masturbating with a bottle of lubricant by his side. It had the same sickly sweet smell that was in his car. Motionless with eyes fixed straight ahead, I could see this rapid movement from the corner of my eye in the dark as he moaned and kept reaching for the bottle, slapping more on. Each week he would say: 'Don't feel inhibited. If you want to do something do it. Try it,' and every week I would resist.

Eventually I didn't.

It was brief. Just a matter of seconds but I knew what it meant. He reached over to touch me and I removed his hand immediately.

I never went back but I never told my parents either. I lived with the shame and the mind games. It ruined my relationships and took me on a long journey of recovery and discovery. I swore I would never be manipulated and controlled again.

I never thought a situation would arise that would have me feeling bad about myself the way I did back then. Now it all came flooding back.

It seemed ironic that a man who had prevented my story coming out in 2005 was now very much in the papers about the same subject.

When I had heard the news about Max last year on 6 December, I danced round the room. It was that Bruce Willis jig from *The Last Boy Scout*. I hadn't seen it coming and I didn't know if the allegations were true, but I didn't care. In a way I was hoping it wasn't true. I never wanted Max Clifford to get justice, he didn't deserve it. I wanted him to suffer injustice.

Even if innocent, this would cause him trouble that would mean Simon's PR man wasn't working to his best on other matters. What implications it had for all his clients, only time would tell.

He wasn't alone in facing a court date. Andy Coulson, who had done much business with Max, had been arrested in relation to phone hacking in July 2011. The man who said he would bury me, together with one of the editors who facilitated that process, were now reaping what they sowed. I thought it doubtful that either would be convicted but I lived in hope.

This meant I began the year full of optimism, plus it looked odds-on that I would be working with Robert McIntosh. I knew I was ready to make my third album because I was working with the right person.

It's amazing how you can go months or years unmotivated but when the right set of circumstances manifest themselves, you can just pick up where you left off. I'd done a couple of taster gigs last December and Robert had come along and loved them. Now I was down to shortlisting songs and for the most part was happy with the list. We considered a live album and Robert suggested an album of soul classics.

In the end "Soul Classics" was to be the title. It wasn't an ideal situation to make another album of covers but it was all that was on the table, and at least on this occasion I would be able to choose the songs. I didn't want to make the same mistakes I had made with Simon.

Unfortunately, his studios had flooded over the Christmas period and we kept putting back our recording date. Then they flooded again. I had to wait it out but luckily I had some nice gigs coming up, including a guest spot with saxophonist Julian Smith from *Britain's Got Talent*.

Meanwhile, it would take time for the Clifford and Coulson cases to come to court, of course, and, even though Leveson had published his findings in November of the previous year, I knew nothing would change in the short term.

I had a terrible time at the hands of the press as much in 2012 as any other year, and yet it ended with news that made it all worth it. With Max Clifford off the scene and the tabloids questioning themselves as to what to report, it was a good time for me to shake things up a bit.

On 12 March, JJ Anisiobi wrote this for the *Daily Mail:*

"*X Factor* flop Steve Brookstein makes jibe at Simon Cowell as he claims music mogul wants to wear wedding dress."

I was still a flop in the eyes of the world but that's OK now. The press themselves were under the spotlight. Andy Coulson had "bully" next to his name. (After the case with Matt Driscoll leaving the paper with close to an £800,000 pay-off after laying that charge at the then editor's doorstep.) I was convinced things were changing.

This wasn't even a story. It had been lifted straight from my Twitter feed and included a still from a *Comic Relief* sketch in which Simon was at an altar getting married to a bride hidden by her white veil.

I had tweeted: *'Chris Maloney wins the toss and elects to wear white and someone's not happy'.*

The reporter said I was having a dig at Simon's sexuality. I pretended to be outraged that this was a non-story, but I have had much worse and eventually this would work in my favour. 2013 and it still proved something. Somewhere down the line Max Clifford's initial agenda to bury me had left me infamous but not quite six feet under. I've always believed if people love *or* hate you then you'll have a career. If people are indifferent you are finished.

For every person who loved Simon Cowell and *The X Factor* there were people who didn't. If 10 million people were watching (and I'm not sure they were) then 50-odd million weren't. These were now my target audience in the tabloid media. I was still up against it, but I was in the best position since 2004. And this was not about revenge. This remained about reasserting the truth.

By early summer I had finally made it down to Robert's studios. I was stunned to see so many *X Factor* pictures on the wall. I hadn't known any connection but it made me nervous, and then I found out that the show had used the studio, too. That made sense, of course, given the pictures. I was suspicious that a man seemingly so close to the show would want to work with me, though I had found him sincere, professional and in appreciation of what I could do.

I felt the clock was ticking on our album and, like everyone, we were on a budget.

It was now 22 July when I emailed suggesting new dates for 7 August to record what was, after all, to be a live album.

Over in New York, a man called Andrew Silverman was filing for divorce, citing his wife Lauren and a man called Simon. There was another Cowell on the way, it seemed.

On 6 August, the day before I had suggested recording with Robert, an email arrived from Christian who had been at *OK!* previously but had moved to *Now* magazine – would I take part in a ten years of *X Factor* shoot in exchange for *'plugs and stuff'*?

I wrote back asking if stuff meant a fee.

It didn't – but I would get my website listed.

I simply replied, 'It's a no. Sorry fella. Not interested.'

It wasn't about the money. It was about two things: agreeing to the shoot was always going to position me as a loser. I don't suppose Leona had signed up for it. Also, it was just the assumption that any artist would be happy to fuel *their* circulation for a train fare and a mention of their website. People knew where I was if they wanted to find me and were already more than happy to lift from my blog or Twitter feed as I have shown!

Then there was the other side of social media. Sometimes it went wrong. I was extremely disappointed that one of my tweets had upset a lot of people when it was not my intention.

I had tweeted that Jon Venables, who had murdered the toddler James Bulger, should be left alone by the press. Everyone from former contestant Rebecca Ferguson to James's mother attacked me.

There is no way in the world I would defend the Bulger killers. What they did was horrific and sickening. I felt lucky that my childhood was good until I was 14. I don't know how people are affected by personal circumstances. I don't think children grow up wanting to be evil murders.

The point I was trying to make was that it wasn't up to the press to monitor Venables or his partner in crime, Robert Thompson. That was the job of social services and the police. I thought it was appalling that I even knew their names. Yes, at times the press could do a very good job of exposing wrong – as in the MPs' expenses – but they were not judge and jury, and of course I was speaking from personal experience when I felt that they perceived themselves to be.

Despite the pair's undoubted crimes, if you believed in rehabilitation in society (and they would ultimately be released) you could not have the press naming and locating them. If the two boys had committed the crime today we wouldn't know their identities and the press wouldn't be able to keep pushing hate.

That was the point I was trying to make. As a parent I was so upset by the distress that an out of context tweet had caused that I actually wrote to Jamie's mum, Denise Fergus, but the damage had been done. I can't imagine the pain she has been through, and it hurt me deeply that I had added to it.

By August, the Silvermans settled out of court in the USA, therefore avoiding Simon Cowell being called as a witness. Simon banned his ex-girlfriends from his yacht, *X Factor USA* was in free fall, and I had another stick to poke him with. In the UK, the tenth series of his show was about to begin and there was plenty of time ahead for court action at home.

Musically, nothing was happening with my album.

I felt something else had got in the way, as though Robert was dragging his feet. On the TV, Sharon had returned. It seemed a strange decision so far down the line in the DNA of the show. One of the problems was that Tulisa had been arrested in an undercover sting, accused of supplying Class A drugs.

Amongst the contestants this year, one had a criminal past and another was five months pregnant and received a bye to the next round after collapsing on the show. The producers had also returned to the audition room concept, which had been a mainstay of the process in the early years, and a new 'flash vote' was introduced at the end of the Saturday night show where the voting lines opened for eight minutes and the act with the fewest votes faced the sing-off. The flash vote wasn't used again after week three. Lorna Simpson, the first contestant to be eliminated, complained it was unfair and exploited to get her out of the competition.

These were tough times for the show – they were in a fierce battle with *Strictly Come Dancing* on BBC1.

It was also tricky that this was the tenth year. That was a major opportunity for the show and for anyone who had ever been on it. No wonder journalists wanted to write about it.

On 17 October, I began to tweet about the anniversary, after seeing the track listing for the Greatest Hits album they were releasing.

'I've not made the album,' I announced. 'Thanks for the 1ˢᵗ ever *X Factor* number 1 and 6 million votes. Just wasn't enough, I guess.'

Leon Jackson was also omitted. The comedian Jimmy Carr piled in, whilst at the same time bigging up the Paul Potts movie:

"Steve Brookstein's not on *X Factor* Greatest Hits album. It's doubly painful for Steve as when someone buys it, he has to scan and pack it."

He had assumed the narrative.

At the same time, I called off Robert McIntosh:

To: Robert McIntosh
From: Steve Brookstein

Hi Robert

Hope you are well.

Our original discussions in late-2012 made me believe that this simple album would be done fairly quickly. The delays and lack of communication are very frustrating for me and I am unable to comment indefinitely when things are so vague. I know you have a lot on with the theatre and that takes priority but I need to move forward.

As I've not been able to get hold of you and due to how late in the year it is, I've decided to start again and re-record it elsewhere.

It's been a real pleasure meeting and getting to know you and I hope that when I get this album finished in the new year we can talk about doing something.

Best wishes

Steve

Crashed and burned. I've no explanation and I was left with no alternative. I didn't like relationships ending badly. In life, I had always tried to get them back but I didn't want to fight and I didn't want to beg. The negative was that a man whom I respected and wanted to work for had gone quiet. The positive was that meeting Robert had given me the impetus to do a new album either way. I could now call the album what I wanted and add some original songs. It wasn't a desperate situation.

I turned to the one group of people who could get me over the line – my fans.

Aware, of course, that if I didn't raise the required amount of money, I would get slaughtered by the press and the chances of that were high. I had dismissed now as virtually none my chances of getting publicity on the radio or TV with the new material, but it made perfect business sense to empower those people who wanted the album and to share the whole experience with them. I would know exactly how many copies we would make, and, in exchange I would auction off launch party tickets, handwritten lyrics, my "Worst Album" award – anything of perceived worth to a genuine fan. I signed the deal with PledgeMusic. It was a perfect match.

I even had an odd pair of Gucci shoes that I wore to the Brits in 2005. My stylist, who was also looking after Will Young, could only spare me five minutes. She ran into the hotel room I was in near Kensington, dropped off half a dozen suits, a pair of shoes and some white shirts, and then she was gone!

Only one suit fitted me, the shoes were uncomfortable and none of the shirts were my size. I had to rush down the road and buy a shirt from Zara. I had always wanted to go to the Brits and it was a disaster before I had even got there!

It wasn't until I got home in agony that I realised that one shoe was a size 9 and one was a size 7.

Those shoes were now signed and a pledge item for raising money to make an album.

I was the act, the product and the salesman, but I loved it because it set me free and I was now only really selling to people who wanted to hear my music. I felt, loyalty, confidence and happiness.

Nobody reported it, of course, because it was a success. It was also the modern way – there was nothing to be ashamed of in self-funding. It was a sensible business model that made the fan feel directly responsible for making it happen – and they were. I could move forward without fear. I was finally in control.

The press attacks had also calmed down, though not completely:

On 21 November, Joel Golby at *Heat* magazine wrote:

> **"James Arthur has gone 'full Brookstein', so let's look back at his top ten worst moments …**
>
> OH DEAR James Arthur. It's not going too well this week, is it, chicken? Not having 'too good a week', by all accounts. To briefly recap: what started as an incredibly ill-advised rap battle with UK MC Micky Worthless has pirouetted and spiralled out into James being called out for homophobia, quitting Twitter in a spectacular blaze of glory, texting abuse to Lucy Spraggan. OH DEAR James Arthur."

I felt a lot of sympathy for him. James was young and naïve. He did a couple of things that were stupid, but as an *X*

Factor contestant were unacceptable. I found it unfair that, soon after making a homophobic comment, he was described as going "full Brookstein". It implied I was a mental condition.

I complained almost immediately to the Press Complaints Commission.

Holly Pick at the PCC replied, saying that the magazine did not accept a breach of the Code.

"It believes that the reference to you was clearly comment and not a statement of fact. It does not believe that the article implies that you have ever used the term 'fucking queer' or have similar sexual habits to James Arthur; it says the comparison implied that James Arthur has not toed *The X Factor* line."

I decided not to fight this. I had raised the money for my new album and was surrounded by positivity. Getting involved in a long email exchange while I was recording my album would not bring out the best in me.

Maybe, I was finally putting that ghost to bed.

2014

"Every year it gets harder and harder for any person of principle to be in tabloid newspapers, because if you don't do it you're sacked and they'll get someone else in." Max Clifford

I had spent the last two weeks of 2013 in the studio and the new year couldn't have had a better start. The recording was going better than I had hoped, and I was excited that it was going to be very special.

In the States on 7 February, Fox pulled the plug on *X Factor USA* the day after Simon announced he was returning to the UK version of the show. Spin to the last – it had only aired for three seasons and declined year on year to ratings reported to be lower than *Countryfile* in the UK. This was music to my ears.

James Arthur was being publicly told to "shut up" by Simon Cowell, while newspapers claimed the hunchback rapper in the forthcoming *X Factor* musical "I Can't Sing" was based on James, though Simon would not confirm or deny this. His record deal looked doomed.

On 23 March "Forgotten Man" was released. It was a low-key, soft launch, which basically means nobody knew about it. We had spent all the money making the album and had nothing left to promote it. Did I care? The best thing about doing the crowdfunding was how the success of raising the money meant I had won before the release. I had just made my best album to date.

It remained the case that my music wouldn't make news. My character would, as per the first audition, though this wasn't the inspiration for the album title. In one of my many late nights watching old soul videos on YouTube I stumbled upon the track "The Forgotten Man" by David Ruffin. David was the lead singer of The Temptations on such hits as "My Girl", "Ain't Too Proud To Beg" and "I Wish It Would Rain".

Although the song itself didn't make the album, it made me think about some of the great soul singers of the past, some well known and some less so.

He was one of the greatest soul singers of all time and yet he died at the age of 50 with a drug addiction. It was a sad end for a legend, and I couldn't help thinking that "The Forgotten Man" was a reference to his career. Soul music gave my individual soul the outlet that, through no fault of my own, other emotions had left vacant. I included "Dark End Of The Street" by James Carr, "Hey Girl" by Freddie Scott, and "Sadie" by The Spinners, with Philippé Wynne on lead vocals. It was a chance to acknowledge these outstanding soul singers and their influence on my entire life.

I did a beautiful version of Marvin Gaye's "If This World Were Mine" with Eileen, and I also included the bonus track of "Dance With My Father". My only regret was that this wasn't my debut album. There wasn't a single song that I wasn't proud of. It was soulful, classy and even had two original songs that I had written with Livingstone Brown and Katie Jackson. It was a long time coming but I had got there. I had made it almost a decade on.

On 26 March, "I Can't Sing – *The X Factor* musical" opened in London.

By 10 May, the show was closed.

On 28 May, Richard Hillgrove, the PR man who had issued an inaccurate press release about me without my consent about an earlier attempt at the book which I felt misrepresented me, was sentenced to fifteen months in prison, suspended for two years. The judge told him 'you were servicing a lifestyle you could not afford'.

On 21 July, Tulisa's trial over drugs allegations collapsed after it emerged that there were strong grounds to believe that a key witness had lied. That witness was Mazher Mahmood, known to many as the *News of the World's* Fake Sheikh – a man who had turned over many high-profile individuals, from the English football manager Sven-Göran Eriksson to Sophie Wessex of the Royal family. He was suspended by News International instantly.

Just the previous month on 24 June, Andy Coulson, his former editor at the paper, who went on to spin for the Government, was found guilty of conspiracy to hack phones, and a month later one of their reporters, Jules Stenson, was charged with similar. (It was Stenson who took me to task on 5 Live only to have nothing to say when I mentioned that they had killed a story about me after the *Closer* incident.)

At Coulson's trial, Dan "Pizza Express" Evans was sentenced on two counts of phone-hacking, as well as making illegal payments to officials and perverting the course of justice.

You couldn't make it up. Partly because it was all true and documented in a court of law.

However, the key date remains 2 May. Max Clifford was found guilty of eight charges of indecent assault against women and girls as young as fifteen between 1977 and 1985.

The offences themselves, of course, have nothing to do with his relationship as a PR consultant with me, but anybody who has been abused understands that you are dealing with individuals who exert mental control in equal amounts.

Even to the last, Clifford seemed to feel invincible, famously mimicking a Sky reporter behind his back as he delivered a piece to camera. Sky, for legal reasons or because they knew the impact, held the piece back until the trial was over. If ever there were a shot that underlined the man's arrogance and deluded self-belief, it was on Tom Parmenter's footage.

When Eileen and I saw the news, everything flooded back.

I remembered each call and every meeting – how he had asked me if I had anything in my closet so he could own my secrets.

'Talk to the press and we'll bury you,' he had said in August 2005. Only now did I question whether he had meant talk to the press about the show or about the contents of the *Closer* story. I had always assumed it was the former. Finally, it made sense why he wouldn't want me going there.

I thought of the charity event he took me to, disbelieving how he had created this altruistic front for himself.

'I can't believe he's gone,' I said in true shock.

I have held Eileen many times since that phone call from Max, but had never felt as free as I did then.

I wiped the tear from her eye. This hadn't just affected me.

I wondered what Simon was thinking. The man he looked to for the last twelve years – the guru – was no longer there to protect or promote him.

So much of the show's machine was about its PR engine. Its ability to generate the sob story and play out wars between judges, in a press that knew it served them well to be onside, had been key to the brand. And now the man who talked to the press more than any would be getting buried himself.

The constant anxiety I had felt for years; the depression I sank into; the fear of doing anything at all for the public ridicule it brought, were being lifted.

People were now willing to speak out about historic abuse and their strength gave me mine.

And I was back gigging. Feeling good again and ten years on from playing a lady called Jane's 50th birthday party at Wentworth Golf Club, I was now performing for her 60th. Some familiar faces, some not, but all remembered what happened after the first time around. I remember that Sir Michael Parkinson wasn't at the 50th, but here he was a decade later. Jane said that he wanted to say hello at some point. I had better put on a good show.

Some guests reminded me that they had told me I would win *The X Factor* and how proud they were. For once, I didn't feel like I had let anyone down. Like that boy with a £20 secret, it wasn't my fault. I could see it for what it was – a set of circumstances. I had made choices and it led me here. I was happily married with two beautiful children and still doing what I love. Who knows where that Lionel Richie gig would have led me?

And Louis was right. He had said that I didn't want it enough and it was true. I didn't want 'it'. I wanted something else.

I had experienced an unbelievable and unpredictable decade and I was still going, still making music and now, out of the blue, I was handing my new album to Sir Michael Parkinson.

'Sorry, I haven't got a business card,' I said, 'but please let me know what you think of this.'

First Sir Tom and now Sir Parky.

He thanked me for the CD and we continued to speak for a few moments more before he left.

It was lovely to be myself again.

There was no point making sense of it and no dream to be taken from it. Like reaching for a plain white envelope on the floor, one small decision can change everything.

A Word From The Ghost

I must declare my hand.

As a ghostwriter I help people find their voice when any number of factors prevent them from doing so. From lack of ability or time, to sheer procrastination, or, in the case of my dear, late friend PC David Rathband, blindness.

It's a wonderful pleasure seeing someone else's story come to life in print, and for me, having lived my life in the public eye as a breakfast radio host on major shows in the Northwest and Northeast of England, believe me, it's a fantastic feeling to be involved with something high-profile without putting yourself out there.

That's why I am putting my cards on the table.

I didn't know Steve before 31 May 2014. I only knew what I had read in the paper, and I, of course, read some of it out on the air. This happens almost every day in broadcasting somewhere in the world and it's a disgrace.

As you turned every page of this memoir, particularly in the second section after the TV show has finished, you will have seen the accumulative process that such actions of disc jockeys can have.

Next time you hear someone on your local station say 'Apparently, in the papers today…' please question every word of it.

I did that once, and I am not a stupid person. Nor am I a broadcaster without a considerable track record. But I got that one wrong. I became part of the vehicle that spun the narrative against my subject. It's only now that we have pieced it together over a decade later that I realise the accumulative effect.

As the story unfolded, you will have drawn your own conclusions, but I hope you have read the story of a decent family man who has proved his talent many times over, only to fall foul of an industry called the press which has been severely discredited in recent times. If some pages didn't leave you open-mouthed at their cruelty then I've not done my job properly.

I make a friend for life in every book I ghost. This was no different. It has been an absolute pleasure. I'd like to thank Steve and Eileen for the trust and you for reading and welcoming us into your world with a very open mind.

Tony Horne
September 2014